D1458239

RESEARCH IN

READING
RECOVERY

CHICHESTER INSTITUTE OF
HIGHER EDUCATION

WS 2123730 1

AUTHOR

TITLE | CLASS No.

RESEARCH | 372.413

MY98 TES

RESEARCH IN

READING RECOVERY

EDITED BY

Stanley L. Swartz & Adria F. Klein

FOREWORD BY

Gay Su Pinnell

HEINEMANN · Portsmouth, NH

Heinemann
A division of Reed Elsevier Inc.
361 Hanover Street
Portsmouth, NH 03801-3912

Offices and agents throughout the world

Copyright © 1997 by Heinemann.

All rights reserved. No part of this book may be reproduced in any form or by any electronic or mechanical means, including information storage and retrieval systems, without permission in writing from the publisher, except by a reviewer, who may quote brief passages in a review.

This book includes articles originally published in *Literacy, Teaching and Learning* (1994–1996), the journal of the Reading Recovery Council of North America and reprinted with permission. All authors' royalties from the sale of this book will be donated to the Council.

Library of Congress Cataloging-in-Publication Data
CIP is on file with the Library of Congress.
ISBN 0-435-07239-0

Cover design: Darci Mehall
Manufacturing: Louise Richardson

Printed in the United States of America on acid-free paper
00 99 98 97 EB 1 2 3 4 5 6 7 8 9

to Marie M. Clay

CONTENTS

FOREWORD

Nothing is more important than the education of our children. More than ever we must assure every child a good start in learning to read and write. Whether or not children acquire skills and knowledge depends to a great extent on their early literacy, which becomes their foundation for later learning and their impetus to develop the complex literacies they will need in the challenging future.

Innovations with which to meet immediate educational needs and/or increase educational effectiveness are many: district and county offices offer workshops; textbook publishers provide new materials and guides; national training programs are developed and advertised; universities set up graduate programs and introduce special courses; thousands of new professional books are printed and marketed every year.

Approaches based either on research or on common sense are invented and reinvented, but history shows that most new programs and initiatives are short-lived. They are put into general practice with varying degrees of fidelity to their originators' vision. Most are not examined with any kind of rigor; they come and they go. Nothing seems to change very much, at least when measured in terms of student achievement. Even programs that *have* been rigorously tested on a small scale with a narrowly defined population seldom include effective designs for their ongoing analysis and improvement.

Research and development are the keys to forward movement, but they appear to have little value in education. We do not bother to investigate the conditions under which promising programs work and under which they will surely fail. The usual solution is to throw them out when their original effectiveness appears to wane and to install new ones in their place.

Innovative programs typically start small, the product of the intimate involvement of a few like-minded people. As these programs expand, they must change to accommodate larger numbers of participants with varied backgrounds in different geographic areas. Their support systems must be continually revised.

The journal *Literacy, Teaching and Learning* was founded by the Reading Recovery Council of North America to support teachers who use Reading Recovery and to introduce Reading Recovery to the larger educational community. Articles in the journal acquaint individual implementers with new research that will inform their work. It is one of several means to ensure that Reading Recovery remains self-renewing, continually reeducating itself.

The book you hold in your hand is a summary volume that brings together significant articles published in the first three volumes of *Literacy, Teaching and Learning*. It makes it easier for interested teachers, administrators, and researchers to find these articles, and it compiles Reading Recovery research in a format suitable for use in a college or university classroom.

A number of the articles deal with the effects of Reading Recovery. Askew and Frasier explore sustained effects of the program on children's cognitive behavior, while Rowe's longitudinal study examines factors affecting students' progress in reading. Hobsbaum reports Reading Recovery results in England, and Yukish describes the effect the program has had on Old Order Amish children in the midwestern United States. Escamilla reports a study of Latino children who participate in Descubriendo La Lectura, as Reading Recovery in known in Spanish.

Other articles fuel our understanding of learning and the educational process. Pinnell explores

Reading Recovery's unique teacher-education model and summarizes research on teacher learning. Lyons explores the issues, challenges, and implications of Reading Recovery as it relates to learning disabilities and special education. DeFord details a study of early writing within the Reading Recovery program, while Jones cites insights from Reading Recovery as she explains theoretical aspects of learning to read. Gentile examines the critical aspect of oral language assessment and development within the program. Finally, Gaffney and Paynter address the larger question of the role of early literacy intervention in the transformation of education.

Taken as a whole, this volume brings together a rich array of investigations by a number of prominent researchers and prompts a thoughtful examination of educational programs and larger systems. By studying Reading Recovery, we can learn how to create and manage educational approaches that will make the program more effective. More important, we can learn to create systems that are self-renewing and continually improving.

Gay Su Pinnell

ACKNOWLEDGMENTS

This book collects and reprints original research on Reading Recovery from the first three issues of *Literacy, Teaching and Learning*, the journal of the Reading Recovery Council of North America (RRCNA). We are indebted to Marie Clay for her encouragement in all of our efforts and her specific support in the development of the new journal. The combination of her enormous intellect with a gentle spirit and her ability to both challenge and nurture serves as an inspiration to us all.

Our gratitude is extended to our colleagues who provide editorial support to *Literacy, Teaching and Learning*, their hard work resulted in both an important new journal and the articles collected in this book. They include: Phylliss Adams; Richard Allington; Billie Askew; Rebecca Barr; Courtney Cazden; Joanne Daniels; Diane DeFord; Mary Anne Doyle; Kathy Escamilla; Irene Fountas; Dianne Frasier; Mary Fried; Janet Gaffney; Celia Genishi; Claude Goldenberg; Judy Grayson; Margaret Griffin; Noel Jones; Pamela Jones; Peter Johnston; Patricia Kelly; Martha King; Blair Koeford; Carol Lyons; Stuart McNaughton; Judith Neal; David Pearson; Gay Su Pinnell; Jean Prance; Yvonne Rodriguez; Olivia Ruiz; Maribeth Schmitt; Barbara Schubert; Robert Schwartz; Rebecca Shook; Lee Skandalaris; Bobbie Sievering; Vladimir Sloutski; Pauline Smith; Trika Smith-Burke; Susan Stoya; Robert Tierney; Barbara Watson; and Joseph Yukish.

We would also like to thank, for their support of the journal and the book, RRCNA Publications committee members Mary Anne Doyle, Chairperson; Janet Bufalino; Susan Burroughs; Diane DeFord; Rose Mary Estice; Mary Fried; Carlos Manrique; Judith Neal; Maribeth Schmitt; and Trika Smith-Burke.

All of our work benefits from the important support of our staff in the Department of Educational Research and Policy at California State University, San Bernadino. We always profit from the input of our colleagues from the Reading Recovery in California project, Becky Shook and Bev Hoffman. Our appreciation also goes to Virginia Evans-Perry, Amie MacPherson, Kimberly McDonald, Lillian Wlasiuk, and Donita Remington. From this group, our special thanks to Patricia Hays, editorial assistant for *Literacy, Teaching and Learning*.

Jean Bussell, Executive Director of RRCNA, provided support for this project from the planning stage to its completion. Our thanks to her and her staff.

Our thanks to members of the Heinemann staff, Mike Gibbons, Renee Le Verrier, and Maura Sullivan. It was a pleasure to work with such an efficient and professional group.

Projects like this book have a way of intruding into the time usually reserved for family and friends. Our thanks to Janet Maule Swartz and all other faithful friends for their support.

The decision to dedicate the proceeds from the sale of this book to the Reading Recovery Council of North America was an easy one. It is our firm belief the RRCNA will provide the necessary leadership to ensure the prosperity of Reading Recovery into the next century. It deserves the support of all of us.

Stanley L. Swartz
Adria F. Klein

READING RECOVERY:
AN OVERVIEW

STANLEY L. SWARTZ and ADRIA F. KLEIN
California State University, San Bernardino

Reading Recovery is an early intervention program designed by Marie M. Clay (1979, 1985) to assist children in first grade who are having difficulty learning to read and write. Children eligible for the program are identified by their classroom teachers as the lowest in their class in reading acquisition. Children who are not taking on reading and writing through regular instruction receive a short-term, individually designed program of instruction that allows them to succeed before they enter a cycle of failure. Reading Recovery is designed to move children in a short time from the bottom of their class to the average, where they can profit from regular classroom instruction. The goal of Reading Recovery is accelerated learning. Children are expected to make faster than average progress so that they can catch up with other children in their class.

Reading Recovery provides one-to-one tutoring, five days per week, 30 minutes a day, by a specially trained teacher. The daily lessons during these 30 minute sessions consist of a variety of reading and writing experiences that are designed to help children develop their own effective strategies for literacy acquisition. Instruction continues until children can read at or above the class average and can continue to learn without later remedial help. Reading Recovery is supplemental to classroom instruction and lasts an average of 12-20 weeks, at the end of which children have developed a self-extending system that uses a variety of strategies to read increasingly difficult text and to independently write their own messages.

The Reading Recovery Lesson

Reading Recovery uses supportive conversations between teacher and child as the primary basis of instruction. This teacher-child talk has been found to be an effective method for experts (teachers) to help beginners (students) take on complex tasks (such as reading) (Cazden, 1988; Kelly, Klein, & Pinnell, 1994) and is a particular need of children having difficulty in school (Clay & Cazden, 1990). The Reading Recovery lesson follows a routine framework of activities that are individually designed based on a daily analysis of student progress by the teacher. Each lesson has seven distinct parts:

1. Child rereads several familiar books. These stories come from a variety of publishers and represent a wide range of narrative and expository texts of varying difficulty levels.

2. Child rereads a book introduced the lesson prior while teacher observes and records the child's reading behaviors.

3. Child does some letter identification and learning how words work.

4. Child writes a story with teacher providing opportunities for the child to hear and record sounds in words.

5. Child rearranges his or her story from a cut-up sentence strip provided by the teacher.

6. Teacher introduces a new book carefully selected for its learning opportunities.

7. Child reads the new book orchestrating his or her current problem-solving strategies.

Teacher Training

Reading Recovery uses a trainer of trainers model. University professors (trainers of teacher leaders) prepare district-level staff developers (teacher leaders) who in turn train teachers in the Reading Recovery teaching techniques. This model ensures that Reading Recovery will have the support at the school district and site levels necessary for successful program implementation. It also sets the stage for systemic reform of how we teach reading and writing and how we provide access to good first teaching for all children.

Experienced teachers are provided professional development in a yearlong curriculum that integrates theory and practice and is characterized by intensive interaction with colleagues. Teachers-in-training conduct lessons behind a one-way glass and are observed and given feedback by their colleagues. In addition, Reading Recovery teacher leaders visit teachers at their sites and help them reflect on and improve their teaching and observing of children. There are three main elements in the Reading Recovery professional development program:

1. Teachers and teacher leaders participate in an extensive training program that combines child development and early literacy theory with practice in the observation and discussion of Reading Recovery lessons that are taught behind a one-way glass.

2. Teachers and teacher leaders work with four children in Reading Recovery each day during their training year and in subsequent years. Teachers are observed and coached by teacher leaders during school visits.

3. Teachers and teacher leaders participate in ongoing professional development as long as they continue to teach in Reading Recovery. Teachers are visited and coached, and they participate in inservice training sessions where demonstrations are observed and critiqued using the one-way glass.

Terminology

Much of the research on Reading Recovery uses various terms that need further clarification and definition:

Observation Survey (Clay, 1979, 1985) contains six measures of a child's attempts on reading and writing tasks and provides information about what the child knows and can control in his or her learning. The components of the survey are:

1. *Letter Identification* - a list of 54 different characters including upper and lower case letters and the printed forms of *a* and *g*.
2. *Word Test* - a list of 20 words most frequently used in early reading materials.
3. *Concepts about Print* - a variety of tasks related to book reading and familiarity with books.
4. *Writing Vocabulary* - children are given an opportunity to write all of the words they know in ten minutes.
5. *Dictation Test* - a sentence is read to the child who writes the words using sound analysis.
6. *Text Reading Level* - a determination of reading level based on actual books organized by a gradient of difficulty.

Roaming around the known refers to the first two weeks of a child's program in which the teacher explores the child's known set of information and helps establish a working relationship, boost the child's confidence, and share some reading and writing opportunities.

Running records are a systematic notation system of the teacher's observations of the child's processing of new text.

Discontinued refers to the decision by the teacher to exit a child from the program based on the readministered Observation Survey scores and observations of the strategies used by the child during reading and writing, as well as reaching at least the average of the classroom performance in first grade.

Program children are those who received sixty or more lessons or who were successfully discontinued from the program prior to having received sixty lessons.

Continuing contact refers to inservice training provided after the initial training year.

Research on Reading Recovery

Reading Recovery has a rigorous research design that continuously monitors program results and provides support to participating teachers and institutions. Data are collected on all students who participate in the program. Findings of these studies include:

1. Approximately 75-85 percent of the lowest 20 percent of children served by Reading Recovery achieved reading and writing scores in the average range of their class and received no additional supplemental instruction (Pinnell, DeFord, & Lyons, 1988; National Diffusion Network, 1993; Swartz, Shook, & Hoffman, 1993).

2. The progress in reading and writing made by children in Reading Recovery is sustained and their performance in the average band has been measured up to three years after the children were discontinued from the program (Pinnell, 1989; Smith-Burke, Jaggar, & Ashdown, 1993).

3. Studies have shown Reading Recovery to be more effective in achieving short-term and sustained progress in reading and writing than other intervention programs, both one-to-one tutorial and small group methods (Pinnell, Lyons, DeFord, Bryk, & Seltzer, 1994; Gregory, Earl, & O'Donoghue, 1993).

4. Reading Recovery has been found to be cost-effective when compared to remedial reading programs, special education placement, and primary grade retention (Dyer, 1992; Swartz, 1992).

Key Elements of Reading Recovery

Reading Recovery has a number of key elements that we believe make the program an important opportunity to reform how we teach young children to read and write. They are provided in summary form.

1. Reading Recovery is an early intervention program that supports early literacy. Reading Recovery focuses on early intervention, the benefits of which have been paid "lip service" for years. Spending the money early—before problems begin rather than on later remedial programs or even on incarcerating criminals—has been talked about but not seen in public schools. Reading Recovery is designed to concentrate resources on first graders as they begin to read.

Reading Recovery also supports accelerated learning. Most of our remedial programs consider themselves successful even when some progress is made. Unfortunately, children making only some progress will always be behind their class. Only acceleration can help a child catch up to the average of his peers and allow participation in the regular class program.

2. Reading Recovery serves the lowest achieving children. The lowest achieving children in first grade, without exception, are selected to receive the program. None of the historic reasons used to explain non-achievement (e. g., likely referral to special education, lack of parental support) are used to exclude children from the program.

3. Reading Recovery is effective with diverse populations. Data collected on program success from different geographical regions (throughout the United States, Australia, Canada, the United Kingdom, and New Zealand) and from various groups of children (those with ethnic, language, or economic differences) are comparable. Preliminary data from the more recently developed Descubriendo La Lectura/Reading Recovery in Spanish are also similar to children receiving the English program.

4. Children develop a self-extending system of learning to read and write. Children learn the skills to be independent learners who will just need the support of regular classroom instruction rather than remedial programs.

5. Student outcomes are sustained over time. Research on students after program completion has demonstrated continued growth in reading and writing without continued Reading Recovery support or other specific interventions.

6. Reading Recovery teachers serve children as part of their training. Teachers in the program learn by doing and use the Reading Recovery lesson framework throughout their training year. Students served by these teachers-in-training show comparable progress to those served by more experienced teachers.

7. Reading Recovery provides continuous professional support for teachers. The continuing contact for trained teachers is provided as long as the teacher participates in Reading Recovery. Unlike other teacher education programs which have little contact with students after the training period, Reading Recovery has ongoing inservice opportunities designed to maintain teaching effectiveness.

8. All Reading Recovery teachers, staff developers, and university professors work with children daily. This ongoing teaching of children by personnel at all levels is the practice that is generally credited with maintaining the effectiveness of the training. Professors can relate instruction in the university classroom to a recent event rather than something from the distant past. This novel aspect of Reading Recovery deserves serious examination by other teacher trainers.

9. Program success is directly tied to student performance. And by implication, success as a Reading Recovery teacher is related to student outcomes. Teachers are accountable for the amount of progress in reading and writing made by children in the program.

10. Reading Recovery is cost-effective. Though Reading Recovery is a supplemental program it remains cost-effective because of its short-term nature. Comparable programs (e. g., Title I, special education) are much more expensive because they are typically long-term. Reading Recovery has been found to be both less expensive and more effective. Public school administrators still express concern about the expense of Reading Recovery. The best response is that the problem is a hard one and the solution will be just as hard. Educators have been searching in vain for cheap and easy answers for many years. A less expensive program that serves more children but has limited outcomes (or does not even attempt to measure outcomes) is no bargain.

11. Reading Recovery is a nonprofit program. Unlike a host of other programs offered to the public schools, Reading Recovery has no royalties, sells no materials, and makes no profits. The Reading Recovery name is trademarked only to protect the integrity of the program. This nonprofit status allows us to promote the program with impunity.

Those of us involved with Reading Recovery do so because its success with children has been continually demonstrated. Reading Recovery is a children-first-and-foremost view of the educational system. As such, the strength of its results with children, both short-term and long range, and its teacher professional development component provide avenues of much needed reform. To those truly interested in genuine school reform that provides access to good first teaching for all children, careful review and consideration of Reading Recovery is recommended.

References

Cazden, C. B. (1988). *Classroom discourse: The language of teaching and learning.* Portsmouth, NH: Heinemann.

Clay, M. M. (1979; 1985). *The early detection of reading difficulties.* Auckland, NZ: Heinemann.

Clay, M. M., & Cazden, C. B. (1990). A Vygotskian interpretation of Reading Recovery tutoring. In L. Moll (Ed.), *Vygotsky and education: Instructional implications and applications of sociohistorical psychology* (pp. 206-222). Cambridge, UK: Cambridge University Press.

Dyer, P. C. (1992). Reading Recovery: A cost-effectiveness and educational outcomes analysis. *Spectrum: Journal of Research in Education, 10*(1), 110-119.

Gregory, D., Earl, L., & O'Donoghue, M. (1993). A study of Reading Recovery in Scarborough: 1990-1992. *Annual Site Report of the Scarborough School District*. Ontario: Scarborough School District.

Kelly, P. E., Klein, A. F., & Pinnell, G. S. (1994). Reading Recovery: Teaching through conversation. In D. F. Lancy (Ed.), *Children's emergent literacy*. Westport, CT: Praeger.

National Diffusion Network. (1993). *1992-93 discontinuation data* (Research rep.). Columbus: Reading Recovery National Data Evaluation Center.

Pinnell, G. S. (1989). Reading Recovery: Helping at-risk children learn to read. *The Elementary School Journal, 90*(2), 159-181.

Pinnell, G. S., DeFord, D. E., & Lyons, C. A. (1988). *Reading Recovery: Early intervention for at-risk first graders*. Arlington, VA: Educational Research Service.

Pinnell, G. S., Lyons, C. A., DeFord, D. E., Bryk, A. S., & Seltzer, M. (1994). Comparing instructional models for the literacy education of high-risk first graders. *Reading Research Quarterly, 29*(1), 9-38.

Smith-Burke, M. T., Jaggar, A., & Ashdown, J. (1993). *New York University Reading Recovery project: 1992 follow-up study of second graders* (Research rep.). New York: New York University.

Swartz, S. L. (1992). *Cost comparison of selected intervention programs in California*. San Bernardino: California State University.

Swartz, S. L., Shook, R. E., & Hoffman, B. M. (1993). *Reading Recovery in California. 1992-93 site report*. San Bernardino: California State University.

AN INQUIRY-BASED MODEL
FOR EDUCATING TEACHERS OF LITERACY

GAY SU PINNELL
The Ohio State University

Knowledge is constructed by the individual who investigates his or her world. In the investigation of literacy, children discover many things for themselves. The evidence supporting self-discovery and constructive learning leaves teachers with important and practical questions. For example: What is my role as a teacher? What can I show and explain to the child without undermining independence? How do I support children's efforts to discover? Such questions are woven through daily teaching and are an element of daily learning on the part of teachers who hold a tentative theory of constructive learning.

Learning to teach has been described as the acquisition of a craft (Tom, 1984), an accumulation of generalizations derived from process-product research (Gage, 1985; Rosenshine & Furst, 1973), the learning of skills (Cruickshank & Metcalf, 1990), or acquiring a body of pedagogical knowledge (Shulman, 1987). Carter (1990) suggested that in addition to formal knowledge of content areas, teachers' knowledge includes information processing (the mental processes used to make decisions), practical knowledge (classroom situations and ways of addressing everyday problems), and pedagogical-content knowledge (ways of representing subject matter to students). Carter's analysis illustrated the complexity of learning to teach; different levels and types of knowledge are required.

Acknowledging the situational nature of teaching and the constructive nature of learning to teach raises dilemmas for teacher educators that parallel general questions about teaching children. What is the best way to assist teachers' learning? How much can be told, explained, transmitted, or demonstrated? What should teachers discover for themselves? Ultimately, a theory of teaching and learning must be reconstructed by every teacher. Duckworth (1986) suggested that the process of inquiry is a context within which the understandings related to teaching can be built. Reading Recovery, usually described as a tutoring program for children, also presents a unique preparation program that Alverman (1990) has described as inquiry oriented and that has been documented through research on student outcomes. This article draws together existing research on an inquiry-based teacher education model, Reading Recovery, and explores its implications for supporting teachers' work.

Background

To inquire is to ask questions or to investigate in search of truth. Inquiry can be applied to a scientist's systematically structured experiments or to exploring a nearby woods, because similar cognitive processes are usually involved (e. g., information gathering, analyzing, predicting, testing, reflecting, confirming, and interpreting). Often, inquirers talk over their hypotheses with others, using language communication to solidify ideas and generate new ones. Inherent in the process is learning. The inquirer who tests hypotheses and reflects on the results gains more than the accumulation of information and even more than learning the answer to a particular question. The act of investigation contributes to expansion and reformation of the original ideas; change in conceptual understandings—or learning—is the result.

Carter (1990) suggested that investigations go beyond what teachers learn to a consideration of what it means to learn to teach. It is evident that "teachers' knowledge is not highly abstract and propositional nor can it be formalized into a set of specific skills or preset answers to specific problems. Rather it is experiential, procedural, situational, and particularistic" (p. 307). Carter added that the teacher education process must provide opportunities for novices to practice problem-solving and develop new ways of thinking about problems.

Research in reading has focused on finding empirical links between student achievement and teacher actions. In a review of the literature, Tom and Valli (1990) pointed out the fallacies of formulating research-based rules for practice. These rules do not always apply within the complex environment of the classroom and do not provide teachers with the flexibility they need to make good judgments while teaching (Clark, 1988; Fenstermacher, 1982). Further, handing down rules dangerously oversimplifies the process of making teaching decisions and does not account for the on-the-spot decisions that teachers need to make. They proposed a view of craft knowledge, grounded in the wisdom of practice as a systematic way of knowing which methods of inquiry, rules of evidence, and forms of knowledge are inherent.

The National Council for Accreditation of Teacher Education (NCATE, 1987) recognized two kinds of knowledge: formal inquiry and theory-built knowledge based on connections to practice. These standards apply both to preservice and inservice teacher education. In this time of educational change, staff development for teachers has been considered by policymakers and administrators to be a key aspect of school reform. In a review of the research on staff development, Sparks and Loucks-Horsley (1990) identified five models: (1) individually guided staff development, in which teachers initiate and carry out their own learning activities; (2) observation/assessment, which involves teachers receiving feedback that can be reflected on and analyzed with the goal of improved student achievement; (3) development/improvement, acquisition of skill, or knowledge to address a particular problem or improve performance in a certain area; (4) training, workshops, or courses designed to impart effective teaching practices and help teachers change their behaviors; and (5) inquiry, which involves teachers in formulating questions about their practices and seeking answers to those questions.

Each approach, according to these authors, has its advantages. They cited evidence from research to support all five. The first approach recognized individual interests and motivations (Hering & Howey, 1982); the second has the advantage of specific observational data, transfer of skills to classroom practice, and ongoing support (Joyce & Showers, 1988). The development/improvement approach is often combined with training and has the advantage of offering specific ways to address problems or improve schooling. Advocates of the inquiry approach (Glatthorn, 1987; Glickman, 1986; Lieberman & Miller, 1986) said that research is an effective avenue through which teachers can develop new understandings. Like all researchers, as teachers formulate and seek answers to particular questions, other questions arise leading to a continual expansion of knowledge and applications to new settings and circumstances.

Sparks and Loucks-Horsley (1990) also suggested that while all models or combinations of approaches have potential for supporting teacher learning, they also all require a supportive organizational context to achieve success. Climate, leadership and support, policy adjustment, and participant involvement are all important factors. As staff development leads to change, the system must also change (Fullen, 1982). The evidence is compelling that organizational factors both affect and are affected by staff development processes, regardless of the model.

Although other models are gaining credibility and use, training is the most frequently used and researched model for staff development. The application of a single model, however, may not capture the complexity of human learning that exists among any group of teachers. Blended models that also give attention to organizational characteristics may have more promise for meeting the complex needs of education today, especially if staff development initiatives are measured not only by qualitative examination of teacher change but are linked to student change and learning.

Teacher Education in Reading Recovery

The key component and the delivery system for Reading Recovery is a staff development model that has some unusual features. The program for children is not a package of materials and step-by-step instructions for teachers. While the program involves teachers learning some specific procedures, these are considered to be a repertoire rather than a prescribed list of teacher actions (Clay, 1993b). Using the procedures means making decisions based on an analysis of the child's strengths and behavioral evidence of shifts in learning over time. Reading Recovery teachers see their own teaching as an opportunity to learn and extend that learning through observation and interaction with others.

The emphasis is on fast analysis; the live lesson goes by rapidly and cannot be retrieved. Teachers are required to concentrate and respond quickly during behind-the-glass sessions, an activity that sharpens their ability to observe and respond to children's behavior *on the run* while teaching. After the lesson there is time for reflection; the teachers work as a group to *get back to* critical moments in the two lessons observed. They reconstruct examples for each other and relate those examples to theoretical concepts they are building. They consult references, but essentially the process is one of social construction of knowledge. Occasionally, for a particular purpose, Reading Recovery teachers may view and analyze a videotaped lesson. However, nothing replaces the intensity of a live lesson.

In Reading Recovery teachers often say that they "learn to teach," but they could just as easily say that they "teach to learn." Each young student represents an individual investigation through which teachers learn as they follow the child's progress and make hypotheses about the nature of his or her learning. The teacher uses opportunities that arise from several sources:

- texts children encounter,
- their responses to those texts,
- the conversations in which they engage, and
- messages composed and written.

From those sources, teachers craft teachable moments; those powerful examples that will have the best chance of demonstrating processes to the child. A core concept is that each child constructs inner control of reading and writing processes by engaging in successful problem-solving while reading or writing extended texts. As they construct literacy, they connect it to their own lives.

Clay and Watson (1982), creators of the program in New Zealand, said, "The key word in the development and implementation of this inservice program was again observation and the unique feature was the potential for multilevel observation and learning that was embedded in the situation" (p. 192). They described an inservice session in which observing teachers were watching for evidence of the child's learning but were themselves being tutored by the leader. In this instance, the leader was being observed by a trainer who would later analyze the session. Thus, the situation represented layers of training. In one situation an observer could see individual guidance, observation/assessment, development/improvement, training, and inquiry.

Support System for Teacher Education

The model is implemented within a support system that is clearly specified from the beginning of implementation. The system includes the training and support of a teacher leader, the key staff developer in the program; the provision of a facility; university credit to support the course structure for teachers; and ongoing professional development for the initial training which takes an academic year, and subsequent years of participation for teachers. A site coordinator is appointed to provide administrative support for the program and to work with the teacher leader to solve problems related to program implementation.

Teacher leaders provide the initial class for teachers and continue to support trained teachers through individual visits and continuing contact sessions in subsequent years. Regional training sites at universities provide professional development for teachers and teacher leaders, including conferences and institutes. Program evaluation data is gathered to determine the progress of every child who participates in the program. These data also support program implementation by providing the information necessary to identify problems and enhance the quality of implementation.

First, teachers learn the observation procedures that they will use to identify children and assess their progress (Clay, 1993a). Then, they begin to learn a repertoire of procedures while simultaneously beginning to teach children. As they act, they reflect on their teaching in light of the observational data they are collecting daily from children. Learning is supported by the teacher leader through individual visits and coaching, but the key process is conversation among peers. Members of the teacher class take turns teaching an individual child behind a one-way glass screen while others in the group observe. They are guided by the teacher leader to state their observations and make inferences about the internal processing that behaviors might signal. This talking while observing process supports teachers' development of internal theories out of which instructional decisions are made.

The whole process takes time. At first, teachers may find the program overwhelming. They concentrate on the logistics of taking on and applying the procedures of teaching. As they participate in the experience and learn to drop their defenses with their peers, they begin to analyze not only children's behaviors but the teaching decisions and their potential impact on learning. After the observation, teachers gather for a reflective discussion with the demonstrating teachers.

These two components—talking while observing and the reflective discussion—make up the major part of the teacher education program. Each case example or demonstration presented gives every teacher a chance to reflect on his or her own teaching. This reflective/analytic experience helps teachers to construct and refine their theoretical explanations and to go beyond procedures. Through shared experiences, a culture is created in which teaching and learning are interwoven. Gaffney and Anderson (1991) provided a description of Reading Recovery as a two-tiered scaffolding model in which teaching and learning are congruent processes.

Research on the Effects of Reading Recovery Staff Development

A discussion of learning to teach in Reading Recovery must be foregrounded by talking about the nature of teaching. Lyons, Pinnell, and DeFord (1993) asserted that the training model as well as continuing contact among teachers are critical factors in assuring children's success. Reading Recovery emphasizes the role of the teacher as an informed, autonomous decision-maker who is responsible for creating a curriculum for each student. To provide opportunities for the development of independent readers and writers, the teacher must follow the student's thinking, recognize 'teachable moments,' and attend to the most memorable and powerful examples that will help learning to occur. The ability to understand and conceptualize learning and instruction at the cognitive and sociolinguistic levels takes reflection, practice, and time. Reflective opportunities, over time, with knowledgeable colleagues are inherent in the Reading Recovery training program and the system of support that surrounds teachers who participate. (Lyons, Pinnell, & DeFord, 1993)

The above statement is extended and illustrated by Elliott's (1994) study of one experienced Reading Recovery teacher who had a history of excellent results. For a period of one academic year Elliott followed this teacher's decision-making relative to two children. After each lesson the expert teacher engaged in stimulated recall to produce a think aloud protocol at regularly scheduled intervals throughout the year. Lessons were recorded by audiotape and videotape. The teacher's analysis of her decisions followed and were also recorded. Elliott described Reading Recovery teaching as a responsive process of which observation is the heart. She described the teacher as "looking for and noticing the *aha* and then acting on it" (p. 26). The process moves from observation to conscious awareness and transaction to decision-making to evaluation; but pedagogical reasoning underlies and permeates all elements. The teacher uses three knowledge sources: knowledge of child, pedagogical content knowledge, and knowledge of content in an integrated way during the reasoning process. Such descriptions are compelling evidence of the situational and dynamic nature of teaching in this individual setting, however, the complexity implies that learning to teach will be difficult.

Relationship to Student Outcomes

Evaluation of the effects of the program on students has been a priority in all implementations. A series of studies has documented the success of the Reading Recovery program for the young students served (Clay, 1990, 1993a; Kerslake, 1992; Pinnell, 1989; Lyons, Pinnell, & DeFord, 1993; HMSO Publications Centre, 1993). Program evaluation data from hundreds of implementation sites in five countries demonstrated the replicability of the positive outcomes for students. These studies, however, did not separate components of the program such as staff development, the teaching procedures, or the materials.

A statewide study (Pinnell, Lyons, DeFord, Bryk, & Seltzer, 1994) followed a group of children for one year and compared four treatments:

1. Reading Recovery, the traditional Reading Recovery with the yearlong staff development program and observation using the one-way glass screen;

2. Reading Success, an adaptation that collapsed training into two weeks with ongoing support from an expert;

3. Reading/Writing Group, a group adaptation using traditionally trained Reading Recovery teachers; and

4. Direct Instruction Skills Plan, a skills tutoring approach.

The two treatments of interest here are Reading Recovery and Reading Success. Both treatments provided one-to-one tutoring using the same framework; however the training for teachers differed considerably, with inquiry components missing for the Reading Success teachers. Results of the study showed that the results of Reading Recovery were superior to all other treatments and that, in fact, the second most effective treatment was Reading/Writing Group, with traditionally trained Reading Recovery teachers. Quality of training emerged as the most powerful component related to student success. Results suggested that the yearlong training program with its unique features is highly related to student success and to the way teachers organize and conduct lessons.

Impact on Teachers as They Learn to Teach

Early in the United States' implementation, a yearlong qualitative study of one group of teachers revealed continuous shifts in their focus of attention throughout the training period (Pinnell & Woolsey, 1985). For a full year, the researchers transcribed informal discussions that occurred after the teacher class. An analysis of the oral language transcript revealed that at the beginning of their training, teachers tended to focus on the mechanics of teaching. They wanted to be told how to do it, how to use the procedures, and how to organize and use materials. They wanted the right answers from their trainers and were dissatisfied when specific answers were not forthcoming.

Gradually, the focus of descriptions shifted to descriptions and interpretations of children's behavior. They told stories about their teaching and members of the group got to know each other's students. They asked about children as individuals and followed their progress. As teachers gained teaching experience and participated in behind-the-glass sessions, they began to link their case-by-case knowledge into broader generalizations. This process took a long time; theoretical statements were not evident until near the end of the training year. Informal conversations with members of that teacher class indicated that even during a year's training, the learning was at a somewhat superficial level. Four years later, one member said:

> Looking back, it almost seems as though I knew so little that first year. I was learning a
> lot, but now we are going so much deeper into the processes. There are new

understandings. I see much more when I observe behind-the-glass and participate in the discussion following the observation session. I think my teaching is getting better because I am noticing new things and understanding the reading process at a different level. (Personal interview with Ann James, 1992)

Geeke (1988) interviewed teachers while they participated in their first year of training. Geeke described the culture created in the Reading Recovery teacher class:

The interview data show that most of the participating teachers had their existing beliefs shaken during the early inservice sessions. They were quickly persuaded that their current methods of teaching reading and writing were based on false assumptions about teaching and learning. Subsequently, on the basis of their observations of children and their experiences during the inservice sessions, they developed new beliefs about teaching and learning. This set of beliefs then acted as a framework into which the specific teaching practices of Reading Recovery could be placed . . . the teaching procedures were not given to the teachers as a set of 'ideas' for teaching literacy. Instead, the teachers were expected to use the procedures in a way that reflected the set of basic beliefs which were being developed at the same time. The ultimate aim of the training program seems to have been the development of a dynamic relationship between belief and practice, with belief acting as an individualizing influence on instruction. (p. 144)

. . . it seems that real teacher change is unlikely to be achieved by simply introducing a 'new method of instruction' in some curriculum area. The new 'method' will only be really effective if teachers have thoroughly accepted the underlying principles of the program as well as its teaching practices. The techniques employed by Reading Recovery to achieve this result deserve close examination, especially as it appears to have been much more successful than usual in achieving teacher change in the group immediately involved. (p. 145)

Geeke (1988) also found that the inservice course had a profound impact on teachers' views. Like the U. S. teachers, Australian Reading Recovery teachers expressed discomfort with the intensity and demands of the inservice program, particularly the behind-the-glass experience; yet, they indicated that they strongly valued the experiences and the learning that occurred. Geeke identified six beliefs that teachers said they had developed from their involvement in Reading Recovery:

1. Effective learning depends on the child assuming responsibility for learning.
2. Effective learning is built on the child's current knowledge and skills, and depends on the child understanding what is expected of him or her.
3. Effective learning leads to an awareness of one's mental processes, self-monitoring of the cognitive strategies being employed, and the development of a self-correcting system.
4. Effective teaching depends on accurate observation and sensitive response, within a framework of coherent beliefs and effective practice.
5. Effective teaching depends on the quality of interaction with the child. In particular, it depends on astute questioning which shows the child how to solve his own learning problems.
6. Effective teaching depends on the teacher's understanding of the learning process, checked against the actuality of children's observable learning behaviors. Only if the teacher really knows how children learn will he or she be able to adapt teaching methods appropriately in response to the children's demonstrated needs. (p. 145)

Power and Sawkins (1991) described a first year implementation in another geographic area. The study affirmed the impact of the program as well as its intensity. Logistic concerns such as teaching loads and scheduling arose in teacher interviews. Teachers also expressed some frustration with the high expectations for independence. Here are two illustrative quotations from teacher interviews (Power & Sawkins):

I don't know about anyone else . . . . I wish that I'd had a lot more answers or a lot more direction . . . . If I was doing something wrong to be just told straight out "look you did this, this was wrong, try this way." (p. 91)

We were never given an answer you know. She used to say, 'there are no answers in

Reading Recovery.' There are no answers. You were fed to the lions. You had to find it out for yourself. And that's what we did. We sat amongst ourselves and sussed it out for ourselves. But she put in all the information. The input was fantastic . . . . But she wouldn't feed it back so we simply had to find an answer. It was like being locked in. Until you found the key you couldn't get out. (p. 89)

In the same study, the tutor (teacher leader) commented:

In a couple of instances I guess they would like me to answer their questions straight out rather than saying, 'Well, where could you go to find out about it?' 'What do you think?' 'Right . . . now what do you think about it?'. . . . And again these teachers have got to be thinking teachers. They've got to work through these things in their mind and I'm not always going to be beside them so it's that independence again. They have to know how to go about solving their own problems. (p. 90)

Power and Sawkins' results indicated that the group of teachers found the inservice sessions "intense," "exhausting," and "stressful," but they were positive about the amount of learning they were experiencing and the results that were showing for the children.

Pinnell, Lyons, DeFord, Bryk, and Seltzer's (1994), Geeke's (1988), and Power and Sawkins' (1991) studies focused on a first group of teachers in a country or region. Two other studies, also of first year training classes, examined language used by participants. Wilson (1988) studied the use of language in behind-the-glass and discussion sessions. Her results indicated that over the course of the year, teachers interacted more and were more likely to challenge each others' assertions. They also grew in their ability to describe specific behavior as evidence. She summarized her results as follows (Wilson, 1988):

This study showed that as teachers are involved over time (1) in the articulation and interpretation of their observations of children and children's learning, and (2) in the integration of new perspectives into pedagogy, they do change in their ways of using language to describe these phenomena. These changes were in a positive direction, indicating a more supportive view of children, a less restrictive view of the reading process and reading instruction, and a higher percentage of high quality utterances with regard to emergent reading. (p. 160)

Rentel and Pinnell (1987) examined teacher participants' language in the discussion following the observation. They recorded discussions at two different points in time, one near the beginning of the training and one several months later. They categorized the language into claims or statements and then assessed the degree to which claims were grounded in evidence or supported by research. Results of this study indicated that from the first to the second observation, teacher participants produced significantly more grounded statements, indicating growth in the ability to support their statements with behavioral evidence.

Lyons (1992) studied six Reading Recovery teachers-in-training. The teachers collected and analyzed observation notes of student behavior, running records of oral reading, and writing samples to determine shifts in student learning. The teachers also used journals to record personal reflections about the effects of their teaching decisions on student learning, and they tape-recorded, analyzed, and evaluated their interactions (verbal and nonverbal) with students throughout the inservice course. The teachers and the researcher met weekly to analyze and evaluate the consequences of their instruction. Lyons' analysis of the audiotaped lessons and of teachers' personal reactions as documented in journals and conversations with colleagues suggested that as teachers became more sensitive to emerging behaviors signalling student change, they began to tailor their own behaviors to meet the students' developing abilities. The study suggested five general principles of learning and teaching (Lyons, 1992):

1. Assisted performance by an expert helps individuals—both students and teachers—expand and reorganize their understandings.

2. The language that surrounds events within a Reading Recovery lesson mediates performance and creates systems of change.

3. Conversation has an important role in teachers' learning; ongoing discussions provide a scaffold for the growth of understandings and a way to mediate performance by providing

bridges between what the teacher already knows and what he or she needs to know to effectively teach.

4. The major shifts in teacher theory development are given impetus by learning the Reading Recovery teaching procedures and are greatly influenced by the inservice course. Lyons (1992) concluded that her study provided evidence that "learning is socially constructed, not only for children, but for adults as well" (p. 13).

The previous studies offer evidence that the initial training results in teacher change. As they are challenged to make their implicit ideas explicit, to examine them and to link them to practice, their theories typically shift. Program evaluation data, collected over the years on training classes, suggest a tendency for teachers to move from a skills orientation toward a more holistic view of literacy learning (The Ohio State University, 1993). More research is needed that follows teachers for longer periods of time, going beyond the initial training. It is possible that once the intensity of the training year wanes, teachers will find it difficult to sustain ongoing development of their understandings and concepts, learning will diminish, and old models that are pervasive in the school system may prevail. Little research has documented the role of continuing contact as it exists in the Reading Recovery network.

Only one study has followed teacher learning over several years. Lyons (1993) described one Reading Recovery teacher's developing knowledge of how to effectively teach beginning reading and explored the effects of this developing knowledge on the teacher's ability to plan and conceptualize teaching. Her observations, analyses of videotapes, and interviews over a three year period suggested that the teacher continued to grow over time in her understanding of how to prompt and ask questions that enabled a student to construct learning. Her approach to instruction became more skillful and complex throughout the investigation period. Lyons identified Phase 1 as trying out the prompts and questions suggested by Reading Recovery training, Phase 2 as using prompts and questions to test her hypotheses about the child's behavior and then to support the student's problem-solving, and Phase 3 as prompting and questioning in response to students' behaviors. The teacher moved from the first phase, in which by her own account she was "parroting questions according to the book" to the third phase when she demonstrated her ability to respond to unexpected answers, to reframe the situation, and to step out of her original perspective in order to recognize the student's perspective. Research is needed on larger numbers of teachers to define patterns and individual paths of growth and change. There is evidence that with system support and an inquiry approach, learning is continuous across time and at every level, as illustrated by this statement from a university professor. In an address to a group of teachers, DeFord (1991) talked about the continual learning process:

> When I first read, or attempted to read Clay's book, *The Patterning of Complex Behavior* (1979), I was immediately put off by the cognitive psychologist language and terms like *confusion*. Consequently, in 1980, I put this book away on my shelf. In 1985, I was asked to observe a Reading Recovery lesson at Ohio State University. I was fascinated as I observed the half-hour lesson, and by turns, brought up short by things I *didn't like*. I could see the child in front of me had made startling gains in both reading and writing, was happy, excited about books, and engaged in learning new things. When his teacher talked about his early reading and writing a different picture emerged, a child who was passive in new learning settings and who, the classroom teacher felt, would fail first grade. My curiosity overcame my initial discomfort with aspects of the program, and I became actively involved in learning about Reading Recovery. At first, the practices I agreed with were easy, and I tried to find ways around using the practices I disagreed with. But during the six years I have been teaching children in Reading Recovery, I have put my disagreements on hold to try to see the sense of particular practices with some children. Daily, I am forced to reconsider my beliefs in light of what I see children and teachers doing, but I have also continued to fill out my beliefs about early literacy learning. I had to take off my 'theoretical high heels,' so to speak, and replace them with walking shoes that are now quite comfortable. (p. 3)

An open-ended survey of 205 Reading Recovery teacher leaders revealed their perspectives on their own training and their role as teacher leaders (Pinnell, Lyons, Constable, & Jennings, 1994). The value of talk with colleagues emerged as a major factor in their learning. During the first year of training, they reported that reflection, dialogue, and the opportunity to articulate new understandings increased learning. The support of colleagues was valued by teacher leaders, especially after the training year. For these leaders, learning to teach is facilitated through talk with others who share their mission and vision.

The Potential of an Inquiry-Oriented System for Staff Development

Describing the opportunities for making implicit theories explicit both in the behind-the-glass talk and during individual school visits by a teacher leader, Alverman (1990) characterized Reading Recovery training as an inquiry-oriented model for teacher education. Inquiry-oriented is an apt description because all components of the staff development model involve teachers in searching and reflection. New Zealand teachers call this process sifting and sorting, referring to the sessions in which they work together to reflect on teaching, describe student behavior, and search for explanations and possible teacher responses. Teachers expect to engage in these sessions throughout their tenure in the program. Sifting and sorting implies that teachers hold a tentative theory; one that is incomplete. Their understandings are always under construction. A tentative stance and ongoing investigation are made possible through the strong content of the Reading Recovery lesson, the built-in research and evaluation, and the strong group support, all components that could be implemented in staff development or teacher education programs.

Records

Investigation takes place at every level of the Reading Recovery program. Data are systematically collected on scan sheets and reported by site and by state. But the investigation that pays off in teacher learning is undertaken by individuals. Teachers keep detailed records of students' progress which they use for analysis as they go. Anecdotal lesson records and running records of text reading are recorded daily and these documents provide a way for teachers to reflect on and analyze children's progress. The lesson notes include not only children's responses but teachers' prompts and questions so that the interaction between the two can be examined.

Running records provide another source of data for teacher investigation. It takes only a few minutes to record the child's reading behavior on a text that has been introduced and read once before. Over several days and weeks, the running records provide information to trace shifts in the student's processing; information that teachers find valuable in their decision-making with regard to individual students. Teachers also consolidate data on individual children in graphs and charts that help them become aware of progress. These records provide a visual profile of individual readers that feeds decision-making while teaching. To Reading Recovery teachers, knowledge of the child must be constantly updated and constantly available.

Dialogue with Colleagues

Analytic and reflective processes are supported by the weekly meetings of the initial training course and in subsequent years by the continuing contact sessions. In behind-the-glass sessions, teachers are freed from teaching. They have the opportunity to become observers, picking up details of behavior and quickly analyzing and interpreting it as they go. Teachers are encouraged to advance hypotheses as the lesson proceeds and to quickly gather evidence to confirm or disconfirm their assumptions and predictions. They have learned a language to talk together in the construction of knowledge.

The Role of Curiosity

Duckworth (1986) has identified two aspects to teaching:
> The first is to put students into contact with phenomena related to the area to be studied—the real thing not books or lectures about it—and to help them notice what is interesting; to engage them so they will continue to think and wonder about it. The second is to have the students try to explain the sense they are making and, instead of explaining things to students, to try to understand their sense. These two aspects are, of course interdependent: when people are engaged in the matter they try to explain it and in order to explain it they seek out more phenomena that will shed light on it. (p. 261-262)

Duckworth's comments illustrate a basic concept underlying teaching in Reading Recovery—teachers are curious about their students' learning. They are always trying to figure out what children are thinking about, how they see things, how they interpret teachers' comments and directions, and what is going on in their heads.

Support From the Teacher Leader

Analysis and reflection are supported in the one-to-one visits a teacher leader makes to both trained and in-training teachers. As teachers become more experienced they begin to assist each other through colleague visits. The interaction is different from the clinical supervision model described in the literature. Teacher leaders and teachers engage in analysis of the lesson viewed and investigate alternative explanations for student behavior and teacher response. Coaching is used and may be quite helpful especially when teachers are beginning their training; but visits primarily function to support the teacher's own thinking.

Although individual teachers engage in inquiry, the process and the learning that accompanies it is supported by the social group. Teachers depend heavily on interaction with their training class to extend their conceptual understandings. Each teacher is expected to contribute to the learning of others in the group and can, in turn, expect to receive assistance. Teacher leaders work to help the group ask questions of each other, challenge, and form chains of reasoning. Learning how to teach reading is a complex and demanding process, but it is made less so when the learning is shared.

Summary and Implications for Teacher Education

The Reading Recovery model provides: (a) an activity structure that builds strong content knowledge, (b) observation of phenomena important to participants and which they encounter daily in their work, (c) guidance from an expert, (d) daily work of an investigative nature, (e) careful records to guide investigation, (f) case examples for the group to consider, (g) a group of professional colleagues who work together over time, and (h) recognition of the central role of language in learning. Teachers who are at the same time learners construct a language to talk with each other about their work and to create a learning community. These characteristics of Reading Recovery could be the foundation of new models for educating and nurturing our nation's teachers.

References

Alverman, D. E. (1990). Reading teacher education. In W. R. Houston, M. Haberman, & J. Sikula (Eds.), *Handbook of research on teacher education: A project of the Association of Teacher Educators.* New York: Macmillan.

Carter, K. (1990). Teachers knowledge and learning to teach. In W. R. Houston, M. Haberman, & J. Sikula (Eds.), *Handbook of research on teacher education: A project of the Association of Teacher Educators.* New York: Macmillan.

Clark, C. M. (1988). Asking the right questions about teacher preparation: Contributions of research on teacher thinking. *Educational Researcher, 17*(2), 5-12.

Clay, M. M. (1979). *Reading: The patterning of complex behavior.* Auckland, NZ: Heinemann.

Clay, M. M. (1990). The Reading Recovery programme, 1984-88: Coverage, outcomes and education board district figures. *New Zealand Journal of Educational Studies, 25,* 61-70.

Clay, M. M. (1993a). *An observation survey of early literacy achievement.* Portsmouth, NH: Heinemann.

Clay, M. M. (1993b). *Reading Recovery: A guidebook for teachers in training.* Auckland, NZ: Heinemann.

Clay, M. M., & Watson, B. (1982). An inservice program for Reading Recovery teachers. In M. M. Clay (Ed.), *Observing young readers: Selected papers.* Exeter, NH: Heinemann.

Cruickshank, D. R., & Metcalf, K. K. (1990). Training within teacher preparation. In W. R. Houston, M. Haberman, & J. Sikula (Eds.), *Handbook of research on teacher education: A project of the Association of Teacher Educators.* New York: Macmillan.

DeFord, D. E. (1991. Fall). Reading Recovery teachers as lifelong learners. *The Running Record, 8*(1), 3.

Duckworth, E. (1986). Teaching as research. *Harvard Educational Review, 56,* 481-495.

Elliott, C. (1994). *Pedagogical reasoning: Understanding teacher decision-making in the cognitive apprenticeship setting.* Unpublished doctoral dissertation, Texas Woman's University, Denton.

Fenstermacher, G. D. (1982). On learning to teach effectively from research on teacher effectiveness. *Journal of Classroom Interaction, 17*(2). Reprinted from C. Denham & A. Liebermann (Eds.) (1980). *Time to learn* (pp. 147-168). Sacramento: California Commission for Teacher Education and Licensing.

Fullen, M. (1982). *The meaning of educational change.* Toronto: OISE Press.

Gage, N. (1985). *Hard gains in the soft sciences: The case of pedagogy.* Bloomington, IN: Phi Delta Kappa.

Gaffney, J. S., & Anderson, R. C. (1991). Two-tiered scaffolding: Congruent processes of teaching and learning. In E. H. Hiebert (Ed.), *Literacy for a diverse society: Perspectives, programs, and policy.* New York: Teachers College Press.

Geeke, P. (1988). *Evaluation report on the Reading Recovery field trial in Central Victoria, 1984.* Australia: Centre for Studies in Literacy, University of Wollongong.

Glatthorn, A. (1987). Cooperative professional development: Peer-centered options for teacher growth. *Educational Leadership, 45*(3), 31-35.

Glickman, C. (1986). Developing teacher thought. *Journal of Staff Development, 7*(1), 6-21.

Hering, W., & Howey, K. (1982). *Research in, on, and by teachers' centers* (Occasional Paper No. 10). San Francisco: Teachers' Center Exchange, Far West Laboratory for Educational Research and Development.

HMSO Publications Centre. (1993). *Reading Recovery in New Zealand: A report from the office of Her Majesty's Chief Inspector of Schools.* London: Author.

Joyce, B., & Showers, B. (1988). *Student achievement through staff development.* New York: Longman.

Kerslake, J. (1992). *A summary of the 1991 data on Reading Recovery, Research and Statistics Division Bulletin* (No. 5). Ministry of Education, Wellington, New Zealand.

Lieberman, A., & Miller, L. (1986). School improvement: Themes and variations. In A. Lieberman (Ed.), *Rethinking school improvement: Research, craft, and concept.* New York: Teachers College Press.

Lyons, C. A. (1992). *Reading Recovery teachers learning to teach effectively through following.* Paper presented at the meeting of the National Reading Conference, San Antonio, TX.

Lyons, C. A. (1993). The use of questions in the teaching of high risk beginning readers: A profile of a developing Reading Recovery teacher. *Reading and Writing Quarterly, 9,* 317-327.

Lyons, C. A., Pinnell, G. S., & DeFord, D. E. (1993). *Partners in learning: Teachers and children in Reading Recovery.* New York: Teachers College Press.

National Council for Accreditation of Teacher Education. (1987). *NCATE standards, procedures, and policies for the accreditation of professional education units: The accreditation of professional education units for the preparation of professional school personnel at basic and advanced levels.* Washington, DC: Author.

The Ohio State University. (1993). *The executive summary: 1984 to 1993, Reading Recovery.* Columbus: Author. (Available from Reading Recovery program, The Ohio State University, Ramseyer 200 — 29 W. Woodruff, Columbus, OH 43210.)

Pinnell, G. S. (1989). Reading Recovery: Helping at-risk children learn to read. *The Elementary School Journal, 90*(2), 159-181.

Pinnell, G. S., Lyons, C. A., Constable, S., & Jennings, J. (1994). *The voices of literacy leaders: A survey of Reading Recovery teacher leaders.* Presentation to the National Reading Recovery Teacher Leader Institute, Columbus, OH.

Pinnell, G. S., Lyons, C. A., DeFord, D. E., Bryk, A., & Seltzer, M. (1994). Comparing instructional models for the literacy education of high-risk first graders. *Reading Research Quarterly, 29,* 9-39.

Pinnell, G. S., & Woolsey, D. (1985). *Report of a study of teacher researchers in a program to prevent reading failure* (Report to the Research Foundation of the National Council of Teachers of English). Urbana, IL: NCTE Press.

Power, J., & Sawkins, S. (1991). *Changing lives: Report of the implementation of the Reading Recovery program on the North Coast, NSW.* Northern Rivers: University of New England.

Rentel, V. M., & Pinnell, G. S. (1987). *A study of practical reasoning in Reading Recovery instruction.* Paper presented at the meeting of the National Reading Conference, St. Petersburg Beach, FL.

Rosenshine, B., & Furst, N. (1973). The use of direct observation to study teaching. In R. M. W. Travers (Ed.), *Second handbook of research on teaching.* Chicago: Rand McNally.

Shulman, L. (1987). Knowledge and teaching: Foundations of the new reform. *Harvard Educational Review, 57*(1), 1-21.

Sparks, D., & Loucks-Horsley, S. (1990). Models of staff development. In W. R. Houston, M. Haberman, & J. Sikula (Eds.), *Handbook of research on teacher education: A project of the Association of Teacher Educators.* New York: Macmillan.

Tom, A. R. (1984). *Teaching as an oral craft.* New York: Longman.

Tom, A. R., & Valli, L. (1990). Professional knowledge for teachers. In W. R. Houston, M. Haberman, & J. Sikula, (Eds.), *Handbook of research on teacher education: A project of the Association of Teacher Educators.* New York: Macmillan.

Wilson, V. (1988). *A study of teacher development in an interactive inservice setting.* Unpublished doctoral dissertation, The Ohio State University, Columbus.

SUSTAINED EFFECTS
OF READING RECOVERY INTERVENTION
ON THE COGNITIVE BEHAVIORS
OF SECOND GRADE CHILDREN
AND THE PERCEPTIONS
OF THEIR TEACHERS

BILLIE J. ASKEW and DIANNE F. FRASIER
Texas Woman's University

Reading Recovery (Clay, 1982, 1991, 1993b) is an early intervention program beginning with first grade children. The children identified as the lowest in the first grade cohort work one-on-one with a specially trained teacher for an intensive 30 minutes daily for approximately 12 to 20 weeks. As the child reads and writes whole text, the teacher responds in ways that support the development of a self-extending system. The ultimate goal is to enable these children to use reading and writing strategies effectively and independently so that they can function successfully in an average reading setting within the regular classroom. Sustained effects of the program should provide some evidence that the child has gained inner control of the strategic processes needed for an independent system that extends itself every time the child reads (Clay, 1991).

Evidence indicates that Reading Recovery has positive outcomes for first grade children already failing to progress at the same rate as their average classmates (Clay, 1982, 1990, 1993b; DeFord, Lyons, & Pinnell, 1991; Lyons, Pinnell, & DeFord, 1993; Pinnell, Lyons, DeFord, Bryk, & Seltzer, 1994). Each Reading Recovery site in the United States maintains local data collection procedures and prepares an annual report of program results. These data also feed into a national data bank at The Ohio State University to be aggregated across a growing, diverse population. There is also evidence of sustained gains in the extensive follow-up studies in New Zealand (Clay, 1993b) as well as the Columbus Project in Ohio (DeFord, Pinnell, Lyons, & Place, 1990; Lyons, Pinnell, & DeFord, 1993). Many individual sites have designed their own follow-up studies to explore the longitudinal benefits of this early intervention.

The general purpose of this study was to examine the sustained effects of the Reading Recovery intervention on second grade children who successfully completed the program by meeting established criteria (called discontinuing). First, they were observed while performing on literacy tasks a year or more following the intervention. Beyond the scores on these literacy tasks, evidence of the comprehending behaviors of the children as they read contributed to an understanding of their cognitive processes. Finally, the perceptions of classroom teachers about the literacy behaviors and school performance offered insights about program effects across time.

The following questions guided the study:

1. How do scores on three literacy tasks (text reading, dictation, and spelling) of second grade children who were successfully discontinued from Reading Recovery compare with scores of their second grade peers one year or more after the termination of the intervention?

2. In what ways are oral reading behaviors on text similar and different for the two groups?

3. Are there differences between the two groups (former Reading Recovery children and second grade peers) on measures of story retellings?

4.   Are there differences between the two groups on measures of fluent reading during oral reading of text?

5.   Are there differences in the ways these groups are perceived by second grade classroom teachers?

A consistently high percentage of the children who have an opportunity for a full program are successfully discontinued from the program into an average classroom setting annually, with the average percent discontinued ranging from 83 percent to 87 percent nationally (Lyons, Pinnell, & DeFord, 1993). Only discontinued children who met Reading Recovery criteria for successfully returning to an average classroom setting during the first grade year were included in this sample.

If a goal of Reading Recovery is to bring children up to average classroom achievement, an important question must be considered. What does it mean to bring them up to average and how does this affect the classroom teacher's perception of the range of reading behaviors among her students? Are the literacy behaviors of former Reading Recovery children expected to match those of children who required no intervention? These children began their first grade year with the lowest literacy profiles in their classrooms. Therefore, the notion of accelerated progress resulting in successful performance within an average classroom setting calls for an exploration of this phenomenon relative to children's performance and teachers' perceptions.

Exploring Comprehending Behaviors

Reading Recovery teachers are frequently questioned about the role of comprehension in the program. Rather than addressing comprehension as a separate process, Reading Recovery developer Marie Clay (1991) assumed that comprehension is an inherent focus in a meaning-based program. A person taking running records of text reading is observing for behavioral evidence of the reader's understanding. Evidence of the comprehending process in Reading Recovery has been examined in both theoretical and research settings (Askew, 1991, 1993).

Goodman (1985) argued that a distinction exists between comprehension as a product and comprehending as a process. He suggested that comprehending is a constructive process in which readers make sense of the text. It goes on during reading and long afterward as readers reconsider and reconstruct what was comprehended:

> The relationships between comprehending and comprehension are not simple and isomorphic. What one knows after reading is the product of what one knew beforehand plus how well one read the text. So, effective comprehending is essential to effective comprehension, but not sufficient. Correlations between measures of the two . . . are moderate and significant, but not high. (p. 831-832)

Tierney (1990) suggested that four major developments since the 1970s have contributed to an expanded conception of comprehension. First is that reading involves constructive processes, with a view of meaning-making tied to key postulates: (a) the desire of readers to make sense drives comprehension processes, (b) understandings are essentially inferential, (c) background knowledge connects with expectations to develop meanings, and (d) interpretation and comprehension are both idiosyncratic and stylized. Tierney cited other developments contributing to a new view of comprehending: reading as writing, reading as engagement, and reading as situation-based. Clay (1991) also suggested that reading and writing acquisition involves the active construction of a network of strategies, with comprehending having a central role.

In the study reported here, comprehending was examined as evidence of a process of constructing meaning from text. Views of assessing meaning-making with young subjects vary in the literature. Three indicators assumed to show evidence of the comprehending process are explored here: processing behaviors during the reading of continuous text, retelling behaviors, and fluency behaviors.

Analysis of Oral Reading

Analysis of oral reading errors has been explored relative to the notion of reading comprehension. Although Leu (1985) cautioned against using oral reading to estimate the kind of linguistic processing going on inside the head of a reader, there is evidence that with young children the analysis of oral reading can be quite informative (Johnston, 1992).

Goodman (1985) contended that evaluation of reading has generally focused on comprehension as a product measured by a post reading test of knowledge. Typical formats include explicit text-based questions, general questions, open-ended retellings following reading, and a combination of these. Since these follow the reading, they are limited by what the reader is willing and able to report as well as what has been comprehended. Comprehension may be changed in the course of testing on the basis of questions which invite particular responses and views.

Miscue analysis is a means of examining comprehending as it takes place during reading (Goodman, 1985). Goodman contended that readers utilize three information systems in comprehending: the graphophonic system, the syntactic system, and the semantic system. Oral reading miscues are examined. "The extent to which miscues result in meaningful text or are self-corrected if they disrupt meaning gives strong indications of the reader's concern for and ability to make sense of the text" (p. 831).

As a tool for observing young readers' oral reading behaviors, Clay (1993a) developed the running record of text reading described in her book, *An Observation Survey of Early Literacy Achievement*. When a child is reading out loud, the recorder simply takes a blank sheet of paper and records the child's reading behaviors in a controlled and systematic way. Advantages of the running record include its flexibility for use at any time and on any book as well as its lack of relationship to a testing setting (Johnston, 1992). Analysis of oral reading errors provides insight into whether children are using sources of information flexibly and strategically.

When examining oral reading errors, the recorder can find consistencies in information about how the child gathers up the cues—from the structure of the sentence, the meaning of the message, the visual cues of the letters, or letter order. The recorder can infer from the kinds of errors and self-corrections that children make, along with their comments during the reading, much of what they are attending to and understanding (Clay, 1993a).

Retellings

Behaviors called upon in retelling events offer evidence about the child as a meaning-maker. Irwin and Mitchell (1983) argued that retellings indicate not only what readers recall from the text, but what they view as important as well as how they organize what they recall. Retellings may provide insights into the product and the process, yielding information about what is comprehended as well as the processes used in comprehending. Mitchell (1988a) suggested that retellings reveal other things about a child's comprehension: sensitivity to text genre, awareness of author's organizing strategies, language fluency, ability to organize retellings in a coherent fashion, ability to identify the important aspects of the material read, and evidence of miscomprehension.

Johnston (1992) outlined limitations frequently cited for using retellings as an assessment of comprehending behaviors. First, he challenged the typical audience for the retelling. It is an unusual social situation in which a child has to retell a shared story to the person who just heard or read it. He suggested that there are ways to make retellings more socially appropriate: retelling to a teacher who has not read the story and who may question the reader, storytelling, dramatization using props or representations, and a variety of additional options and combinations of options. Johnson further argued that some children may be shy in a performance situation. Although he reported studies that indicated that more able readers tend to give more retelling responses than less able readers, Johnson suggested that the able readers are more likely to recognize and fit into a testing situation while the less able readers tend to give a shorter but more socially appropriate response.

Garcia and Pearson (1991) called for contextualized retellings that include all children, inviting them to respond in comfortable and familiar ways. They also suggested that bilingual children may need to present their retellings in their first language.

Fluency

Although the term fluency is widely used in the literature, it is difficult to find precise definitions of it. Common usage ranges from an emphasis on the mechanical aspects of rapid reading to an emphasis on the connections between fluency and the expressions of thought (Hoffman & Isaacs, 1991).

Slayter and Allington (1991) argued that discussions of dysfluency too often focus on slow or deficient decoding or word recognition abilities. They contended that even in initial stages of acquisition, oral reading fluency is more directly linked to text comprehension processes than to word recognition.

"Nothing destroys the meaning more rapidly than droning through the phrases and punctuation marks, pausing at points which break up the syntactic groups and the sense" (Clay, 1991). Clay and Imlach (1971) studied pause and stress behaviors of children at a grade placement comparable to second grade in the United States. They found that good readers were operating at the sentence and phrase level, moving to the word level when necessary. They appeared to gain speed and understanding from anticipating whole stretches of text and checking their predictions visually. Low progress readers, however, seemed unable to use cues beyond the syllable and word level and were overcommitted to the notion that reading was recognizing or sounding out words.

Based on Clay's work, DeFord (1991) suggested that flexibility in using all information sources when reading is the goal of fluency instruction, not just increased pacing of text reading. If fluent reading is influenced by a reader's facility and flexibility in monitoring and searching actively for sources of information, in checking one source of information against another, and in solving problems, then it seems that the study of fluent reading behaviors should provide some evidence of comprehending behaviors while reading text (Clay, 1993b):

> Fluent reading in young, beginning readers has been associated with the process of comprehending or meaning-making. When the reading is phrased like spoken language and the responding is fluent (and some people say fast), then there is a fair chance that the reader can read for meaning, check what he reads against his language knowledge, and his attention can go mainly to the messages. (p. 51)

Clay (1993b), however, cautioned that two essential kinds of learning must be balanced: successful reading of familiar material which strengthens the decision-making processes, and independent problem-solving on new and interesting text with supportive teaching.

The relationship between fluent oral reading and comprehending is a tenuous one. Dowhower (1991) compared the relationship to the chicken-and-the-egg dilemma. She argued that it is not possible to know which comes first or if one is necessarily an indicator of the other. It does, however, appear that comprehension and fluent reading are linked, but it is unclear how they are related.

Pilot Study

A comprehensive pilot study was conducted to explore ways of comparing former Reading Recovery children who had successfully discontinued from the program in grade one with their second grade peers on a variety of measures: literacy tasks, retelling tasks, fluent reading measures, and perceptions of second grade teachers. At the end of their second grade year, 50 discontinued Reading Recovery children were randomly selected from the total list of discontinued children in three sites. A random group of 50 children was also selected from all regular first grade classrooms in Reading Recovery schools in the same three sites. Children in both groups were selected from the total eligible population using a table of random numbers. Any children formerly served in Reading Recovery were ineligible for membership in the random group, making comparisons more rigorous for the Reading Recovery group. In both groups the numbers of males and females were similar and ethnic representation included Anglo, African American, Hispanic, and Asian.

Tasks and Procedures

Literacy performance was assessed using measures of oral reading of text, dictation, and spelling. The Reading Recovery test packet, used nationally for program data collection, was used as the test of text reading. The packet comprises a series of selections that have been leveled according to gradients of difficulty. Books and selections have been tested for levels of difficulty across large numbers of children through the Reading Recovery project at The Ohio State University. (See Table 1 for an explanation of text reading levels.) Running records (Clay, 1993a) were used to determine book level scores and to document oral reading behaviors.

The dictation task, developed by DeFord (DeFord, Pinnell, Lyons, & Place, 1990), consisted of a two sentence passage that was read to the child first as whole text and then reread as needed for the child to write each word. The child was reminded to say each word slowly and

Table 1
Correspondence Between Text Reading Levels and Traditional Grade-Level Designations

Text Reading Level	Grade Level Designation[a]
1-4	R
5-8	Preprimer
9-12	Primer
14-16	First Reader
18-20	Second Reader
22-24	Third Reader
26	Fourth Reader
28	Fifth Reader
30	Sixth Reader
32	Seventh Reader
34	Eighth Reader

[a]Materials representative of commercially graded reading series.

to write anything he or she heard. Dictation scores represented the number of sounds heard and recorded from a possible 64 sounds. The same task was used to obtain a spelling score. A point was assigned for each word written correctly, with a possible score of 18.

Two tasks were used to document evidence of comprehending behaviors. The first was an oral retelling following each text reading for which the oral reading accuracy was 90 percent or higher. Working on the assumption that retellings can yield information about the comprehending process, investigators explored a variety of retelling scoring options. An important criterion was the use of a system that viewed comprehending as both text-based and reader-based. Therefore, the holistic system proposed by Mitchell (1988b) was used with some modification. The following categories provided the basis for scoring retellings in this study: (a) text-based comprehension (including attention to explicit information, inferred information, important information, and relevance of content and concepts); (b) reader's response and reactions to text (including use of prior knowledge, application of generalizations, use of creative reactions to text, and affective involvement with text); and (c) reader's language use (including language fluency and organization abilities). Two of Mitchell's indicators from the third category: evidence of the reader's sense of audience or purpose and evidence of the reader's control of the mechanics of speaking or writing, were excluded because of the nature of this study.

The second measure of comprehending behaviors was fluent oral reading. The system chosen for the scoring of fluency measures on text reading was a multidimensional fluency scale (Zutell & Rasinski, 1991) rather than some of the more traditional, single dimension scales often used. Zutell and Rasinski's multidimensional scale consists of three dimensions: pace, smoothness, and phrasing. Within each dimension, four levels are described serving as a scoring rubric. Although the three aspects of pace, smoothness, and phrasing influence each other, they are somewhat distinct. This multidimensional scale was selected to add descriptive data about the strengths and weaknesses of the readers.

In order to tap the perceptions of classroom teachers, a questionnaire was developed. In addition to information about grades, reading group placement, placement in any other programs, and basal/text placement, the instrument included questions about teacher perceptions of each child's performance on a number of factors and predictions for each child's future reading and writing performance.

All testing was completed in May by Reading Recovery teacher leaders approaching the end of their training year. All text readings, along with retellings, were audiotaped. Retellings were transcribed verbatim. Questionnaires were collected from the classroom teachers of the Reading Recovery children. Although general questions were asked of teachers of the random sample group, these teachers did not complete questionnaires on random group children, a clear limitation of the pilot study.

Pilot Results

Literacy scores were examined to determine if mean scores of Reading Recovery children fell within an average band, measured as a standard deviation above and below the mean, of the mean scores of the random group. Mean scores on the three literacy tasks (text reading, dictation, and spelling) are shown in Table 2. Reading Recovery children scored within average range for their peer group in second grade. The mean text reading level for the Reading Recovery group indicated that, on an average, children successfully (at 90 percent accuracy or above) read a passage taken from a fourth grade reader. Mean scores for the random sample group reflected successful oral reading performance on a passage from a fifth grade reader.

No significant differences ($p < .05$) were found between the Reading Recovery and the random group on any of the three retelling indices or when all three indices were considered together (See Table 2 for means and standard deviations on retelling measures.). Although responses were generally short and not elaborated, children in both groups revealed the main idea or general theme of the selection. Their facts and inferences were generally relevant. Most retellings, again across both groups, were organized sequentially or in a way to be easily understood. Very few children volunteered more information as the result of a teacher prompt to continue. It is possible that the decision to score the retellings on the highest level passage read at 90 percent or better influenced the scores. Children were frequently retelling passages taken from materials considerably above their grade level assignment. Conceptual load may have been a factor in retelling measures. For example, one of the higher passages was about a maestro/virtuoso.

There were no significant differences ($p < .05$) between the two groups on any of the three measures of reading fluency or when the three measures of fluency were considered together. Fluency scores were not generally very high for either group (see Table 2). Very few children were fluent on all three dimensions perhaps because these were first readings of novel texts. It should also be noted that fluency measures were based on the highest text level read at 90 percent accuracy or higher. Frequently these text levels were considerably higher than a typical second grade passage. Therefore, conceptual load and/or text characteristics may have affected the children's attempts at fluency and may have influenced findings in this pilot study.

Because complete questionnaire data were collected only on Reading Recovery children, results reflecting teacher perceptions were of limited value. It seems important, however, to report status of discontinued children relative to referrals for additional support services. Of the 50 children in this study, 42 received no additional remedial support. Chapter 1 continued to serve four children, while four were served for learning disabilities.

Teacher-reported data also indicated that a dramatic number of high text readers may be under-placed in basal/text materials in both the random and the Reading Recovery groups. Most children were placed in texts identified as on-level, regardless of group assignment. Therefore, membership in a high group did not correlate strongly with basal/text level placement.

On a five-point scale of reading behaviors and attitudes, teachers perceived that most of the discontinued Reading Recovery children were average in reading ability. Teachers also perceived that the children generally had positive attitudes about reading, chose books when time allowed, worked diligently on school tasks, and responded well to discussion. When predicting reading progress for these children in third grade, teachers indicated that 24 of the children should continue to make good to excellent progress. They predicted that 16 would make steady progress while five would make cautious progress.

Table 2

Pilot Study Means, Standard Deviations, and Average Band for Scores on Literacy Tasks, Retellings, and Fluency Measures

Task Score	Maximum	Reading Recovery (*n* = 50)	Random Sample (*n* = 50)	Average Band (1 SD)
Dictation Task	64	60.32 (3.50)	61.20 (4.19)	57.01-64.39
Spelling Task	18	12.26 (2.86)	13.90 (3.17)	10.73-17.07
Text Reading Task	34	25.78 (5.75)	28.42 (6.85)	21.57-35.27
Fluency: Pacing	4	2.09 (.97)	2.43 (.93)	1.50-3.36
Fluency: Smoothness	4	1.93 (.89)	2.30 (.79)	1.51-3.09
Fluency: Phrasing	4	2.07 (.89)	2.30 (1.03)	1.27-3.33
Retelling: Text-Based	16	8.84 (2.25)	9.12 (2.94)	6.18-12.06
Retelling: Prior Knowledge	16	4.07 (.34)	4.15 (.42)	3.73-4.57
Retelling: Language	8	4.23 (1.07)	4.39 (1.32)	3.07-5.71

Limitations of Pilot Study

Findings in the pilot study were influenced by the following limitations: (a) the population lacked diversity, including suburban districts with records of achievement levels well above the national average; (b) text levels used for fluency and retelling data may have included conceptual and vocabulary loads that were inappropriate for the children, affecting comprehending behaviors; (c) questionnaires were completed only for Reading Recovery children, with limited data about random children coming from informal dialogue with teachers; and (d) running records were not analyzed for evidence of reading behaviors during the processing of continuous text.

A replication of the study considering the limitations as well as refinement of procedures was considered important. Establishment of scoring criteria for retellings and fluency was an important result of the pilot study. The main study was intended to include a more diverse population and to include additional analyses.

The Main Study

Method

Subjects

At the end of their second grade year, 54 children who had been successfully discontinued from the Reading Recovery program during their first grade year were randomly selected in nine school districts. Another group of 53 children (random group) was randomly selected from all second graders (excluding all former Reading Recovery students) in the same schools. The nine school districts were characterized by a wide range of socioeconomic levels and ethnic groups. Six districts were large suburban districts, while three were classified as urban.

In the Reading Recovery group, 30 children were male and 24 were female. Ethnic representation included 26 Anglos, nine African Americans, 15 Hispanics, three Asians, and one other. In the random group, 27 males and 26 females were involved in the study. Thirty-two were Anglo, nine African American, seven Hispanic, four Asian, and one other.

Tasks and Instrumentation

The three literacy tasks (text reading, dictation, and spelling) were identical to the pilot study. Mitchell's (1988b) holistic rubric was used to analyze retellings and Zutell and Razinski's (1991) multidimensional fluency scale was used to analyze fluency behaviors. Running record data were added to describe oral reading behaviors for both groups.

The classroom teacher questionnaire was modified slightly following the pilot study (see Figure 1). An effort was made to obtain the following data for all children in May of their second grade year: ethnicity, gender, types of services that children may be receiving, reading group membership, reading grade on most recent report card, and level of placement in basal or other text. Teachers were also asked to make predictions for the child's progress in reading and in writing in third grade. In addition, teachers completed a five-point Likert scale to describe behaviors (both literacy and school behaviors) of each child. Additional teacher comments were invited. The teacher questionnaire was completed in May, the last month of the school year.

Procedures

Near the end of the school year, both groups of second graders were given a text reading task (oral reading) using a series of leveled selections, while the tester completed a running record (Clay, 1993a) of text reading. All children were also given a two sentence dictation task that was

Figure 1. **Follow-Up Questions for Classroom Teachers: Second Grade.**

DISTRICT:_____SCHOOL:_____TEACHER:_____

Please complete the following information about _____

1. Check the appropriate ethnic description:
   ____ Anglo   ____ Hispanic   ____ Other
   ____ African American   ____ Asian   _____

2. Is this child   ____ male?   ____ female?

3. Is this child currently receiving any of the following services? (Check all that apply.)
   ___ Chapter 1   ___ ESL   ___ Resource (LD)
   ___ Speech   ___ Other _____
                                          (Please describe)

4. In what reading group is this child currently placed? (Circle below) If reading groups are not used, estimate placement if groups were formed.

   Low   Low   Average   High   High
                  Average   Average

5. What information did you use to place him/her in this group?

6. What grade did this child receive in reading on the last report card?

7. In what basal reader is this child currently reading? (Circle below.)
   P   P1   PP2   PP3   P   1   2-1   2-2   3-1   3-2   4   5   6

   If no basal is used, what approximate text level is the child currently reading?
   Is there a literature book that would characterize the level at which this child can read?

6. How do you predict this child will perform in third grade as a reader?

7. How do you predict this child will perform in third grade as a writer?

8. Rate the attributes that best describe this child by circling the appropriate numbers.

	Weak--Strong				
Reading ability	1	2	3	4	5
Writing ability	1	2	3	4	5
Attitude toward reading	1	2	3	4	5
Attitude toward writing	1	2	3	4	5
Chooses to read when time allows	1	2	3	4	5
Selects books on his or her own	1	2	3	4	5
Independent in class work	1	2	3	4	5
Tries hard	1	2	3	4	5
Completes work	1	2	3	4	5
Attends well in class work	1	2	3	4	5
Responds in group discussions	1	2	3	4	5

9. Other comments

scored for sounds recorded and for accurate spelling. Although these were not a major focus of the present study, results will also be reported.

If level 20 (on-level text) on the text reading task was read with an accuracy rate of 90 percent or higher, the reading was followed by a request for the child to retell the story in his or her own words. The decision to ask for the retelling on grade-level material based on pilot study results attempted to control for concept load within higher level texts. The children had been told prior to the reading of each story that they may be asked to tell about the story after reading it. The tester prompted twice after the child stopped the retelling: "Can you think of anything else?"

All testing was completed by Reading Recovery teacher leaders approaching the end of their training year or by experienced teacher leaders and teachers in the field. All text readings, along with retellings, were audiotaped. Retellings were transcribed verbatim.

Teacher questionnaires were collected for all children in both groups. Although classroom teachers were not informed about group membership of the children, it is possible that they were already aware due to prior communication about particular children with Reading Recovery teachers in the school.

Analyses

Means and standard deviations were used to describe scores of literacy tasks for the two groups. Multivariate analyses of variance (MANOVA) were used to test for significance between the groups on three retelling measures and three fluency measures. Running records for both groups were analyzed for processing behaviors on the oral reading of continuous text. Correlational and descriptive data were analyzed for factors related to teacher perceptions based on responses to questionnaires, as well as literacy and comprehending behaviors.

In contrast with the pilot study, texts representing the end of second grade (level 20) or the beginning of third grade (level 22) were used when possible for analyses of oral reading behaviors, retellings, and fluency. If a child's highest text reading was lower than those levels, the highest level at which the reading accuracy was at least 90 percent was used. Care was taken to remove any mark of group identification on retellings or fluency tapes. All scoring was completed without knowledge of group membership.

As a result of the pilot study, fluency data were analyzed using several predetermined criteria. First, the length of the selection to be analyzed was defined with consideration given to time for comprehending the major ideas and for building momentum. Therefore, all tapes were analyzed at the same point in the text. Some dialogue was included in the level 20 tapes so that fluency could reflect a child's reading of dialogue. Each tape was played twice before scoring unless the fluency was clearly outstanding on all three factors during the first playing.

Interrater reliability for scoring the retellings using Mitchell's (1988b) categories was .81. Using the Zutell and Rasinski (1991) scale, interrater reliability was established at .79 for scoring oral reading fluency. On the fluency scale, raters agreed when scores were at extremes (i. e., scores of 4 and scores of 1 on the 4-point scale). However, differences were noted when scores of 2 or 3 were assigned.

Main Study Results

Performance on Literacy Tasks

Mean scores on three literacy tasks (text reading, dictation, and spelling) are shown in Table 3. When Reading Recovery scores were considered within an average band of the random sample using one standard deviation, Reading Recovery children scored within the average of their second grade peers. The mean text reading level of 26 for Reading Recovery children paralleled a basal reader level of fourth grade. All but three children in the Reading Recovery group were able to successfully read materials at or above second grade level. The random sample group mean text level score of 29 compared with fifth grade level materials. Both groups indicated the ability to read oral passages considered to be above level at 90 percent accuracy or better.

When compared with the pilot study, comparison data on the three literacy tasks revealed similar findings (see Table 2). In both studies, Reading Recovery children had high dictation scores that almost matched those of the random group. Also, in both studies both groups were successfully reading text designated at above grade level.

Oral Reading Analyses

Running records of oral reading behaviors were examined for both groups of children. When possible, levels 20 and 22 (grade-level texts) were analyzed most closely (See Table 1 for explanation of text levels.). The mean accuracy rate for text reading on level 20 was 95.83 percent for Reading Recovery children and 96.55 percent for the random group, revealing no significant differences between groups. If those levels were read with extremely high accuracy rates by an individual child, higher text levels were used in order to observe error and self-correction behaviors. Texts examined were generally read at an accuracy rate of 94-96 percent.

Table 3

Main Study Means, Standard Deviations, and Average Bands for Scores on Literacy Tasks, Retellings, and Fluency Measures

Task	Maximum Score	Reading Recovery (n = 54)	Random Sample (n = 54)	Average Band (1 SD)
Dictation Task	64	59.35 (3.37)	61.15 (2.92)	58.23-64.07
Spelling	18	12.56 (2.46)	14.57 (2.16)	12.41-16.73
Text Reading	34	26.04 (4.69)	29.51 (4.94)	24.57-34.45
Fluency: Phrasing	4	2.94 (.54)	3.10 (.74)	2.36-3.84
Fluency: Smoothness	4	3.06 (.70)	3.24 (.77)	2.47-4.01
Fluency: Pacing	4	2.87 (.66)	3.16 (.71)	2.45-3.87
Retelling: Text-Based	16	8.01 (2.48)	8.61 (2.42)	6.19-11.03
Retelling: Prior Knowledge	16	4.18 (.72)	4.33 (.82)	3.51-5.15
Retelling: Language/ Organization	8	4.02 (1.37)	4.33 (.82)	3.51-5.15

Attention was given to evidence of the following behaviors: self-monitoring, the detection and self-correction of errors, and use of information sources in errors as well as self-corrections. For both groups, there were generally a high accuracy rate and a high self-correction rate on grade-level texts. Errors that changed meaning were generally self-corrected. However, on higher level texts, both groups tended to shift more to focus at the word level. They appeared to be trying to pronounce difficult words and meaning appeared to suffer.

While the reading behaviors for both groups revealed high self-correction rates and meaning-driven construction of text, the Reading Recovery children demonstrated more reading work. There was overt evidence of reading behaviors. For the random group, most of the reading work was not audible but resulted in accurate reading. However, for the Reading Recovery group it was possible to observe the reading process more clearly. For example, there seemed to be more repetitions, self-corrections, and multiple attempts. Interestingly, however, even though there were more overt reading behaviors for the Reading Recovery children, the work must have been processed rapidly because the fluency measure of smoothness was not affected. It is possible, however, that pace was affected by the overt evidence of reading processing by Reading Recovery children.

Retelling Responses

There were three retelling indices: text-based comprehension, reader's response and reaction to text, and reader's language use. MANOVAs showed no significant differences ($p < .05$) between the Reading Recovery children and the random group on any of the three retelling indices or when all three indices were considered together. Retelling data for both groups failed to correlate significantly with the following factors: literacy task scores, teachers' reading and writing predictions, or fluency factors. For both groups retelling data correlated significantly but not strongly with basal reader placement. For the random group, there was a significant though weak correlation between retellings and group placements. Usefulness of correlational data may be questionable due to the limited potential range of scores in categorical data including group placement, and basal/text level placement (See Table 3 for means and standard deviations on retelling data.).

Retelling responses for both groups were generally short and not elaborated. However, most children in both groups revealed the main idea or general theme of the selection. Facts and inferences were generally relevant.

To illustrate the variety of retelling data, some examples follow. The text is about a proud mouse who thinks he is the master of the forest. His uncle warns him that the elephant is the king and will be angry. The mouse goes to find the elephant and meets a lizard, thinking he is the elephant.

Most retellings for both groups indicated an understanding of the topic, the main idea, or the gist of the text. A low scoring, not elaborated example follows:

Child: Okay. Once there was a small proud mouse — that had heard about a big giant elephant. That's as good as I can get it!

The following example represents a typical elaborated story retelling for text comprehension:

Child: Okay. Once there was a mouse and he was so proud he liked to, he liked to show off and, and say that he was the master of this forest until one day his uncle said that the elephant was — had, had heard about his showing off and was mad because he, because he was bigger than him and, and he was the master of the forest and he went off to, to show the elephant he was the master of the forest. Then he came to a lizard and he, and he said, and the mouse said, "Are you the mo . . . the elephant?" And the lizard said, "No." "Well, you're lucky because when, because when I find the elephant, I'm going to break him to bits."

Although most retellings were expressed in their own words, several children offered the language of the book when the comment was particularly unusual. Many children used dialogue in their retellings. The following example demonstrates the child's use of book language and dialogue:

> *Child:* Once there was a, um, a mouse who thinks she was *proud*. One day, uh, his uncle said, "The elephant is angry. So you should not be proud." "I'll teach that elephant." So he, *off he went*. He came to a lizard. The mouse said, "Are you, are you a elephant?" "No, *not I*," said the lizard. "You are lucky. If you were an elephant, *I would break you to bits!*"

There were few retellings that tied the text with the child's prior knowledge or touched affective behaviors. This is not surprising because the prompt did not invite personal comments. An exception follows.

> *Child:* Well, there's an elephant. There's a mouse who thinks he's the master of the forest, and he's going to try to teach the elephant a lesson and he's going to break the lizard into bits."
> *Teacher:* Can you think of anything else you want to add?
> *Child:* He should've, he should've listened to his, to his, uncle.
> *Teacher:* Can you think of anything else you want to add?
> *Child:* You shouldn't try to beat up or take up for yourself when the other person's bigger. You should ask somebody to help you or tell the teacher or something.

Although many retellings were fairly nonfluent renderings, generally retellings across both groups were organized sequentially or in a way to be easily understood. Few children volunteered much additional information as the result of a teacher prompt to continue. Testers reported that the retelling task appeared to be uncomfortable for many of the children, possibly because of the lack of familiarity with the task.

When compared with results of the pilot study, retelling data were similar. This is particularly interesting because in the earlier study, retelling data were gathered on the highest level at which the child read at 90 percent or higher. Means were similar across both studies indicating no differences due to text difficulty.

Fluency Behaviors

Three holistic measures of fluency were included in the analyses: phrasing, smoothness, and pace. MANOVAs showed no significant differences ($p < .05$) between groups when fluency was considered as a single factor or when considering phrasing or smoothness as factors. However, there was a significant difference between the two groups on pacing, with the random group demonstrating a faster pace in oral reading of text.

An interesting finding was that fluency mean scores were noticeably higher for both groups in this study (see Table 3) than in the pilot study (see Table 2). The change from fluency ratings based on the highest level text read to fluency ratings based on texts designated as second grade texts seemed to increase oral fluency across groups. Text difficulty seemed to affect fluency for both groups of readers.

Relatively few children were rated as highly fluent on all three dimensions. Fifteen random children had perfect scores on all three dimensions while six Reading Recovery children had perfect scores. Descriptive patterns paralleled those of the pilot study. However, an interesting and unexpected finding was noted. Because several children were not native English-speakers, there were differences in intonation and phrasing patterns. In these cases, discourse patterns did seem to affect the expected fluency patterns making scoring more difficult. These discourse patterns deserve additional attention in future research efforts.

For the Reading Recovery group, fluency scores correlated significantly ($p < .05$) though not strongly with dictation scores, spelling scores, and teachers' predictions for reading progress. Fluency scores for the random group correlated significantly ($p < .05$) with all literacy scores, group and basal placements, report card grades, and teacher predictions for reading progress and writing progress.

Individual data provided insights that were lost with aggregated data. Of the six Reading Recovery children and the 15 random children with perfect fluency scores, teacher predictions for their progress in reading were also very high. Four of the six Reading Recovery children and 11 of the 15 random children with perfect fluency scores also received the highest teacher predictions for progress in reading. Only one child with a perfect fluency score was predicted to have difficulty in third grade. Children in both groups with the lowest combined fluency scores were generally predicted to experience average to low progress in reading. Only three out of 20 children across both groups with low fluency scores were predicted to have above average progress in reading in third grade.

Teacher Perceptions

Data from questionnaires completed by classroom teachers of both groups of children were used to describe teacher perceptions. Results are categorized.

Perceived Need for Continued Services.
Descriptive data revealed information about services received by both groups of students during their second grade year. Chapter 1 services were received by four Reading Recovery children and three random children. One child in each group was served in a setting for learning disabilities. Speech services were received by three children in each group, while eight Reading Recovery children and three random children received ESL services.

Reading Groups, Materials, and Report Card Grades.
Correlational data were influenced by the narrow range of possibilities within categorical data, with large numbers clustering in the middle range of most categories. Therefore, interpretations of these data must take this limited potential for variance among the sample population into consideration.

Reading group placement did not correlate significantly with any of the literacy tasks for the Reading Recovery group. However, placement in reading groups was significantly correlated with all three literacy tasks for the random group. Most former Reading Recovery children were in average reading group placements, with five children in the lowest group and two in the highest group. In the random group, four children were in the lowest group while 12 were in the highest group. The remainder were in average groups.

Significant, though not particularly high correlations were shown for the random group between basal reader/text level placement and literacy tasks. No significant correlations between basal/text level placement and literacy tasks were shown for Reading Recovery children. Perhaps the correlational data on basal placements are misrepresentative because so many children were placed in on-level materials regardless of text reading performance. Very few children in either group were in material leveled higher or lower than grade level. Of the 54 Reading Recovery children studied, 49 were placed in materials graded at second grade or above. For the random group, 53 of the 54 were receiving instruction at materials leveled at second grade or above. While the relationship between each literacy score and reading report card grades assigned by teachers was positive and significant for the random group, only the text reading score correlated significantly with grades for the Reading Recovery group.

Perceptions and Predictions.
On a five-point Likert scale of literacy behaviors and attitudes (see Figure 1), teachers perceived that former Reading Recovery children were within an average range in reading ability; mean score on the five-point scale was 3.0. The ratings for Reading Recovery children clustered in the middle range while ratings for random children showed more children in the higher range. The stratified nature of the random group may have been an influencing factor. Teacher perceptions of writing ability were lower than reading perceptions for both groups.

Classroom teacher predictions for reading progress for the random group correlated significantly and strongly with all other factors except retelling measures. For Reading Recovery children, however, predictions correlated only slightly with spelling and more strongly with group placement, basal placement, reading grade, and writing predictions. In other words, teacher predictions for successful reading progress for Reading Recovery children did not match the child's performance on reading and writing tasks very well. Instead, the correlations were with other measures of teacher perceptions rather than measures of child performance.

Teacher predictions of reading progress of Reading Recovery children revealed a perception of average. Five children were expected to make excellent progress in third grade, five should be closely monitored, and the remainder were expected to make average progress. Seventeen random children were predicted to make excellent progress, five should be closely monitored, and average performance was predicted for the others. For both groups, teachers perceived children to be stronger in reading than in writing. Their comments, however, indicated considerable differences among teachers' notions of writing.

Additional descriptive data were analyzed from teacher comments on questionnaires from second grade teachers. Specifically, comments were examined to determine any behavioral trends among those children in either group who were perceived by the teachers to be less successful in literacy tasks. The following general categories emerged. Specific descriptors by teachers are in quotations after each category:

1. speed: "pacing," "slow;"
2. focus: "focusing on task," "attention span, " "gives up," "doesn't apply himself;"
3. personal behaviors: "motivation," "emotional problems," "immaturity," "absenteeism," "work habits," "unpredictable behaviors," "talkative;" and
4. skills: "comprehension," "vocabulary," "mastery of skills," "study skills," "low grades." Very few of the teacher comments about children perceived by the teacher as less successful were directly related to literacy behaviors.

Discussion

Literacy Measures

Based on findings in both the pilot study and the main study, it appears that discontinued Reading Recovery children sustain their literacy gains at least a year or more after receiving Reading Recovery. They are able to read materials at or above their grade level and compare well with their peers on three literacy measures: text reading, dictation, and spelling.

Consideration should be given to additional or revised instruments for measuring literacy behaviors in future studies. The mean text scores in this study were extraordinarily high for both groups. An examination of appropriate assessment texts/passages seems to be in order. Additional literacy assessments may include some standardized measures, including assessment of responses to silent reading tasks.

Comprehending Measures

On measures of oral reading analysis, retelling tasks, and fluency scores, Reading Recovery children appear to compare well with their classroom peers at the end of their second grade year. Oral reading analyses indicated that both groups were reading for meaning. There were no significant differences between the two groups on the comprehensive measures of retelling or fluency tasks, although there was a difference between the two groups on the pacing factor within fluency measures.

Oral Reading Behaviors on Continuous Text. Analyses of oral reading behaviors through running records support the usefulness of the instrument for making inferences about what children are attending to and comprehending based on the kinds of errors and self-corrections they make (Clay, 1993a). From oral reading analyses, it can be argued that both groups of children were reading for meaning and strategically problem-solving on text. If evidence of "reading work" moves across a continuum of overt to covert, Reading Recovery children were still operating at a more overt level than random group children whose reading behaviors were more covert. Although pace may have been affected slightly, the important issue is that the former Reading Recovery children were able to engage in reading work and problem-solve successfully on text. The intricate relationship between reading work and fluency will be discussed later in this section.

Use of the running record, along with other instruments for systematically observing the reading behaviors of children, should enable teachers to continue to monitor these children who were initially hard to teach. Observations of children's reading work allow teachers to make specific decisions about how these children view the reading process, what strategic behaviors they control, and in what areas they continue to need supportive instruction.

Retelling Behaviors. Former Reading Recovery children seem to compare well with their peers on oral retelling tasks. However, correlations between retelling measures and other factors were low and insignificant. Interestingly, in spite of the lack of correlation of retelling factors with other literacy and perception factors, children in both groups seem to be able to report the *big picture*—either the topic, the theme, or the main idea of the selection. It is also interesting that mean scores on retelling factors in this study were similar to mean scores in the pilot study. Pilot scores were based on the highest level read at 90 percent accuracy or better, while scores for the study were based on grade-level materials. Text difficulty, as controlled in these studies, did not seem to be a factor in explaining the phenomenon of retelling data.

Future studies should take into account some of the problems noted with retelling data in the present study. First, most of the children in both groups did not appear to be familiar with the task. Supporting Johnston's (1992) concern, they may have also seen the task as socially inappropriate, without a logical audience for the retelling. The testers did not elicit anything but text-based information, and the scores represented only one passage type—fanciful fiction.

Future studies, then, should include various ways of eliciting children's understandings. Retellings with appropriate audiences (Johnston, 1992) and engagement activities (Tierney, 1990) are two possibilities for consideration. Refinement of rubrics and scoring procedures for these interactive tasks is also needed.

Fluency Behaviors. Findings in this study indicated that former Reading Recovery children compare well with their second grade peers on fluency indicators with the possible exception of pace. Phrasing and smoothness were similar for both groups. In both groups, children's fluency scores were highest when text levels were near grade-level assignments. This finding indicated that fluency is influenced by text difficulty and supports the need for appropriate texts (Allington, 1983; Clay, 1991, 1993b).

Interestingly, in the pilot study there was no difference between groups on pace when the text level was much higher; both groups of children responded similarly to materials leveled considerably above their grade level placement. Also, the reading work of Reading Recovery children as evidenced through running record data may have influenced pace. Perhaps the evidence of problem-solving on novel text should supersede attention to fluent oral reading at this time for these children.

As indicated earlier, the relationship between fluency and comprehension is a complex one. While there seems to be general agreement that oral reading fluency has become a feature in defining good reading, the role of oral reading fluency in comprehension is ambiguous (Allington, 1983; Dowhower, 1991). Dowhower argued that there is a relationship between fluency and comprehension, but that we are not sure which comes first or if one is necessarily an indicator of the other. Based on Clay's work, DeFord (1991) suggested that rather than just increased pacing of text reading, the role of fluency involves the use of all information sources in the reading process flexibly. It is this flexibility which promotes more fluent processing in general, in turn, facilitating fluency in oral reading.

The scoring of oral reading fluency behaviors is also problematic. Although the scale used in this study was multidimensional, it failed to appropriately account for such dimensions as prosodical features—reading in expressive rhythmic and melodic patterns. Further, fluency measures in this study were obtained only on the first reading of novel text. Findings in this study also revealed that children whose first language is not English often display different prosodical patterns than native English-speakers. Considering the multitude of linguistic differences, fluency is a difficult behavior to assess.

It seems that there are three major areas of discussion about fluency resulting from the findings in this study:

1. Is fluency a suitable variable for study? Is there a generally accepted definition? Does the term confuse people? Are measures of fluency probing surface level factors, without revealing underlying processes within the reader? Perhaps the complexity of the notion of fluency is reflected in DeFord's (1991) six factors that "may impinge upon the fluent use of the reading process: (a) the material being read, (b) the flexibility of the reader's strategies, (c) the reader's knowledge about the topic, (d) the match between the language of the reader and that of the author, (e) the reader's purposes, and (f) other contextual factors" (p. 203). Simplistic definitions of fluency tend to ignore the complex relationships of these factors with fluent processing of text.

2. Fluency is very difficult to measure. The measures used in this study were clearly not comprehensive. Again, measures will be elusive as long as there is no accepted definition of fluency.

3. In spite of the lack of evidence linking fluency and comprehending, results of this study suggest that classroom teachers are influenced by children's fluency on oral reading tasks. There were significant correlations between classroom teachers' predictions for reading progress and scores on fluency measures for both groups. The correlations are even stronger when examining individual data as opposed to aggregated data. According to Lipson and Lang (1991), judgments about reading ability are frequently made on the basis of oral reading fluency. Placement and group decisions also emanate from these judgments. Readers who are not fluent often find themselves relegated to the low reading group for instruction (Hoffman & Isaacs, 1991).

If fluency has a strong influence on readers and their teachers, it seems important to consider classroom practices for promoting fluency. The following list represents a composite of frequently suggested practices (Allington, 1983; Askew, 1991, 1993; Clay, 1991, 1993a, 1993b; DeFord, 1991; Dowhower, 1987): (a) teacher modeling of good expressive reading through read-alouds and shared readings, (b) meaning oriented instruction, (c) increased opportunities for reading, (d) rereading of familiar text, and (e) selection of appropriate texts. One practice that has received wide attention in the literature is that of rereading familiar texts (Allington, 1983; Dowhower, 1987; Herman, 1985; Rasinski, 1990; Samuels, 1979). Dowhower (1987) reported evidence that multiple readings resulted in improved rate, accuracy, comprehension, and prosodical readings among second grade transitional students.

Askew (1991, 1993) found that first graders' control over strategic behaviors increased across multiple readings of familiar text. Findings revealed that (a) evidence of monitoring, error detection, and self-correction behaviors increased as text became more familiar; (b) children began to take more initiative in solving problems with each reading of the text; and (c) fluency or flexibility in using all information sources increased dramatically across multiple readings of texts.

Although the term repeated reading is generally used in the literature, Clay (1991) used the term familiar reading to refer to the revisiting of books previously read. She argued that children should practice the skills that they have on easy materials and build up fluency, as defined by the orchestration of flexible processing (Clay, 1991):

> If children can return frequently to reread a wide variety of familiar material they have two opportunities: first, to orchestrate the complex patterns of responding to print just as the expert musician practices the things he or she knows; and second, to read those texts with increasing levels of independence. (p. 184)

Clay (1993a) further suggested that readers need opportunities to engage in two types of reading: (a) successful performance on familiar text which strengthens the decision-making processes of the reader and (b) independent problem-solving on new and interesting texts with supportive teaching. Reading Recovery lessons include both opportunities daily. Classroom opportunities for both types of reading should affect both fluency and problem-solving on text.

Teacher Perceptions

A major implication of this study is that teacher perceptions about literacy and literacy learners are important. In many instances, the literacy performances of children in both the Reading Recovery and random groups did not match the teachers' perceptions of literacy abilities. Perhaps the nature of the questionnaire influenced the responses of teachers. Perhaps there are flaws in the literacy measures, or perhaps other factors were at work (Wood, 1988):

> When teachers are asked to evaluate a child's likely potential in a particular subject or discipline, their answer is likely to relate to a specific feature of the child's classroom behavior: the child's willingness or capacity to concentrate on tasks relevant to that subject. Those children who spend most time on task in the classroom are most likely to be judged capable of doing well in the subject or discipline being taught. More importantly, if we monitor the children's progress we will find that teacher predictions are, more often than not, borne out. (pp. 55-56)

Wood proposed that children may be limited because they do not possess the relevant experience and expertise needed for success. Children are often able to perform, with help, tasks that they are unable to perform alone. These gaps between unassisted and assisted competence are referred to as the zone of proximal development (Vygotsky, 1978).

Teachers who apply the expert-novice metaphor in their teaching help children to construct their own expertise. Well-built scaffolds help children to learn how to achieve heights they are unable to scale alone (Wood, Bruner, & Ross, 1976). The teacher's role continues to be crucial throughout the academic lives of children.

Attention and concentration are not natural capacities that can be used to account for a child's inability to succeed on school tasks (Wood, 1988). Rather, processes of self-regulation include aspects which have to be learned. Children may seem to be incompetent when they are still struggling with the problem of making sense to other people. Children's learning takes time and creates challenges for them and their teachers. When school demands on children are greater than their current level of understanding, we cannot expect to find the child focusing on what is being said and done. Therefore, attention should be given to the match, or mismatch, between what children understand and what they are being required to do. Teachers' sensitivity to these notions may significantly reduce the number of children who are regarded as unsuccessful.

In this study, teachers' perceptions and predictions may have been influenced by an educational phenomenon that can occur when the *bottom* is removed. Because teachers in these studies were forced to rank children on numerical scales, it is possible that ratings were relative to current perceptions of the comparative performance of the members of the class. Children perceived as low may have been labeled as such due to their relative performance in a classroom. Persistence of old concepts may be keeping teachers from realizing how close to average these children are actually operating. Additional study from multiple perspectives is needed relative to classroom perceptions about literacy behaviors of children.

Challenges

The following challenges to teachers, administrators, and researchers may help to contribute answers to Clay's (1993b) question, "What is possible when we change the design and delivery of traditional education for the children that teachers find hard to teach?" (p. 97).

As in this study, when most children are performing satisfactorily on grade-level literacy tasks, classroom teachers are facing a new concept of average. All of the former Reading Recovery children studied here began their first grade year with the lowest literacy profiles in their classrooms. Accelerated progress in Reading Recovery resulted in successful performance wthin the average range in a classroom setting as measured by a range of assessments. That does not mean that all students are alike. The results of this study reveal that the idea of average is a complex one. It may be that programs like Reading Recovery push the curve so that the lower group is removed, and a large group make up the mainstream of classroom work, with a few children moving out ahead. In this situation a new concept of average may be considered, not as the exact middle of any one group of children, but as gathering up children to progress together, bringing their different competencies to bear on the curriculum, with no one being left behind. When all children are full participants in the mainstream of classroom education, individual differences can most readily be noticed, and when necessary, given special attention.

A new and exciting dialogue among teachers is needed to focus on the success of these children rather than on old expectations that some children must be classified as low. Opportunities to collaborate on children's strengths, to explore potentially biased perceptions of children, and to problem-solve on the scaffolds needed by children to support their continuing learning should be the challenge for educators.

It is important to acknowledge that the former Reading Recovery children in both of these studies continued to work effectively within the average band of their grade-level peers. The accomplishment of these children does not preclude the need for teacher attention and support, especially when facing novel tasks. Learning how to learn, think, and communicate is related to the acquisition of various kinds of expertise. If instruction is at the heart of human development (Vygotsky, 1978), the teacher's role as expert is a critical component of schooling and it must continue throughout a child's educational experience.

There are also challenges to the researchers. Follow-up studies with children previously served by Reading Recovery are needed that continue to look at comprehensive measures across diverse populations. Future studies may need to include some standardized measures as well as some classroom observation case studies. Because of the impact of classroom teacher perceptions, it is crucial to explore the behaviors of children in classrooms as well as the behaviors of classroom teachers with children of differing needs.

In all follow-up studies of early intervention programs, care must be taken not to attribute the literacy success or failure of children to any one single factor. Although external social, linguistic, and cultural factors must be considered, it is most crucial to continue to explore the factors for which schools can be held responsible. While searching for those factors, opportunities for children to experience early literacy success must continue (Slavin, Karweit, & Wasik, 1992):

> Success in the early grades does not guarantee success throughout the school years and beyond, but failure in the early grades does virtually guarantee failure in later schooling. If there is a chance to prevent the negative spiral that begins with early reading failure from the start, then it seems necessary to do so. (pp. 11-12)

Although it is the responsibility of the school to offer supportive and appropriately challenging opportunities for all children, the responsibility is perhaps greatest for those children for whom the road to literacy has been more difficult. The challenge is there for all educators. The systemic changes brought about by successful early intervention may be just beginning.

References

Allington, R. L. (1983). Fluency: The neglected reading goal. *The Reading Teacher, 36,* 556-561.

Askew, B. J. (1991). Analysis of the comprehending process within the setting of Reading Recovery lessons: New insights. In S. McCormick & J. Zutell (Eds.), *Learner factors/teacher factors: Research and instruction* (pp. 229-237). Chicago: National Reading Conference.

Askew, B. J. (1993). The effect of multiple readings on the behaviors of children and teachers in an early intervention program. *Reading and Writing Quarterly, 9,* 307-315.

Clay, M. M. (1982). *Observing young readers.* Portsmouth, NH: Heinemann.

Clay, M. M. (1990). The Reading Recovery programme, 1984-1988: Coverage, outcomes and education board district figures. *New Zealand Journal of Educational Studies, 25,* 61-70.

Clay, M. M. (1991). *Becoming literate: The construction of inner control.* Portsmouth, NH: Heinemann.

Clay, M. M. (1993a). *An observation survey of early literacy achievement.* Portsmouth, NH: Heinemann.

Clay, M. M. (1993b). *Reading Recovery: A handbook for teachers in training.* Portsmouth, NH: Heinemann.

Clay, M. M., & Imlach, R. H. (1971). Juncture, pitch and stress as reading behavior variables. *Journal of Verbal Behavior and Verbal Learning, 10,* 133-139.

DeFord, D. E. (1991). Fluency in initial reading instruction: A Reading Recovery lesson. *Theory into Practice, 30,* 201-210.

DeFord, D. E., Lyons, C. A., & Pinnell, G. S. (Eds.) (1991). *Bridges to literacy: Learning from Reading Recovery.* Portsmouth, NH: Heinemann.

DeFord, D. E., Pinnell, G. S., Lyons, C. A., & Place, A. W. (1990). *The Reading Recovery follow-up study* (Technical Report, Vol. III). Columbus: The Ohio State University.

Dowhower, S. L. (1987). Effects of repeated reading on second grade transitional readers' fluency and comprehension. *Reading Research Quarterly, 22,* 389-406.

Dowhower, S. L. (1991). Speaking of prosody: Fluency's unattended bedfellow. *Theory into Practice, 30,* 165-175.

Garcia, G. E., & Pearson, D. P. (1991). The role of assessment in a diverse society. In E. H. Hiebert (Ed.), *Literacy for a diverse society* (pp. 253-278). New York: Teachers College Press.

Goodman, K. S. (1985). Unity in reading. In H. Singer & R. B. Ruddell (Eds.), *Theoretical models and processes of reading,* (pp. 813-840). Newark, DE: The International Reading Association.

Herman, P. A. (1985). The effect of repeated reading on reading rate, speech pauses, and word recognition accuracy. *Reading Research Quarterly, 20,* 553-565.

Hoffman, J. E., & Isaacs, M. E. (1991). Developing fluency through restructuring the task of guided oral reading. *Theory into Practice, 30,* 185-194.

Irwin, P. A., & Mitchell, J. N. (1983). Assessing retelling assessments: Review and analysis. Unpublished manuscript.

Johnston, P. H. (1992). *Constructive evaluation of literate activity.* New York: Longman.

Leu, D. J. (1985). Oral reading error analysis: A critical review of research and application. *Reading Research Quarterly, 17,* 420-437.

Lipson, M. Y., & Lang, L. B. (1991). Not as easy as it seems: Some unresolved questions about fluency. *Theory into Practice, 30,* 218-227.

Lyons, C. A., Pinnell, G. S., & DeFord, D. E. (1993). *Partners in Learning: Teachers and children in Reading Recovery.* New York: Teachers College Press.

Mitchell, J. N. (1988a). *Procedures for using retellings for assessment and instruction.* Unpublished manuscript.

Mitchell, J. N. (1988b). *The reader retelling profile: Using retellings to make instructional decisions.* Unpublished manuscript.

Pinnell, G. S., Lyons, C. A., DeFord, D. E., Bryk, A. S., & Seltzer, M. (1994). Comparing instructional models for the literacy education of high-risk first graders. *Reading Research Quarterly, 29,* 8-38.

Rasinski, T. V. (1990). Effects of repeated reading and listening-while-reading on reading fluency. *Journal of Educational Research, 83,* 147-150.

Samuels, S. J. (1979). The method of repeated readings. *The Reading Teacher, 32,* 403-408.

Slavin, R. E., Karweit, N. L., & Wasik, B. A. (1992). Preventing early school failure: What works? *Educational Leadership, 50,* 10-19.

Slayter, F. Z., & Allington, R. L. (1991). Fluency and the understanding of texts. *Theory into Practice, 30,* 143-148.

Tierney, R. J. (1990). Redefining reading comprehension. *Educational Leadership, 47,* 37-42.

Vygotsky, L. S. (1978). *Mind in society: The development of higher psychological processes.* Cambridge: Harvard University Press.

Wood, D. (1988). *How children think and learn: The social contexts of cognitive development.*

Cambridge: Basil Blackwell.

Wood, D., Bruner, J. S., & Ross, G. (1976). The role of tutoring in problem-solving. *Journal of Child Psychology and Psychiatry and Allied Disciplines, 17,* 89-100.

Zutell, J., & Rasinski, T. V. (1991). Training teachers to attend to their students' oral reading fluency. *Theory into Practice, 30,* 211-217.

Special acknowledgments to the following Texas Woman's University doctoral students for their assistance in data collection, data analysis, and literature searches: Doreen Blackburn, Ann Bullion-Mears, Cynthia Clinger, Linda Dorn, Cynthia Elliott, Diana Geisler, and Linda Mott. Appreciation is also expressed to Texas Reading Recovery teacher leaders for their support in data collection.

SUCCESS OF OLD ORDER AMISH CHILDREN IN A STRATEGY-ORIENTED PROGRAM FOR CHILDREN AT RISK OF FAILURE IN READING

JOSEPH F. YUKISH
Clemson Universtiy
JOHN W. FRAAS
Ashland University

Since the 1984–85 school year, Teachers in school systems throughout Ohio have helped a high proportion of *at-risk* first grade children achieve in reading through successful implementation of the Reading Recovery program (Huck & Pinnell, 1984/1985; Lyons, Pinnell, McCarrier, Young, & DeFord, 1987; Lyons, Pinnell, Short, & Young, 1986; Pinnell, Fried, & Estice, 1990; Pinnell, Short, & Young, 1986). Reading Recovery teacher training sites are located throughout Ohio, the first state in the United States to implement a statewide Reading Recovery program. This article describes a study of the Reading Recovery program with an Old Order Amish population of first grade students from the East Holmes Local School District (EHLSD) in Holmes County, Ohio, who were taught by teachers from the Ashland College Reading Recovery training site. Given this particular population, this study examines the results of the implementation of a Reading Recovery program with culturally and linguistically diverse children.

Reading Recovery is an early intervention program developed in New Zealand by Marie M. Clay, a developmental child psychologist (Clay, 1979, 1985, 1993). The program is designed for the lowest achieving readers in the bottom 20 percent of first grade classrooms who are identified with an individually administered Observation Survey and by teacher recommendation. The daily, thirty-minute individual Reading Recovery lessons supplement regular classroom reading instruction and enable the vast majority of children to be discontinued from the program in a 12- to 20-week period by achieving reading performance comparable to their classroom average. Students who are successfully discontinued from the program are defined as having reached the average performance of their classroom or better (if the classroom average is lower than expected) and having developed a self-extending system that allows students to continue to grow in their reading ability through ongoing interactions with reading text in an effective classroom environment.

Rather than placing emphasis on mastery of isolated reading skills, Reading Recovery teachers assist students in developing a set of self-regulatory metacognitive reading abilities similar to those described by Brown (1985). The ultimate goal of the program is the development by the students of a strategy-oriented, self-extending system in students that enables them to continuously achieve at or above the average in reading of their classmates throughout their educational endeavors.

During the 1986-1987 school year, 23 teachers from 14 school systems in six counties were trained at the Ashland College Reading Recovery site. Six of these teachers were from elementary schools in the EHLSD which serviced the world's largest population of Amish children who attend public schools (Miller & Aguilar, 1984; Lifer, personal communication, 1988). This article will present an analysis of the progress of the Old Order Amish children in the Reading Recovery program. After highlighting several characteristics of the Old Order Amish subculture which might provide challenges to progress in learning to read standard English, statistical analyses will be used to address the following four research questions:

1. Do the Amish discontinued Reading Recovery students in the EHLSD achieve end-of-year mean scores on the Diagnostic Survey (Clay, 1979, 1985) (revised by Clay in 1993; name of instrument was changed to Observation Survey) that fall within the mean-band scores of the (a) Amish non-Reading Recovery first grade students from EHLSD, (b) non-Amish non-Reading Recovery first grade students from EHLSD, and (c) the Ashland College Reading Recovery site?

2. Do the non-Amish discontinued Reading Recovery students in the EHLSD achieve end-of-year mean scores on the Diagnostic [Observation] Survey that are located within the mean-band scores of the (a) Amish non-Reading Recovery first grade students from EHLSD, (b) non-Amish non-Reading Recovery first grade students from EHLSD, and (c) non-Reading Recovery first grade students throughout the Ashland College Reading Recovery site?

3. Is the mean number of lessons required to discontinue Amish students less than the mean number of lessons required to discontinue (a) non-Amish discontinued Reading Recovery students in the EHLSD and (b) the discontinued Reading Recovery students from the school systems located outside of Holmes County that are serviced by the Ashland College Reading Recovery site?

4. Does the proportion of Amish Reading Recovery students who are from EHLSD who are discontinued from the program differ from the proportion of non-Amish Reading Recovery students from EHLSD who were discontinued from the program?

Characteristics of the Old Order Amish Subculture

This section describes the characteristics of the Old Order Amish subculture. These characteristics distinguish the Old Order Amish from a new, more liberal sect of Amish that is a branch of the Mennonite faith.

A culture is comprised of several "patterns and products of learned behavior: etiquette, language, good habits, religious and moral beliefs, systems of knowledge, attitudes and values; as well as the material things and artifacts produced—the technology—of a group of people" (Havinghurst & Neugarten, 1975, p. 6). Because the environmental situation of Old Order Amish students is quite different from the characteristics of the dominant, non-Amish culture, these students are influenced by a subculture much like that defined by Wolfson (1976):

> Subcultures exist within the framework of a larger culture. Members of a subculture, although adhering to a greater or lesser extent to the values and social norms of the wider culture, also have their own values and norms, and they may differ in social structure and patterns from the main culture of which they form a part. (p. 121)

The Old Order Amish society exists as an anachronism in the space age. It gives a glimpse of what was abandoned when people left the farms a century ago (Barker, 1986; Wittmer, 1983). The following differences of the Amish subculture exist so the members can maintain a social isolation from the world of the *outsider*, can practice their religion, and achieve their goal of gaining eternal life. They avoid outsiders, or people who are not of the Old Order Amish faith, and their worldly ideas. The Amish may be willing to interact with the outsiders, or non-Amish, on what they see as an equal basis of limited bond (i.e., buyer or seller of goods). Beyond this, they desire limited contact with the world outside their society (Lee, 1984). Modern appliances, including television and radio, and technological advances which encourage contact with or require dependence on members outside their subculture are avoided. The dress of all members is plain and colorless reminding everyone that they are Amish (Ediger, 1980).

To maintain their individuality and isolation as a group, a German dialect similar to Yiddish is spoken in homes (Wittmer, 1983). Amish children score significantly lower on language portions of standardized tests suggesting that these problems may be due to language and cultural differences (Hostetler & Huntington, 1971). Once Amish students adjust to standard English and the school curriculum, their semantic development has been found to match comparison groups of suburban children and exceed the semantic development of black and white inner city children (Entwisle, 1969).

Researchers have shown the importance of language in a facilitative role to serve as a template for interpreting the printed word (Downing & Leong, 1982; Sticht & James, 1984). Therefore, some intervention must occur to help the Amish student develop confidence in speaking standard English before reading instruction begins. Model programs for Amish children which stress extensive language arts intervention, parent involvement in introducing preschoolers to standard English at home, and other literacy events to assure transition to standard English have been recommended (Fishman, 1987; Logan, 1964; Parsons, 1983).

Formal education is important to the Amish because it will enable them to function in the non-Amish society. The Amish believe that all education should focus on knowledge and skills that can be put to practical use. Any other knowledge or skills are frivolous and unnecessary beyond that which can be used in their goal of living a simple life to practice their religion (Bontreger, 1969). Reading is important to the Amish because it enables them to read the Bible; math is important for household/farm management. Sciences and higher learning, however, are considered foolish, unnecessary, and sinful (Hostetler & Huntington, 1971).

The value Amish parents place on education and reading achievement should encourage these parents to express positive attitudes about academic achievement to Amish students. Parental attitudes toward reading were found to be an important influence on their children's own reading attitudes (Ransbury, 1973). When New Zealand groups of white, Samoan, and Maori children were compared, Clay (1976) found that Samoan children made better progress than Maori children in the initial stages of learning to read. The progress of the Samoan children was attributed to frequent experiences of parents reading to them from the Bible and observing the high value placed on reading and writing, and because of letters between parents and relatives in the home country. Reading the Bible with children has an equally high priority in the Amish society.

The Bible and some Amish monthly publications are found in Amish homes (Fishman, 1987; Miller & Aguilar, 1984). Beyond reading of the Bible to practice their religion, researchers found that most Amish adults do not read. Those who do read do so for practical purposes such as machine repair or to answer questions about farming (Miller & Aguilar, 1984). The fact that parents do not appear as wide readers could be detrimental to Amish children's view of the importance of reading. Also, their infrequent use of books may not provide the opportunity for them to teach their children implicit knowledge about book handling suggested by Logan (1964).

The Amish feel that eight years of schooling is sufficient to gain enough practical knowledge and skills for their style of living. The eight-year school career encourages some parents to place even more importance on their children's school work. During interviews conducted by the author, parents stated that their children must learn to read immediately so they can benefit completely from the eight years they have to learn the practical skills and knowledge they will need for future life. After many years of legal struggles, the United States Supreme Court ruled that compulsory, formal education beyond eighth grade would endanger the free exercise of the Amish religious beliefs. Some Amish families, however, choose to send their children to public school and allow them to attend high school (Wittmer, 1972).

Reaction to Change by the Amish Society

Change occurs so slowly in the Amish society that most outsiders do not realize that change is being slowly accomplished. The literal interpretation of the Bible and previously described behaviors aimed at isolation are the focus of most observers of this group; these characteristics have remained relatively constant. However, subtle change is occurring as described in the following examples of the Amish culture:

1. An increased emphasis is being placed on legal means by the federal and state government of regulating Amish behavior. The eight-year school attendance decision and refusal to pay social security taxes are two areas of regulation.

2. The Amish are increasing their use of technical medical services. They will buy medical services, and in some cases, very sophisticated services. For example, recently one Amish man had a heart transplant. Another Amish man bought a hearing aid from the Ashland College Speech and Hearing Clinic.

The Amish can no longer be considered a farm-oriented society exclusively. Different kinds of work are being performed by members (e.g., carpentry, construction, and factory work). It should be noted, however, that even those who have non-farm work continue to farm on a small scale (Barker, 1986).

These changes may eventually require the Amish to allow their children to go beyond the study of the basic subjects. For example, jobs which involve technology will require understanding basic science principles, and courses which stress the legal structure of the outsiders' society may need to be studied.

Some sociologists predict that employment changes may cause a breakdown of the Amish society. Other researchers feel that stabilizing factors like large, close-knit families; strong convictions; personal relationships with other members of the congregation; hard work and thrift; and religious beliefs central to their simple, less complex way of life will maintain the Amish society (Ediger, 1980).

Amish beliefs and behavior have an impact on children's response to educational procedures and how teachers should interact with these children. When Amish attend public schools, they encounter positive results with non-Amish students. However, these same procedures are in direct opposition to many of the beliefs and practices of the Old Order Amish. Wittmer (1983) and Wittmer and Moser (1974) suggested that public school educators must be aware of the following issues when working with the Amish:

1. Promoting individuality, procedures to boost self-concept, and stressing pride in one's work should be avoided. The Amish feel they are members of a group and the group ethic prevails. Therefore, the competitive spirit should be avoided; competition works against the feeling of working for the group. Teachers should also be very selective with praise. "Praise is reserved for groups and not for individuals" (Wittmer & Moser, 1974, p. 182).

2. The Amish are a task-oriented, exact society. Work is a moral directive. One should work slowly and accurately. Therefore, speed should not be stressed or expected.

3. Although some change away from a farm-centered society has been noted, career exploration is not an interest for the Amish student. Units stressing career education may not be applicable in the Amish students' curriculum.

4. To maintain the isolation that is required by their religion, Amish students purposely keep their distance from non-Amish students in school. Encouraging friendships with outsiders should be avoided.

5. Advice and counseling by teachers about church or family matters may be avoided by Amish children, because parents may have warned children not to be swayed by the advice or interest of teachers or counselors in these matters.

Because the dominant subculture usually controls the school system, a hazardous situation which can inhibit learning occurs when students find that the school environment is foreign to the patterns and products of their subculture (Downing & Leong, 1982). Wittmer (1983), a professor of education who was born and raised in an Old Order Amish home, stated:

I often joke about the fact that one entering a public school without knowledge of the

Bobbsey twins or Mother Goose is in immediate danger of failure. But there is much truth to this. The American public schools have often been viewed ideally as one American institution where tolerance of individual difference is much in evidence. However, I can vouch that the contrary is more the norm. The goal is institutionalization and those who don't conform to the social norms and who refuse to be assimilated are in trouble. (p. 180)

Many Old Order Amish communities educate their children in their own parochial schools to avoid the discrepancies between their subculture and the dominant subculture that controls the school system. However, situations occur when parochial schools are not available. The Amish will support a public school education as long as it is rural in nature and does not depart much from the Amish life pattern (Keefer, 1969).

Definition of Terms

Reading Recovery Children — are children who received 60 or more lessons in the Reading Recovery program or who were discontinued from the program. Table 1 contains the number of students in the various groups analyzed in this study.

Discontinued Reading Recovery Children — are children who successfully completed the program and who were officially released during the year or who were identified as having met the criteria for discontinuation at the final testing in May (see Table 1).

Not Discontinued Reading Recovery Children — are those children who were not officially discontinued from the program for various reasons including: (a) the student moved from the school, (b) the student did not have time to complete a minimum of 60 lessons before the end of the school year, (c) the student was referred to another program such as special education, or (d) the student did not respond adequately to the program after a maximum of 20 weeks of instruction. Table 1 lists the number of students not discontinued for the various Reading Recovery groups.

Non-Reading Recovery Children — served as comparisons for the reading performance of the discontinued Reading Recovery groups. The non-Reading Recovery children were divided into three groups. The first groups consisted of Amish non-Reading Recovery children in the first grade classrooms in the East Holmes Local School District (EHLSD). The second group was composed of the non-Amish non-Reading Recovery children in first grade classrooms in the EHLSD. The third group consisted of the students in Groups 1 and 2 as defined plus a group of children randomly selected from the first grade classrooms from every school outside the EHLSD serviced by the Ashland College Reading Recovery site (see Table 1).

Testing

Assessment of the subjects' reading performances was accomplished by administering the Diagnostic Survey (Clay, 1979, 1985) (revised by Clay in 1993; name of instrument was changed to Observation Survey). The Diagnostic [Observation] Survey was designed to capture change during the emergent stages of reading and writing progress. This series of observational tasks includes six assessments. These assessments are:

1. *Letter Identification:* Children identify 54 different characters including upper and lower case letters and conventional, manuscript print for the letter *a* and g (range of scores: 0-54).

2. *Word Test:* Students read a list of 20 words drawn from the most frequently found words in basic beginning reading materials (range of scores: 0-20).

3. *Concepts About Print:* While the teacher reads a book aloud, students are tested on 24 significant concepts about printed language, for example, directionality and one-to-one matching (range of scores: 0-24).

4. *Writing Vocabulary:* Children are asked to write as many words as possible in ten minutes, starting with their own names and including basic vocabulary and other words. General

prompting of categories of words (e.g., color words) by the teacher is used (range of scores: determined by the number of words a child can write correctly in ten minutes).

5. *Dictation:* Children write a sentence dictated word-by-word by the teacher. Credit is given for each phoneme represented by the correct letter (range of scores: 0-37).

6. *Text Reading:* Students read text selections leveled in difficulty to align with texts from the classroom. As the child reads, a running record is made of reading behavior. Children continue reading at higher levels until they reach two levels at which they score below 90 percent accuracy. The score on text level is the highest level read with 90 percent accuracy (range of scores: 1-34).

Table 1
Number of Students in the Reading Recovery (RR) and Non-Reading Recovery Groups

Location and Type of Student	RR Students	Discontinued Students	Not Discontinued RR Students	Non-RR Students
Amish from EHLSD*	26	25	1	82
Non-Amish from EHLSD*	12	8	4	48
Students from school systems outside the EHLSD* serviced by the Ashland RR site	84	64	20	108
All students from the school systems serviced by the Ashland RR site	122	97	25	238

* East Holmes Local School District

Calculating the Average (mean) Band

The goal of the Reading Recovery program is for discontinued Reading Recovery children to reach average levels of performance in their respective classrooms and continue to learn with their peers without any more assistance or remediation beyond regular classroom reading instruction. To determine whether the discontinued Reading Recovery students have reached the average levels of their peers, their mean scores on the Diagnostic [Observation] Survey were compared to the corresponding average bands that were calculated for the subtests of the non-Reading Recovery groups.

An average band for each non-Reading Recovery group was calculated for each subtest by subtracting one-half of a standard deviation unit from the mean and by adding one half of a standard deviation unit to the mean. Average bands were calculated on each of the six subtests of the Diagnostic [Observation] Survey for each of the three non-Reading Recovery groups.

Selection Procedures

Selection of Reading Recovery Students. The 44 Reading Recovery students included in this study were selected from first grade classrooms in five elementary schools of the East Holmes Local School District during the second week of September. Classroom teachers used an alternate ranking procedure in which they identified the two students with the highest and lowest reading ability in their class. Next, the second highest and lowest students were identified. The process was repeated until a class list was developed. Each Reading Recovery teacher developed individual class lists for each first grade classroom from which Reading Recovery children were selected.

Reading Recovery teachers tested the top and middle five percent of the children from each list in addition to the bottom 20 percent. Children from the top and middle five percent provided the Reading Recovery teacher with an estimate of the reading ability of higher functioning children in the class. Beginning of the year comparisons could be made between these children and the Reading Recovery children.

The lowest achieving four children were selected (from the bottom 20 percent of the students). These children formed the first group of Reading Recovery children to be taught in the program. The other children in this bottom 20 percent group were placed on a waiting list. When a child was discontinued, moved, or was referred from the program, the next lowest child entered the program.

Forty-four children from the East Holmes Local School District were instructed in the Reading Recovery program during the school year. Of those 44 students, 29 were Old Order Amish and 15 were non-Amish. Of the 29 Amish children, 26 received a full Reading Recovery program (i.e., they received more than 60 lessons or were discontinued). Of the 15 non-Amish children, 12 received a full program. Only students who experienced a full Reading Recovery program are included in the analysis. Six of the students (three Amish and three non-Amish) will not be included because they had less than 60 lessons, moved from the district, or were referred to another alternative program such as special education. Thus, for the purposes of this pilot study, the total Amish population of program children was 26 and the total non-Amish population of the program was 12.

All Reading Recovery entrants who receive 60 or more lessons are considered program children. The main goal of the program, however, does not focus on the number of lessons. Reading Recovery teachers attempt to enable program children to achieve at least the average level of reading performance accompanied by using independent reading strategies. This level of mastery of the reading process is required before Reading Recovery teachers will discontinue a student from the program. Many children are discontinued before 60 lessons are completed.

Other children may not meet these criteria even though they received 60 or more lessons. When students did not respond to the program, they were not discontinued and were not included in analyses which involves discontinued Reading Recovery students. Therefore, the statistical analyses which follow will contain only 25 discontinued Amish students and eight discontinued non-Amish students.

The Amish children included in this study were Old Order Amish and lived in a subculture similar to that described in an earlier section of this paper. Two of the elementary schools served only Amish children. It should be noted that some Amish parents may have more readily agreed to send their children to these public schools for this reason.

Because the Amish parents of the children in these two schools encouraged their children to speak the German dialect at home, intensive language intervention programs were implemented by the schools during the kindergarten year and the beginning of the first grade year. Therefore, children who had kindergarten experience were selected for the Reading Recovery program at the beginning of the year. If students did not attend kindergarten, they were not included in the first group of four children who entered the program. They could enter the program in the second group of children in first grade, allowing more time for language intervention and experience in school. This selection procedure supports the oracy to literacy research cited earlier. The general principle for selection of students for Reading Recovery is that the lowest achieving children are served (Clay, 1993). The program is intended for children who have shown to be at risk after one year of schooling. Last, Clay suggested that the child have sufficient English to "understand the instructions of the Observation [Diagnostic] Survey" (p. 67) (and presumably, the instructional programmes).

Selection of Non-Reading Recovery Students. Three groups of non-Reading Recovery students were identified. Two of these groups were identified in EHLSD first grade classrooms. One group was made up of all first grade Amish students in the EHLSD first grade classrooms who were not in the Reading Recovery program. This group consisted of 82 students. The second group contained all non-Amish Reading Recovery students from the EHLSD first grade classrooms. This second group consisted of 48 children. The third group consisted of the 130 non-Reading Recovery students from the EHLSD plus 108 non-Reading Recovery first grade students in the 14 school systems outside of the EHLSD serviced by the Ashland College Reading Recovery site.

These three comparison groups were used to establish the average levels of performance for first grade students through the calculation of average bands for the subtests of the Diagnostic [Observation] Survey. According to the tenets of the Reading Recovery program, discontinued Reading Recovery children should be achieving at or above this average level. Thus, the mean postscores of the Reading Recovery groups should fall within the average bands of the non-Reading Recovery groups.

Method of Instruction

After Reading Recovery children were identified and the comparison groups were established, the Reading Recovery program was implemented. Reading Recovery teachers conducted daily lessons for one-half hour, five days per week according to program guidelines. (For a complete description of the daily lesson procedures, see Clay 1985, pp. 56-58.)

Data Analysis

Question 1: Do the Amish discontinued Reading Recovery students in the EHLSD achieve end-of-year mean scores on the Diagnostic [Observation] Survey that are located within the mean-band scores of the (a) Amish non-Reading Recovery students from the EHLSD, (b) non-Amish non-Reading Recovery students from the EHLSD, and (c) non-Reading Recovery students throughout the Ashland College Reading Recovery site?

Question 2: Do the non-Amish discontinued Reading Recovery students in the EHLSD achieve end-of-year mean scores on the Diagnostic [Observation] Survey that are located within the mean-band scores of the (a) Amish non-Reading Recovery students from the EHLSD, (b) non-Amish non-Reading Recovery students from the EHLSD, and (c) non-Reading Recovery students from throughout the Ashland College Reading Recovery site?

To provide information relative to Questions 1 and 2, a comparison was made between the mean scores for the Amish discontinued Reading Recovery students on the six subtests of the Diagnostic [Observation] Survey and the corresponding average bands for the three comparison groups. Data in Table 2 contain the mean pretest and end-of-year scores on the six subtests for the Amish discontinued Reading Recovery children from the EHLSD first grade classrooms and the non-Amish discontinued Reading Recovery children in these classrooms. Table 3 lists the mean and standard deviation values of the end-of-year scores on the six subtests of the Diagnostic [Observation] Survey for the three comparison groups (e.g., the Amish non-Reading Recovery students and the non-Amish non-Reading Recovery students from the EHLSD first

Table 2
Mean and Standard Deviation Values on the Diagnostic [Observation] Survey for the Discontinued Reading Recovery (RR) Groups

Test	Amish Discontinued RR Students from EHLSD*						Non-Amish Discontinued RR Students from EHLSD*					
	Pretest			End-of Year			Pretest			End-of-Year		
	n	mean	SD	n	mean	SD	n	mean	SD	n	mean	SD
Letter Identification	25	36.48	14.60	25	52.88	1.13	8	40.87	13.22	8	53.37	.74
Word Test	25	.64	3.00	25	19.16	1.25	8	.25	.46	8	18.87	1.81
Concepts About Print	25	8.04	3.46	25	20.32	1.70	8	8.37	3.02	8	18.25	3.15
Writing Vocabulary	25	5.04	4.60	25	47.16	11.11	8	1.75	1.04	8	50.87	9.36
Dictation	25	4.16	6.05	25	36.04	1.57	8	5.12	5.92	8	35.75	1.75
Text Reading	25	.44	1.21	25	21.08	5.26	8	0.00	.00	8	24.25	5.60

* East Holmes Local School District

Table 3
Mean and Standard Deviation Values on the Diagnostic [Observation] Survey for the Non Reading Recovery (RR) Students

Test	Amish Non-RR Students from EHLSD*			Non-Amish Non-RR Students from EHLSD*			Non-RR Students from all Schools Serviced by the Ashland RR Site		
	End-of Year			End-of Year			End-of-Year		
	n	mean	SD	n	mean	SD	n	mean	SD
Letter Identification	82	52.97	1.53	48	53.22	.99	238	53.11	1.29
Word Test	82	19.00	2.39	48	19.10	1.28	238	18.91	2.24
Concepts About Print	82	18.61	2.93	48	19.68	2.55	238	19.26	2.71
Writing Vocabulary	82	47.63	15.71	48	50.23	11.41	238	45.47	14.73
Dictation	82	33.79	6.13	48	35.83	1.81	238	34.45	4.88
Text Reading	82	20.41	10.20	48	22.58	7.09	238	19.95	9.35

* East Holmes Local School District

Table 4
End-of-Year Diagnostic Survey Scores for the Discontinued Reading Recovery (RR) Students and Average Bands for the Non-Reading Recovery Groups

| | Mean End-of-Year Score for Discontinued RR Students | | Average Band for Non-RR Students | | |
Test	Amish Students in EHLSD* (n = 25)	Non-Amish Students in EHLSD* (n = 8)	Amish in EHLSD* (n = 82)	Non-Amish in EHLSD* (n = 48)	Average Band for all Non-RR Students (n=238)
Letter Identification	52.88	53.37	52.21-5473	52.74-5372	52.47-5357
Word Test	19.16	18.87	17.81-1994	18.46-1974	17.79-2003
Concepts About Print	20.32	18.25	17.15-2007	18.42-2096	17.91-2061
Writing Vocabulary	47.16	50.87	40.05-5521	44.52-5592	38.11-5283
Dictation	46.04	35.75	30.73-3688	34.92-3673	32.02-3688
Text Reading	21.80	24.25	15.31-2551	19.03-2613	15.28-2464

* East Holmes Local School District

Table 5
Mean and Standard Deviation Values for the Number of Lessons Completed Until Discontinued

| | | Lessons | | Weeks |
Group	n	mean	S	mean
Amish Students from EHLSD*	25	73.2	31.8	14.6
Non-Amish Students from EHLSD*	8	84.1	27.8	16.8
Students outside the EHLSD*	64	70.2	34.5	14.0

*East Holmes Local School District

grade classrooms, and the non-Amish non-Reading Recovery students from the Ashland University site). Table 4 shows the comparisons of the mean end-of-year scores of the Amish discontinued Reading Recovery students to the average bands for the non-Reading Recovery students.

The results contained in Table 4 indicate that all mean end-of-year scores except for the Concepts About Print subtest for the Amish discontinued Reading Recovery students were located in the corresponding average bands for the three non-Reading Recovery groups. The mean Concepts About Print subtest scores exceeded the upper limit of the average band for the Amish non-Reading Recovery group.

Five of the mean scores for the end-of-year non-Amish discontinued Reading Recovery group from the EHLSD first grade class were located within the average bands of the three non-Reading Recovery groups. Only the Concepts About Print mean score of the non-Amish discontinued Reading Recovery group fell slightly below the lower limit of the non-Amish, non-Reading Recovery group.

Question 3: Is the mean number of lessons required to discontinue Amish students less than the number of lessons required to discontinue (a) non-Amish discontinued Reading Recovery students in EHLSD and (b) discontinued Reading Recovery students from the school systems outside of East Holmes Local School District serviced by the Ashland College Reading Recovery site? Table 5 contains the analysis of the number of lessons completed for the Reading Recovery groups from the EHLSD and a group of all discontinued Reading Recovery students from outside of the EHLSD (n = 64).

East Holmes Local School District (EHLSD) Amish discontinued Reading Recovery students were discontinued in an average of 73.2 lessons or 14.6 weeks. East Holmes Local School District non-Amish discontinued Reading Recovery children were discontinued in 84.1 lessons or 16.8 weeks. The average number of lessons calculated for the discontinued Reading Recovery students outside of EHLSD was 70.2 lessons or 14 weeks.

According to common statistical practice, a difference of approximately one third or more of a standard deviation unit would indicate that the difference between two means is practically significant. One third of the weighted average standard deviation value for the number of lessons for the three groups was 11.1 lessons. Since the difference between the mean number of lessons for discontinuation of the Amish and non-Amish discontinued Reading Recovery students from EHLSD is 109, the difference approaches the size of being considered practically significant. The difference in the mean number of lessons for the discontinued Reading Recovery students outside of EHLSD and the Amish discontinued Reading Recovery students was 3.0 lessons. This difference did not approach practical significance.

Question 4: Does the proportion of Amish Reading Recovery students from EHLSD who discontinued from the program differ from the proportion of non-Amish Reading Recovery students from EHLSD who were discontinued from the Program?

Table 6 lists the number of students who were discontinued and not discontinued in the Amish Reading Recovery groups and non-Amish Reading Recovery group from the EHLSD. Only one of these 26 Amish students who had a full Reading Recovery program was not discontinued. She was tested and placed in a special education program. Four of the 12 non-Amish students in the EHLSD who had a full Reading Recovery program were not discontinued. A Fisher's exact probability test indicated that the proportion of Amish discontinued was statistically significantly greater than the proportion of non-Amish Reading Recovery students from the EHLSD who were discontinued.

Table 6
Number and Percent of Students Discontinued from the Reading Recovery (RR) Program

Group	Discontinued from the Program	Not Discontinued from the Program	Percentage Discontinued
Amish RR Students from EHLSD*	25	1	96.2
Non-Amish RR Students from EHLSD*	8	4	66.7

Note. A Fisher's exact probability test produced a probability level of .027.
*East Holmes Local School District

Discussion

The relationship of the school to the environmental zones of culture, subculture, and home directly influence children's success in school. When the school environment does not cut across the areas of subculture and family, the school zone is said to lie outside the children's own territory of subculture and family (Downing & Leong, 1982). Children who experience this phenomena are often called disadvantaged because their language, experiences, customs, attitudes, and values are foreign to those of the school.

Members of the Old Order Amish purposely create a lifestyle that places the characteristics of the public school outside the children's territory of subculture and family. The purpose of this study was to determine if these differences would inhibit progress of Amish children in a one-to-one strategy-oriented program of beginning instruction for at-risk readers. The language difference, limited experiential background, and desire for isolation from the ways of outsiders were viewed as obstacles that would interfere with school progress and make discontinuation from the Reading Recovery program more difficult.

It appears from the results of this study that concerns about the success of Amish children in the Reading Recovery program were unfounded. Amish children were discontinued at an unusually high rate in a shorter period of time than the non-Amish students from the East Holmes Local School District. The average amount of time Amish children spent in the program before they were discontinued was comparable to the average amount of time required to discontinue all discontinued Reading Recovery children outside of the EHLSD.

One implication which can be drawn from these findings related to a feeling voiced by some teachers and parents about the involvement of Amish children in the Reading Recovery program. It was expressed that cultural and language differences exist between Amish and non-Amish students, and these difference would inhibit the Amish students' progress toward discontinuation. It appears that these concerns are unwarranted. The analyses in this study indicates that Amish children may discontinue more quickly and at higher numbers than non-Amish children in the EHLSD.

When performance on subtests in the Diagnostic [Observation] Survey was examined, performance of Amish and non-Amish discontinued Reading Recovery children in the EHLSD elementary school was comparable. On one measure, Concepts About Print, the Amish discontinued Reading Recovery students' *mean performance* surpassed the upper limit of the average band of the non-Amish discontinued Reading Recovery students.

The success of Amish discontinued Reading Recovery students noted in text reading and the development of knowledge about books and printed language noted in concepts about print may be due to the fact that these children were having their first experience with a set of innovative, colorful texts in a strategy-oriented program which stressed concepts about print. It was noted that EHLSD non-Amish discontinued Reading Recovery students had lower average Concepts About Print scores even though their average text reading level was two levels higher than the Amish discontinued Reading Recovery children.

There could be other factors in the Amish home environment, however, that contribute to the success of Amish students in text reading and the development of concepts about print. Emphasis on daily Bible reading in the home has already been cited as one possible factor (Clay, 1976). The Amish Reading Recovery students would experience a similar emphasis on Bible reading. Fishman (1987) has begun to document ethnographic studies of how Amish families in Lancaster, Pennsylvania, prepare their children for literacy demands. A more extensive look for parallels between these works and the literacy environment of Holmes County Amish should be pursued.

In her study on the effect of language and cultural differences on learning to read, Clay (1976) made the following conclusion:

The study of the Samoan child in this research has contributed markedly to new understanding . . . . The Samoan child who speaks two languages, who is introduced to a book and to written message in his home, who is urged to participate fully in schooling, and is generally supported by a proud ethnic group with firm child-reading practice, manages to progress well in the early years of school without handicap from his low scores on oral English tests. It appears from this study that the comprehension of English for the Samoan child was developed in a good instructional program which operated like a monitoring system directing the child's attention to more and more sources of cues to the written message. In both these respects schooling was the source of progress. (p. 341)

It appears that even though the Amish attempt to use cultural and social differences to maintain isolation from those outside their subculture, they realize the importance of education as a means of maintaining their lifestyle. The priority placed on mastering practical knowledge in basic subject areas appears to have a positive supportive effect of encouraging the child to fully participate in schooling in the midst of a family whose firm child rearing practices are rooted in its proud religious heritage. These qualities, combined with the schooling effects of the strategy-oriented Reading Recovery early intervention program, have created a school situation that allows Old Order Amish children at risk of reading failure to achieve success.

References

Barker, R. (1986, February). *The farm experience: Its importance in a child's life*. Paper presented at the meeting of the North American Montessori Teachers Association Regional Conference. (ERIC Document Reproduction Service No. ED 265 958)

Bontreger, E. (1969). What is a good education? In J. Hostetler (Ed.), *Anabaptist conceptions of child nurture and schooling*. Philadelphia: Temple University College of Liberal Arts.

Brown, A. (1985). Metacognition: The development of selective attention strategies for learning from texts. In H. Singer & R. Ruddell (Eds.), *Theoretical models and processes of reading* (3rd ed.) (pp. 501-526). Newark, DE: International Reading Association.

Clay M.M. (1976). Early childhood and cultural diversity in New Zealand. *The Reading Teacher*, 29(4), 333-342.

Clay, M.M. (1979). *Reading: The patterning of complex behavior* (2nd ed.). Portsmouth, NH: Heinemann.

Clay, M.M. (1985). *The early detection of reading difficulties* (3rd ed.). Portsmouth, NH: Heinemann.

Clay, M.M. (1993). *Reading Recovery: A guidebook for teachers in training*. Auckland, New Zealand: Heinemann.

Downing, J., & Leong, C. (1982). *Psychology of reading*. New York: Macmillan.

Ediger, M. (1980). The Old Order Amish in American society. *Education*, 101, 29-31.

Entwisle, D. (1969). *Semantic systems of minority groups* (Report No. 43). Washington, DC: The Johns Hopkins University. (ERIC Document Reproduction Service No. ED030 106)

Fishman, A.R. (1987). Literacy and cultural context: A lesson from the Amish. *Language Arts*, 43(8), 842-845.

Havinghurst, R., & Neugarten, B. (1975). *Society and education*. Boston: Allyn and Bacon.

Hostetler, J., & Huntington, G. (1971). *Children in Amish society: Socialization and community education*. New York: Holt, Rinehart and Winston.

Huck, C., & Pinnell, G. (1984/1985). *The Reading Recovery project in Columbus, Ohio: Pilot year, 1984-1985*. (Tech. Rep.). Columbus: The Ohio State University.

Keefer, D. (1969). *The education of the Amish children in LaGrange County, Indiana*. Carbondale: Southern Illinois University.

Lee, K. (1984, July). *Amish society—In celebration of rural strengths and diversity*. Paper presented at the annual National Second International Institute on Social Work in Rural Areas (Report No. 141). (ERIC Document Reproduction Service No. ED258 746)

Logan, W. (1964). *Language ability: Grades seven, eight and nine* (Project No. 1131). Berkeley: University of California, Berkeley.

Lyons, C., Pinnell, G., McCarrier, A., Young, P., & DeFord, D. (1987). *The Ohio Reading Recovery* project: *Volume VIII, State of Ohio, year 1* (Tech. Rep.). Columbus: The Ohio State University.

Lyons, C., Pinnell, G., Short, K., & Young, P. (1986). *The Ohio Reading Recovery project: Volume IV, pilot year, 1985-1986* (Tech. Rep.). Columbus: The Ohio State University.

Miller, J., & Aguilar, W. (1984). Public library use by members of the Old Order Amish faith. *Reading Quarterly, 23*(3), 322-326.

Parsons, E. (1983). *Factors influencing the teaching of Amish students in public school* (Report No. 131). (ERIC Document Reproduction Service No. ED 233 835)

Pinnell, G.S., Fried, M., & Estice, R. (1990, January). Reading Recovery: Learning to make a difference. *The Reading Teacher, 43*(4), 282-295.

Pinnell, G., Short, K., Lyons, C., & Young, P. (1986). *The Ohio Reading Recovery project: Follow-up study in Columbus, Ohio, Volume II, 1985-1986* (Tech. Rep.). Columbus: The Ohio State University.

Pinnell, G., Short, K., & Young, P. (1986). *The Ohio Reading Recovery project in Columbus, Ohio: Volume III year one, 1985-1986* (Tech. Rep.). Columbus: The Ohio State University.

Ransbury, M. (1973). An assessment of reading attitudes. *Journal of Reading, 17*, 25-28.

Sticht, T., & James, J.H. (1984). Listening and reading. In R. Barr, M. Kamil, & P. Mosenthal (Eds.), *Handbook of reading research* (pp. 293-317). New York: Longman.

Wittmer, J. (1972). The Amish and the Supreme Court. *Phi Delta Kappan, 54*(1), 50-52.

Wittmer, J. (1983). . . . . Be ye a peculiar people. *Contemporary Education, 54*(3), 179-183.

Wittmer, J., & Moser, A. (1974). Counseling the Old Order Amish child. *Elementary School Guidance, 8*, 263-270.

Wolfson, J. (1976). *Cultural influences on cognition and attainment.* Milton Keynes, England: Open University Press.

Research in Reading Recovery

Factors Affecting Students' Progress in Reading: Key Findings from a Longitudinal Study

Kenneth J. Rowe
The University of Melbourne

Abstract

*A*s a basis for policy development, the study reported here was a research initiative of the State Board of Education and School Programs Division of the Ministry of Education, Victoria, Australia. Conducted among a sample of 5,000 students and their teachers, drawn from 70 government and 30 non-government elementary schools and secondary colleges, the study was designed to provide information over a four-year period (1988-1991) about factors affecting students' literacy development (with a particular focus on reading achievement), and to identify key factors affecting that development.

The study had two primary foci, substantive and methodological. The substantive focus entailed an empirical delineation of student level, teacher level, and school level factors that were hypothesised to influence students' achievements and progress in reading, with particular emphasis on the implications of findings for both policy and practice. The methodological focus involved a comparative examination of the adequacy of explanatory modeling techniques to account for the magnitude and stability of these influences over the first three years of the study, and to use the quantitative findings as a basis for intensive qualitative investigations of class/teacher and school level characteristics among a sub-sample of participating schools during the fourth year. Thus, both quantitative and qualitative methods were used.

Following an outline of the policy context for the study, the related research and description of the methodologies employed, the paper presents a nontechnical summary of key findings with particular emphasis on their related policy implications. Specific technical details of findings from various aspects of the study have been reported elsewhere (Rowe, 1990a, 1990b, 1991b; Rowe & Rowe, 1992a, 1992b, 1992c; Rowe & Sykes, 1989).

Policy Context of the Study

Consistent with the adoption of corporate management models in educational governance and the prevailing climate of *economic rationalism* in which such models operate, policy activity since the mid 1980s related to issues of *accountability, assessment, standards monitoring, performance indicators, quality assurance*, and *school effectiveness* have been widespread throughout Australia, Britain, Europe, and North America (e.g., Austin & Reynolds, 1990; Bosker, Creemers, & Scheerens, 1994; Bottani & Delfau, 1990; Broadfoot, Murphy, & Torrance, 1990; Chapman, Angus, Burke, & Wilkinson, 1991; Cuttance, 1992; Floden, 1994; Hewton, 1990; Jesson, Mayston, & Smith, 1987; OECD, 1989, 1993; Reynolds & Cuttance, 1992; Shavelson, 1994; Wyatt & Ruby, 1989). Much of this activity continues to be directed away from concerns about *inputs* of education systems (i.e., curriculum and teacher professional development), towards *outputs* (i.e., student performance, teacher, and school effectiveness).

From the mid-1980s in Australia, focus on standards monitoring, performance indicators, accountability, and teacher and school effectiveness issues were ultimately given impetus by the federal government's financial support for the *Good Schools Strategy* and its related projects, namely, the *National Schools Project* (NSP) and the *National Project on the Quality of Teaching and Learning* (NPQTL) (Schools Council, 1991). "The NSP is a major action research activity of the NPQTL to investigate how changes to work organization can lead to improved student learning outcomes" (Hill, 1992, p. 403). This activity confirmed an increasing national approach to educational governance and accountability by the government, first signaled in the paper entitled, *Strengthening Australia's Schools* (Dawkins, 1988). Above all, the major effect of these initiatives was to signal major shifts in government policy intention ". . . to bring the delivery of professional educational services into public sector accounting, underscored by a concern to ensure that such services represent value for money" (Rowe & Sykes, 1989, p. 129). Reviews of these developments have since been provided by Chapman, Angus, Burke, and Wilkinson (1991) and McGaw, Piper, Banks, and Evans (1992).

Consistent with these shifts in focus, the rhetoric of Australian government reports specifically related to teacher education and professional development during this time (e.g., Joint Review of Teacher Education, 1986; Report of the Inservice Teacher Education Project, 1988; Report of the Quality of Education Review Committee, 1985) emphasised the importance of functional links between teacher professional development and the quality of student educational outcomes. This emphasis was curious given that there was, and continues to be, a serious shortage of empirical evidence to support such links. While there was an expanding local and international literature attesting to the efficacy of inservice professional development for teachers (Eraut, 1985; Guskey, 1986; Harris & Fasano, 1988; Ingvarson, 1987; Ingvarson & Mackenzie, 1988; Joyce & Showers, 1988; Sutton, 1987; Walberg, 1986), evidence for its impact on student outcomes was scarce (for exceptions, see Brophy, 1986; Brophy & Good, 1986). In fact, Ingvarson and Mackenzie (1988) noted with alarm: "A considerable investment is made in further training and development for teachers, but little is known about the impact or benefits of most of what takes place" (p. 139). This comment continues to apply to a dearth of knowledge about *benefits* for students.

However, teacher professional development in Australia during the mid 1980s, particularly in the teaching of literacy, was characterised by intense activity. Major impetus for this came from the 1984 Commonwealth Schools Commission-funded program, *Basic Learning in Primary Schools* (BLIPS), which was to operate between 1985 and 1987. Focused on the early years of elementary education (kindergarten [K] to Grade 3), the central aim of this program was (Commonwealth Schools Commission, 1984):

. . . to raise the achievement levels of primary school children in basic subjects. Particular emphasis is to be placed upon improving students' performance in reading, writing, speaking, and listening. (p. 1)

Three priority areas were identified for program support: (a) inservice teacher professional development programs, (b) home-school relations and parental participation, and (c) curriculum change. However, the major priority area was teacher professional development, ". . . providing intensive programs to improve elementary teachers' understanding of language . . . learning, and developing their skills in teaching and observing children" (Commonwealth Schools Commission, 1984, p. 1).

By the end of 1987 in the state of Victoria, there were at least nine literacy programs operating in both elementary and secondary schools (Rowe, 1987) including the Early Literacy Inservice Course (ELIC), the Later Reading Inservice Course (LaRIC), the Continuing Literacy Inservice Course (CLIC) and Reading Recovery (Clay, 1985). Some of these programs had statewide exposure, involving the training of large numbers of teachers. For example, it was estimated that approximately 4000 Victorian teachers had been trained in the ELIC program by the end of 1987 (Rowe, 1987; Rowe & Griffin, 1988). Other programs were localised (e.g., Reading Recovery) or were specific to Catholic schools (i.e., CLIC). Others were undergoing trial or were in their first stages of operation (e.g., LaRIC and Key Group Literacy).

Although there was a body of qualitative, formative evaluation literature for these programs separately, indicating positive changes in teacher confidence and associated teaching practices (e.g., Charlton & Holmes-Smith, 1987; Felton, 1986; Geekie, 1988; Glen, 1986; Rowe, 1987; Wheeler, 1986), quantitative attempts to examine the impact of professional development (PD) programs on changes to teachers' professional self-perceptions and then to student achievement outcomes were conspicuous by their absence. A notable exception was the study by Smylie (1988) whose findings indicated that changes in teachers' classroom practices due to professional development (PD) were a direct function of teachers' professional self-perceptions (i.e., "personal teaching efficacy," p. 25). However, a longitudinal study of teacher PD effects on student outcomes had yet to be conducted. In spite of the conceptual and methodological difficulties entailed by this kind of research (namely, a multilevel data structure of students nested within teachers and schools over time), it was argued that ". . . the estimation of changes to teachers' professional self-perceptions and practices is crucial to the provision of evaluative criteria for determining the effects of inservice teacher training on student achievement outcomes" (Rowe & Sykes, 1989, p. 130).

Against this background, a formal proposal for a longitudinal study of the impact of inservice teacher professional development programs on students' literacy achievements was formulated (Rowe & Griffin, 1988) and submitted for funding of its operational costs, to be met by a direct grant from the *Commonwealth Resource Agreement 1988: Literacy and Numeracy* allocation. A rationale for the study was expressed in the following terms (Rowe & Griffin, 1988):

> Given the heterogeneity of existing literacy programs, a desirable outcome of the study would be the identification of program effects and their related mediating factors that yield sustained improvement in students' literacy achievements over time. (p. 1)

The original intention of the study was to focus on students' literacy development in *reading, writing,* and *spoken language*. This intention was subsequently modified to focus exclusively on reading. The reasons for this were twofold. First, psychometrically reliable instruments for the measurement and assessment of students' writing and speaking/listening skills spanning the full range of elementary and secondary schooling had yet to be devised. This was especially the case for students in the early years of elementary schooling (Griffin, 1990; Griffin & Nix, 1991). The second reason was that the major thrust common to the literacy PD programs in Victorian schools at the time (as cited) emphasised the development of students' competencies in reading.

Scope and Nature of the Investigation

In a comprehensive review of the reading research literature, Calfee and Drum (1986) noted: "Literacy is the foundation for lifelong learning; thus its importance in practice and in research" (p. 843). The *prima facie* simplicity of this assertion belies the fact that literacy-related research constitutes one of the most vital, vigorous, diverse, complex, and problematic domains of educational and psychosocial inquiry. From a preliminary search of the ERIC files when first beginning their review, Calfee and Drum reported having found more than 25,000 entries identified under the general heading of *reading*. Since that time, the volume of literature has not diminished. To synthesise and evaluate findings from the similarly expanding body of literature related to factors affecting students' reading achievement *per se* is difficult, not only because of the plethora of relationships that have been found, but also because of the range of methodologies that have been employed. Nonetheless, the major factors identified in the literature were classified in four domains: (a) students' cognitive, affective, and behavioral characteristics, (b) sociocultural and home background factors, (c) teacher and/or instructor characteristics, and (d) school organizational and climate characteristics (Rowe, 1991a, 1991b). Some of this literature is reviewed briefly.

From exploratory work in these domains separately and their interactions, many significant associations with students' reading and other academic achievements have long been identified. Bearing testimony to this is the meta-analytic work of Fraser, Walberg, Welch, and Hattie (1987); Fraser (1989); Hattie (1992); and Walberg (1986); and the work of the International Association for the Evaluation of Educational Achievement (Elly, 1992; Lunberg & Linnakylä, 1993; Postlethwaite & Ross; 1992; Purves, 1973). While there was clearly no lack of empirical evidence, the problem remained one of explicating the observed relationships among factors in *explanatory* terms. Further, since little was known about the relative salience of student, home, and school factors affecting reading achievement, or the impact of teacher and school characteristics and the extent to which these factors are in turn modified and changed by achievement, it was not known which of these factors or combinations might best be enhanced to maximise achievement. Thus, the key task confronting the present study was the identification of *alterable variables* (Bloom, 1980) that may have important implications for both the formulation and implementation of policy and practice.

Given this substantial body of exploratory research related to student achievement, it was considered timely for an *explanatory* study to be undertaken to examine the operation of elements in what Keeves (1986a) refers to as the *cycle of performance*. Moreover, due in part to analytical problems in much of the existing research, the direction of effect relationships among the elements was not clear. A guiding proposition of the study was that it is no longer sufficient to merely report simple bivariate relationships (e.g., coefficients of correlation, regression, or effect size) between given factors and specified learning outcomes. Rather, even at the risk of oversimplification, it was considered necessary to develop *explanatory* models based on substantive theoretical grounds that specify the directions and provide estimates of the effects of critical variables in the *cycle* on student achievement (Rowe, 1989, 1991b). By estimating the extent to which a variable acts either directly or indirectly with other variables to influence achievement, it is possible to gain an understanding of how such variables affect learning and to identify practical intervention strategies.

Major Research Question

It was in this context and in the light of this rationale that the present study addressed the following research question:

> To what extent are students' reading achievements over time influenced by factors at the student level (including home background effects, attitudes towards reading, and attentiveness in the classroom), at the teacher level (professional development and teacher affect), and at the school level (including school organization, climate, or school ethos factors)?

Four major features of this question should be noted. First, central to the thesis of the present study was the assertion that each of the factors mentioned, and their interrelations, do in fact influence students' reading achievement. The supporting literature for this assertion is considerable; a brief review of which is presented here. Second, given the importance of these factors, explanatory models were proposed and tested for fit to the relevant student and teacher data by applying three statistical modeling techniques: (a) multiple regression models using ordinary least squares estimation (OLS), (b) structural equation models using weighted least squares (WLS) estimation (Jöreskog & Sörbom, 1989), and (c) multilevel models using iterative generalized least squares (IGLS) estimation (Prosser, Rasbash, & Goldstein, 1991). In the attempt to answer the research question, the investigation focused on a comparison of the parameter estimates obtained from fitting these statistical models to the data in terms of their explanatory utility, as well as the substantive implications for interpretation of the findings.

Third, the research question implies that the related data have a hierarchical or multilevel structure, namely, students within classes/teachers within schools. Under such circumstances it is important to account for variability at the student, the class/teacher, and school levels simultaneously, both in terms of explanatory variables at these levels and the extent to which between-class/teacher/school differences may explain variation at the student level. While learning essentially takes place at the student level, the fact that students are grouped into classrooms and schools demands careful estimation of the variation in student achievement that may be due to group membership influences. To ignore the essential hierarchical nature of the sampling structure, typical of much educational and psychosocial research and to assume that the student, teacher, or school alone is the unit of analysis, leads to gross aggregation bias, heterogeneity of regression, and related problems of model mis-specification due to lack of independence between measurements at different levels (Aitkin & Longford, 1986; Bryk & Raudenbush, 1989, 1992; Burstein, 1988; Cheung, Keeves, Sellin, & Tsoi, 1990; Goldstein, 1986, 1987, 1995; Raudenbush & Willms, 1991; Robinson, 1950; Rowe, 1989; Rowe & Hill, 1995).

In particular, failure to account for the essential hierarchical nature of the data is that traditional single-level analyses invariably lead to an increased probability of committing Type I errors (Aitkin & Zuzovsky, 1991; Rowe, 1992a), with important ramifications for the substantive interpretation of findings. Unfortunately, such errors occur all too frequently in educational and psychosocial research. Recent developments in multilevel analysis provide strategies that make allowance for estimating the effects of variables at different levels of analysis simultaneously, thus providing evidence for teacher/program/school effectiveness (Bryk, Raudenbush, & Congdon, 1992; Longford, 1986, 1987; Prosser, Rasbash, & Goldstein, 1991; Rasbash, Goldstein, & Woodhouse, 1995). Moreover, such evidence is likely to have useful implications for educational policy determination and implementation.

Fourth, the longitudinal nature of the project was a crucial design feature of the study. Fundamental questions in education centre upon issues of growth in individual and group learning. Since it is axiomatic that students enter classrooms in schools to learn, grow, develop, and change, the study of growth in student knowledge and skills in schools is of central interest in a considerable body of educational research. However, in spite of the fact that the very notion of *school learning* implies *growth* and *change* in specific organizational settings and such issues fall quite naturally into a contextual and longitudinal framework, the vast majority of research attempts to determine the salience of factors affecting student learning outcomes have ignored the inherent hierarchical structure of the derived data and have been addressed with cross-sectional designs (Burstein, 1980; Goldstein, 1979, 1987; Raudenbush & Bryk, 1988; Raudenbush, 1989; Willett, 1988).

It should be noted that studies of school and classroom effects on student learning share two key features: (a) the fact that student growth is the object of inquiry and (b) the fact that such growth occurs in groups or natural organizational settings (i.e., classes and schools). These two features correspond, in turn, to two of the most troublesome and enduring methodological problems in educational research, namely, the problem of measuring *change* (Harris, 1963; Goldstein, 1979, Linn, 1981; Rogosa & Willett, 1985) and the problem of analysing *multilevel* data (Aitkin & Longford, 1986; Bryk & Raudenbush, 1989, 1992; Cronbach & Webb, 1975; Goldstein, 1987, 1995). Since students are not randomly assigned to either classrooms or schools, the task of measuring change in student growth is problematic if the effects of classrooms and schools are ignored.

A major criticism of research in schools is that most studies have used cross-sectional designs or have employed, at most, two time points. Since these studies are usually nonexperimental, drawing *causal* inferences is particularly problematic in the absence of longitudinal data (Murnane, 1975), since measures of change based on only two time points are notoriously unreliable (Bryk & Raudenbush, 1987; Willett, 1988). The problem is that studies of student growth involve time-series, repeated measures data on students nested within groups, giving rise to difficulties associated with appropriate levels of analysis, aggregation bias, heterogeneity of regression, and problems of model mis-specification mentioned earlier. Further, Nuttall, Goldstein, Prosser, and Rasbash (1989) offer ". . . a note of caution about any study of school effectiveness that relies on measures of outcome in just a single year or of just a single cohort of students. Long time series are essential for a proper study of stability over time" (p. 775).

To avoid these problems, the present study employed a longitudinal, three-wave panel design involving: (a) repeated measures on four cohorts of students nested within classes/schools to estimate their growth trajectories and (b) repeated measures on schools—to evaluate the stability of school effects over time. The second design involved cross sections of student cohorts nested within schools that were changing over time.

At this point, the key terms of the research question are examined briefly within the context of the related research literature as bases for determining the elements of the proposed explanatory models for the student and teacher data to be tested and as pointers for the investigation of school level factors.

Student Home Background Factors

For the past 30 years, the major theories (or models) of learning processes (e.g., Bennett, 1978; Bloom, 1976; Carroll, 1963; Cooley & Leinhardt, 1975) and the *process-product* research generated by them (Brophy, 1986), have primarily focused on *school learning*, or ". . . holistic conceptions of student learning in classroom settings" (Boekaerts, 1986, p. 129). Such is also the case for reading achievement (Calfee & Drum, 1986) despite consistent findings indicating that school factors including financial and material resources, class size, teachers' qualifications, classroom organization, and teaching methods account for less than ten percent of the variation in student achievement measures (Coleman, et al., 1966; Hanusheck, 1981; Glass, Cahen, Smith, & Filby, 1982; Larkin & Keeves, 1984; Thompson, 1985).

Rather, during these 30 years, highly respected researchers such as Coleman et al. (1966) and Jencks et al. (1972) in the U.S.A. and Bernstein (1971), Peaker (1967), and Plowden (1967) in Britain, ". . . provided evidence that schools and teachers are not effective in enhancing achievement" (Hattie, 1992, p. 9). They unanimously asserted that ethnic and family socioeconomic background factors constituted the dominant determinants of students' educational achievement outcomes. In a comprehensive review of studies of educational production relationships covering many different schooling situations, grade levels, and outcome measures, Hanusheck (1985) concluded: ". . . differences in family backgrounds have dramatic effects on student achievement" (p. 4059). For example, Rutter, Tizard, and Whitmore (1970) and Thompson (1985) reported that the cumulative effects of home background factors consistently account for more than 50 percent of the variance in measures of student literacy performance.

Similarly, from several British studies during the mid 1980s, comparisons of the academic outcomes of local education authorities (LEAs) showed that social, ethnic, economic, and environmental factors accounted for up to 80 percent of the variation in student academic attainment (Department of Education and Science, 1983, 1984; Gray, Jesson, & Jones, 1984). In a review of factors underlying the academic success of Indochinese refugee children in the U.S.A., Caplan, Choy, and Whitmore (1992) found that family sociocultural ["collective obligation"] values and ". . . the family's commitment to accomplishment and education . . ." (p. 21) had strong positive impacts on students' achievements in both literacy and numeracy. Similar findings have since been observed in the IEA *Study of Reading Literacy* conducted by the International Association for the Evaluation of Educational Achievement (Elly, 1992; Lunberg & Linnakylä, 1993; Postlethwaite & Ross, 1992). Reynolds, Hargreaves, and Blackstone (1980) summarised such findings in the following terms: ". . . variations in what children learn in school depends largely upon variations in what they bring to school and not on variations in what schools offer them" (p. 208).

A growing number of researchers, however, have since provided contrary evidence to such claims (Bryk & Raudenbush, 1987; Fraser, Walberg, Welch, & Hattie, 1987; Goldstein, 1987; Hattie, 1992; Lee & Bryk, 1989; Raudenbush & Willms, 1991; Reynolds & Cuttance, 1992; Rowe, 1991b, 1992a). Many of these researchers have been critical of findings from studies such as Coleman, Hoffer, and Kilgore (1982) because the inherent hierarchical nature of the data had not been taken into account. For example, from meta-analytic syntheses of 7,827 studies of factors affecting students' educational achievements, Fraser (1989) notes:

. . . there is little support for the contentions of Jencks et al. (1972) or Coleman et al. (1966) that, relative to home influences, there are no measurable school resources or policies that show consistent relationships to a school's effectiveness in boosting achievement. The effects of the home environment on achievement are neither dramatically more than the effects of the schooling variables, nor do they explain a substantial proportion of the variance. (p. 716)

A major problem in many studies attempting to account for the effects of students' home background factors is the way in which such factors have typically been measured. Whereas numerous studies have included surrogate measures of home background factors, the variables most often chosen have not been measured directly, but rather, have been proxied by other observable attributes such as student self-report estimates of the number of books in the home, access to community and school libraries, and classifications of family social class or socioeconomic status (e.g., Davie, Butler, & Goldstein, 1972; Douglas, 1964; Elly, 1992; Fotheringham & Creal, 1980; McGaw, Long, Morgan, & Rosier, 1989; Postlethwaite & Ross, 1992; Rutter, Maughan, Mortimer, Ouston, & Smith, 1979; Williams & Silva, 1985).

In an Australian study of early reading achievement, the findings of Share, Jorm, Maclean, Matthews, and Waterman, (1983) indicated that the common practice of using proxy measures such as a single index of socioeconomic status (SES) to *measure* home background influences, severely underestimated the relationship between the home and educational achievement. Share et al. showed that although indices of SES were associated positively with reading achievement, specific processes operating within the home such as academic guidance, language models, levels of family literacy, parental participation and aspirations for the child were more directly related to student achievement (Morgan & Lyon, 1979; Topping & Wolfendale, 1985; Winter, 1988). Fraser's (1989) meta-analytic synthesis of related research concluded:

What might be called 'the alterable curriculum of the home' (e.g., informed parent-child conversations about school and everyday events; encouragement; and discussion of leisure reading; . . . interest in the child's academic progress) is twice as predictive of academic learning as is family SES (p. 711) . . . achievement is more closely linked to family psychological characteristics than to social class (p. 712).

Further:

. . . this chapter has provided considerable evidence supporting the effect of home environment (especially intellectual stimulation and home interventions) and the class environment (especially cohesiveness, satisfaction and goal direction) in promoting learning, thus suggesting the important role to be played by teachers and parents in attempting to enhance student achievement through changing classroom and home environments. (p. 717)

Quality home background influences have also been found to be important in the development of positive attitudes towards reading (Beach, 1985; Caplan, Choy, & Whitmore, 1992; Purves, 1973; Walberg & Tsai, 1985).

Recognition of the value of parents as reading tutors for children has been the subject of considerable interest by researchers and education professionals (Scarborough, Dobrich, & Hager, 1991; Wareing, 1985; Webb, Webb, & Eccles, 1985). First described by Morgan (1976) and Morgan and Lyon (1979), practical implementation of the *Paired Reading* (PR) technique for parents, for example, was outlined more fully by Tizard, Schofield, and Hewison (1982) and studied extensively by Topping and coworkers (Topping, 1986; Topping & McKnight, 1984; Topping & Wolfendale, 1985). A local Australian variant of the PR technique is the *School, Home and Reading Enjoyment* (SHARE) program (Turner, 1987), which appears to impact positively on participating students and their school communities (Jones, 1989). However, a review by Winter (1988) indicated that whatever effects PR has upon reading achievement and attitudes may be due to features far from unique to PR as proposed by Morgan and Lyon (1979) and advocated by Topping (1986). Winter argued that whenever parents are actively involved in their child's education, regardless of specific program-related protocols, educational outcomes are maximised. This view has been supported strongly in a collection of papers published in a special issue of the *Elementary School Journal* edited by Hoffman (1991). Nevertheless, such recognition stands in contrast to the bulk of production-function research concerned with factors affecting student achievement, which typically has not included direct measures of parental involvement or related qualitative aspects of family educational inputs. The same can also be said of the bulk of studies concerned with school effectiveness.

Student Cognitive and Affective Factors

The large literature on student factors associated with reading achievement has focused predominantly on *individual differences* in the cognitive, affective, and behavioral domains, as well as their interactions with presage variables such as gender, race, ethnicity, and socioenvironmental factors. The salient finding from research in the cognitive domain, for example, is that early reading achievement is the major determinant of later reading performance (Beck & Carpenter, 1986; Butler, Marsh, Sheppard, & Sheppard, 1985; Share, Jorm, Maclean, & Matthews, 1984; Stanovich, 1986; Tunmer & Nesdale, 1985). This is especially the case for measures of early phonological awareness which consistently correlate more highly with subsequent reading achievement than do omnibus measures of general intelligence or reading readiness (Mann, 1984; Williams, 1984). Results from studies employing structural equation modeling (Torneus, 1984) show that early phonological awareness skills, mediated by home background influences such as quality parental or other adult inputs, lead directly to later superior reading achievement.

Studies of students' affective characteristics such as attitudes and motivations suggest that favourable attitudes towards reading are related to general success in school and contribute towards positive student self-esteem (Ainley, Goldman, & Reed, 1990; Alexander & Filler, 1976; Beach, 1985; Purves, 1973; Walberg & Tsai, 1985; Weiner, 1984). From Purves' (1973) international study of students' attitudes towards reading, the one factor that contributed most strongly towards positive attitudes was the extent to which opportunity to read was provided and encouraged, both at home and at school. The evidence for home influences appears to be particularly important. When students are read to by parents or other adults during their preschool years, such experiences are associated with subsequent positive attitudes towards reading, increased confidence and motivation to read, and are related to enhanced reading and writing skills (Bettelheim & Zelan, 1982; Grimmett & McCoy, 1980; Scarborough, Dobrich, & Hager, 1991; Spiegel, 1981; Wells, 1986).

Student Behavioral Factors

From the theoretical work of Carroll (1963, 1984), Cooley and Lohnes (1976), and Bloom (1976) has come the key operational construct of *active learning time* or its equivalents, *time-on-task*, *engaged learning time, perseverance,* or *attentiveness*. These writers argued that although students may differ in their aptitude for learning, the different amounts of time needed to achieve a given level of proficiency is a direct function of the amount of *attention* or effort invested by an individual in a learning task. Findings from related research provide strong support for this view, indicating that *attentiveness* is directly related to achievement outcomes (deJong, 1993; Fisher, et al., 1980; Keeves, 1986b; Lahadern, 1968; Rowe, 1991b; Rowe & Rowe, 1992b, 1992c, 1993). This work suggested that *attentiveness*, defined as: "purposeful activity showing a sustained attention span, perseverance, concentration and not easily distracted" (Rowe & Rowe, 1992a, p. 349), is a crucial variable associated with student behavior at home and at school, through which the effects of learning experiences and attitudes are mediated to influence learning outcomes.

Evidence from studies investigating the impact of maladaptive student behaviors provides strong support for the importance of *inattentiveness* as a major variable having negative effects on student achievement, particularly in literacy. These studies reflect an enduring concern of teachers, parents, and mental health professionals of the extent to which the major characteristics of *externalizing* behavior problems in the classroom—classified as *disruptive behavior disorders* in

DSM-III-R (APA, 1987) and *DSM IV* (APA, 1994) (i.e., attention deficit/over activity and conduct disorders), adversely affect students' opportunities for learning and educational development.[1] Students whose behaviors are regarded as inattentive, disruptive, or maladjusted have been shown to be at risk of poor educational attainment (Cantwell & Baker, 1991; Davie, Butler, & Goldstein, 1972; Elkins & Izard, 1992; Hinshaw, 1992a, 1992b; Keller, et al., 1992; Maughan, Gray, & Rutter, 1985; McGee & Share, 1988; Rowe & Rowe, 1992a, 1992b, 1993; Rutter, 1985; Silver, 1990). Moreover, in addition to the consequences for an individual, such behavior problems in the classroom diminish educational opportunities for other students and contribute to teacher stress (Brenner, Sörbom, & Wallius, 1985; Otto, 1986; Wearing, 1989). As noted by Hinshaw (1992a), externalizing behavior disorders ". . . are quite refractory to typical interventions and, like severe under achievement, comprise a major psychological, economic, and social problem" (p. 894) (see also Kazdin, 1987; Loeber, 1990; Robins, 1991).

While students' classroom behaviors have been found to be partly dependent on factors such as ethnicity (Dunkin & Doenau, 1985), social background (Kahl, 1985), gender (Bank, 1985), as well as cognitive and affective characteristics (Debus, 1985; Sinclair, 1985), findings from a growing number of correlational studies indicate stronger direct associations between poor attention and reading difficulties—both in general student populations and in identified learning disabled groups (Dykman & Ackerman, 1991; Jorm, Share, Matthews, & Maclean, 1986; Levy, Horn, & Dalglish, 1987; Maughan, Gray, & Rutter, 1985; McGee, Williams, & Silva, 1987; McKinney, 1989; Stanton, Feehan, McGee, & Silva, 1990; Stevenson, Richman, & Graham, 1985). For example, in their longitudinal study in Dunedin, New Zealand, McGee and coworkers have consistently found poor reading achievement to be strongly related to high ratings of inattention. McGee and Share (1988) estimated that 80 percent of their sample of 11-year old children identified with *Attention Deficit Disorder with Hyperactivity* (ADDH), as defined by *DSM-III R* (APA, 1987), had learning disabilities in reading and written language skills. Due, in part, to a variety of methodological and analytical limitations in these studies, however, both the direction and magnitude of *effect* relationships is not clear. For an explication of these limitations, see Rowe and Rowe (1992a).

From interest in the relationship between students' reading disabilities and problem behaviors, Rutter, Tizard and Whitmore (1970) have proposed four alternative *causal* hypotheses, namely: (a) problem behavior leads to reading difficulties, (b) reading disability produces behavior problems, (c) both problem behavior and reading disability are produced by some third factor, and (d) it may be that all of these hypotheses could be partly true. In a review of the related research, McGee, Williams, Share, Anderson, and Silva (1986) noted: "All hypotheses have drawn support from the literature and the proposed mechanisms underlying the relationship between reading disability and behavior disorder appear to be equally plausible" (p. 597).

On the basis of a more detailed review of the literature concerned specifically with the relationship between ADDH and failure to acquire literacy skills, McGee and Share (1988) concluded: "The evidence the authors have reviewed suggests that a substantial overlap exists between ADDH and learning difficulties and that, as yet, no unique pattern of cognitive or attention deficits has been identified that can discriminate between these two types of disorder" (p. 322). (For a detailed discussion, see Fletcher, Morris, & Francis, 1991). Following Kinsbourne (1984), who argued that attention problems are both *context* and *task* dependent, McGee and Share (1988) further concluded that "ADDH behaviors might best be considered as a disorder of conduct in the classroom, because the child with learning difficulties is excluded from much of the normal classroom activity" (p. 322). This view is consistent with the findings of Day and Peters (1989) who suggested that "learning disabled children seem to be better characterized as 'inattentive in the classroom'" (p. 360).

---

[1] The link between academic underachievement and students' externalizing behavior problems has long been noted (Sampson, 1966). For an excellent historical review of this interest and the related research, see McGee, Share, Moffit, Williams, and Silva (1988).

Teacher Professional Development and Affect Factors

As indicated earlier, Australian Government reports on inservice teacher education during the 1980s emphasized the importance of a functional link between teacher professional development (PD) and the quality of educational outcomes for students. While there was an expanding local and international literature espousing the efficacy of inservice professional development for teachers at the time (Eraut, 1985; Freiberg, Prokosch, Treister, & Stein, 1990; Harris & Fasano, 1988; Ingvarson, 1987; Ingvarson & Mackenzie, 1988; Joyce, Showers, & Rolheiser-Bennett, 1987; Joyce & Showers, 1988; Sutton, 1987; Walberg, 1986), there is little evidence for direct effects of teacher PD on student achievement. One exception includes the study by Aitkin & Zuzovsky (1991) which found, using multilevel analysis, that teachers' recent participation in professional development was an important contributor to science achievement for Israeli primary school students drawn from ethnic minority groups.

However, there is growing evidence for the positive effects of PD on teacher affect and changes to their classroom practices (Hill, Holmes-Smith, & Rowe, 1993; Rowe, 1987; Rowe, Hill, & Holmes-Smith, 1994; Rowe & Sykes, 1989; Smylie, 1988). For example, Rowe's (1987) cross-sectional evaluation among teachers trained in the ELIC program documented their claims that participation had markedly improved their competence as "observers of children's learning behaviors," and "notably enhanced their professional repertoires of literacy teaching skills" (p. 10). Above all, typical of the comments from teachers was: "ELIC has recharged my batteries; my confidence as a teacher has grown dramatically" (p. 10). Similarly, findings from Smylie's (1988) study indicated that the effects of PD impacted positively on changes to teachers' classroom practices and on changes in their professional self-perceptions or "personal teaching efficacy" (p. 25). Using structural equation modeling techniques, findings from Rowe and Sykes' (1989) study indicated strong positive effects of professional development on teachers' professional self-perceptions and particularly those concerned with *energy, enthusiasm*, and *job-satisfaction*. Such outcomes point to a need to determine whether these affects are consistent over time and the extent to which they influence student outcomes.

From the research literature there is some evidence for the effects of teacher behavior on student achievement (Brophy, 1986; Brophy & Good, 1986; Lanier & Little, 1986) and mounting evidence that teachers' self-perceptions and related affective factors (i.e., *efficacy*—Stipek & Weisz, 1981) interact with and impact on their professional practices (Ashton & Webb, 1986; Dunkin & Biddle, 1974; Lee, Dedrick, & Smith, 1991; Levis, 1985; Rosenshine & Furst, 1971; Ryans, 1960). A major proposition at the outset of the present study was that teachers' professional self-perceptions are crucial input components of any attempt to evaluate the benefits of inservice programs or to monitor educational outcomes, since both the identification and evaluation of outputs at the student level are necessarily mediated by the relative saliency of *teacher effects*. That is, since inservice program effects on students are not independent of the mediation effects of teachers who deliver them to students, it is important to examine the relative impact of professional development on teacher affect and to estimate, in turn, teacher affect influences on student outcomes.

School Organizational Factors

During the last decade, there has been a growing body of research suggesting that administrative and social organizational features of schools are important factors influencing both teachers and students (Ainley, Goldman, & Reed, 1990; Lee, Dedrick, & Smith, 1991). The current interest in the effects of school organizational factors, focused mostly on student achievement outcomes, stems mainly from two sources: research on effective schools (for comprehensive reviews, see: Bosker, Creemers, & Scheerens, 1994; Reynolds & Cuttance, 1992; Reynolds, et al., 1994; Rosenholtz, 1985; Scheerens, 1992) and the relative effectiveness of public and private schools (Anderson, 1990; Coleman, Hoffer, & Kilgore, 1982; Lee & Bryk, 1989; Steedman, 1983). In fact, organizational factors are increasingly seen as important determinants of effective schools (Chubb, 1988; Chubb & Moe, 1990; McNeil, 1986; Metz, 1986; Newman, Rutter, & Smith, 1989), with frequently cited features including the school's organizational culture, ethos, or climate (Grant, 1988; Lightfoot, 1983; Rutter, Maughan, Mortimer, Ouston, & Smith, 1979).

Many of these studies, however, have had difficulties in demonstrating direct empirical links between school organization or climate and student outcomes. The reasons for these difficulties are both methodological and substantive (Bidwell & Kasarda, 1980; Bossert, 1988; Ecob, Evans, Hutchison, & Plewis, 1982; Goldstein, 1980; Ralph & Fenessey, 1983; Rowe, 1989, 1992a). Briefly, the methodological difficulties stem from ignoring the essential multilevel nature of data at the student level and higher levels, operationalizing teacher level and school level variables as aggregates, and using these aggregates as explanatory variables in single-level regression models to estimate the magnitude of their effects on student level outcomes. The substantive difficulties arise from a general failure to realise that it is more appropriate to conceptualize the link between schools and students as *indirect*, mediated by teachers (Lee, Dedrick, & Smith, 1991).

According to this view, school organization factors influence how teachers view their work and how they teach. In turn, teachers' perceptions and practices influence students' learning. While strong relationships have been demonstrated between student achievement and teachers' levels of *efficacy* (Ashton & Webb, 1986) and *commitment* (Rosenholtz, 1985), these studies are limited because their analyses did not take hierarchical relationships into account. However, using multilevel modeling, Rowe (1990b) showed that teacher energy / enthusiasm—due mainly to participation in inservice professional development programs—had significant effects on students' reading achievement.

The most widely cited summarizations of school organizational characteristics as alterable correlates of educational achievement have been provided by Edmonds (1979a, 1979b, 1981), Purkey and Smith (1983), and Tomlinson (1980). A more recent summary has been provided by Levine and Lezotte (1990). Common to each of these summaries, however, is the tendency to produce *recipes* for effectiveness based on disparate and often anecdotal *findings* reported in the literature, rather than on empirical research evidence. Fortunately, a notable exception is the large-scale empirical work of Postlethwaite and Ross (1992), who provide a list of indicators that discriminate between *more effective* and *less effective* schools in students' reading achievement. Nevertheless, the relevant research literature on effective schools is not extensive, with scholarly comment and critique constituting the major proportion and providing the basis for recipe-like systems of performance indicators of the kind proposed by Hopkins (1991) and Scheerens (1993). Lists provided by these commentators illustrate this approach.

Edmonds listed five ingredients of an *effective* school: strong administrative leadership from the principal, high expectations of student achievement, a safe and orderly atmosphere conducive to learning, an emphasis on the acquisition of basic skills, and frequent monitoring of student progress. For a critique of this five factor model, see Scheerens and Creemers (1989). Tomlinson (1980) agreed with Edmonds, but added (among others) efficient use of classroom time involving an active engagement of students in learning activities and the use of parents or aides to help keep students on task. On the basis of a further review of the effective schools literature, Purkey and Smith (1983) provided a *portrait of an effective school* by making a distinction between nine *organizational and structural variables* and four *process variables*, which taken together, define the climate and culture of the school. They asserted that the most important organization-structure variables are: school site management, instructional leadership, staff stability, schoolwide staff development, parental involvement and support, schoolwide recognition of academic success, maximized learning time, and district support.

Purkey and Smith argued that this first group of variables, which can be set in place by administrative and bureaucratic means, precede and facilitate a second group of process variables, namely: collaborative planning and collegial relationships, sense of community, clear goals and expectations, order, and discipline. They noted, however, that although these variables seem to be responsible for a school climate that leads to increased student achievement, it is ". . . difficult to plant them in schools from without or to command them into existence by administrative fiat" (p. 445). The same can also be said of many conclusions drawn from the research on teacher effectiveness. As Brophy and Good (1986) noted: ". . . what constitutes effective instruction varies with persons and contexts" (p. 370). Such cautions have important implications for policy. On the basis of an intensive empirical study of models of school effectiveness, Banks (1992) has provided a further note of caution:

> Research on effective schools is being used to shape major policymaking initiatives in Australia and overseas, even though what makes some schools more effective than others remains an open question. Because clear and unequivocal messages to educators and policymakers are yet to emerge from the research, unquestioning acceptance of the current findings should be a cause for concern. (p. 199)

Due to the magnitude and complexity of such school organizational factors, quantitative data on these factors were not obtained for the present study. Furthermore, the available evidence for the importance of these factors is not specific to reading achievement per se. Rather, on the basis of the student and teacher data, the approach adopted involved the identification of those schools in which students consistently indicated high levels of reading achievement over a three-year period (1988-1990) followed by qualitative field investigations in those schools (1991). These investigations were designed to identify and describe school level characteristics that had positive impacts on students' reading achievements.

The Explanatory Models

Against this background and in the context of this body of research, the present study was designed to estimate the extent to which students' reading achievements over time are influenced by explanatory factors at the student, teacher, and school levels. To this end, the basic explanatory model tested is schematically presented in Figure 1. This model posits that student Reading Achievement (ACHIEVE) is positively influenced by the effects of five student level variables (Gender [SEX], Family Socioeconomic Status [SES], Reading Activity at Home [READACT], Attitudes Towards Reading [ATTITUDES], and Attentiveness in the Classroom [ATTENTIVE]); and five class/teacher level variables (Teacher Experience [TEXP], Participation in Professional Development [PD], Professional Self-Perception [ENERGY/ENTHUSIASM], whether or not teachers were trained in one or more of three common literacy professional development programs [LITPRG] and School Type [SCHTYP], i.e., government or non-government).

Figure 1, however, does not allow estimation of the interdependent effects among the factors (constructs). To this end and for substantive purposes, the baseline covariance structure model tested in this study is schematically depicted in Figure 2 and the three-wave, latent longitudinal model is shown in Figure 3.

For simplicity, Figure 2 presents the hypothesized structural relationships among the latent constructs of interest at the first time point (baseline). As a means of clarifying the proposed effect relationships, the hypothesized directions of influences are given by unidirectional arrows. Estimation of the effects among the constructs, indicated by plus signs (+) and their relative magnitudes, constituted the initial objectives of the study. At the teacher level, the model posits that teachers' participation in inservice professional development has direct positive effects on their professional self-perceptions (Teacher Affect), which in turn, have positive effects on students' Attitudes Towards Reading, Attentiveness in the Classroom, and on students' Reading Achievement. At the student level, the model posits that Home Background Factors have both direct and indirect positive effects on Reading Achievement, as well as on the mediating latent variables of students' Attitudes Towards Reading and Attentiveness in the Classroom.

Figure 3 presents a schematic version of the proposed three-wave, latent longitudinal model, showing the hypothesized structural relationships among latent factors at the student, teacher, and school levels over three time points (i.e., three years). Several features of this model are worth noting. First, the model requires estimation of the auto regressive effects of the student and school level factors on themselves, over time. Second, the model allows for estimation of the reciprocal effects among the factors. Third, since it is usual for students to be taught by a

Figure 1. Schematic representation of the basic explanatory model.

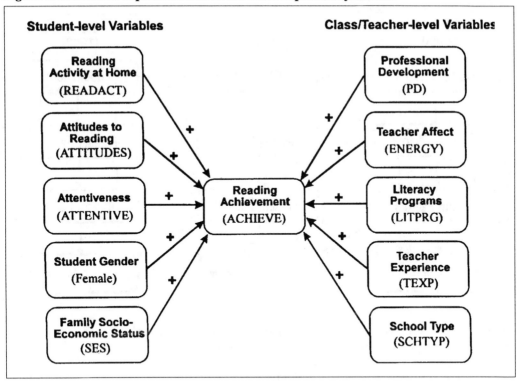

Figure 2. Schematic representation of the baseline structural equation model.

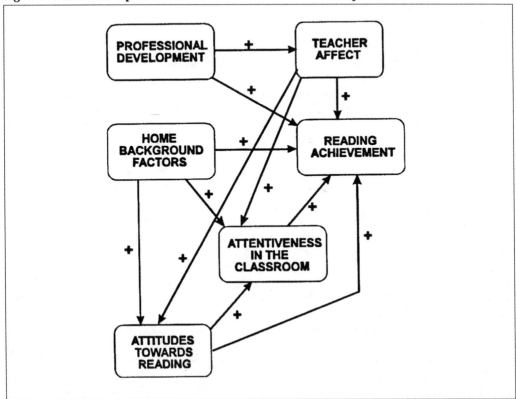

Figure 3. Schematic three-wave model.

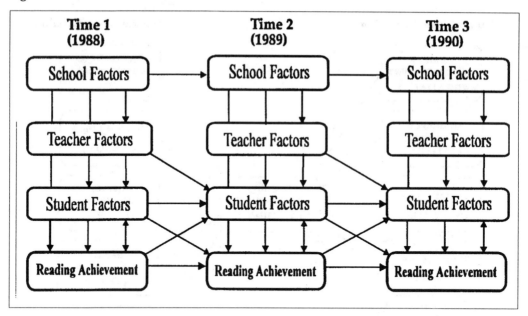

different teacher each year or by multiple teachers during any one school year, the effects of teacher level variables were estimated at each time point only.

Method

Design

Based on the major research question, the following sample design procedures were aimed to address the dual needs of the study, namely, (a) to obtain stable cross sectional baseline data and (b) to provide for the conduct of detailed longitudinal investigations. To this end, the present study employed a longitudinal, three-wave panel design involving: (a) repeated measures on five cohorts of students (initially at grade levels 1, 3, 5, 7, and 9) nested within classes/schools, and (b) repeated measures on schools. The second design involved cross sections of students nested within schools that were changing over time. Hence, the design was both longitudinal and cross sectional as illustrated in Table 1.

Sample Characteristics

For simplicity, specific details of the target populations, sampling strata, and design are not reported here, but are available elsewhere (Rowe, 1990c). In brief, the study was conducted in a stratified probability sample of students and their teachers in government, Catholic, and independent elementary and secondary schools, involving a cohort of students initially in Grades 1, 3, 5, 7, and 9 located in four education regions (two metropolitan and two rural), within and without the teacher professional development literacy programs of interest, (i.e., ELIC, LaRIC, CLIC, and Reading Recovery).

The sample design procedures were aimed to address the dual needs of the study, namely, (a) to obtain stable cross sectional baseline data and (b) to provide an opportunity for conducting detailed longitudinal investigations. Thus, the sample design employed within each of the sample strata was a three-stage cluster design in which schools were selected with probability proportional to their enrollment size (PPS) at the first stage, one intact class selected randomly

Table 1
Sample Cohorts by Grade Level and Date

Date	Grade Levels					
	Cohort 1	Cohort 2	Cohort 3	Cohort 4	Cohort 5	
1988	1	3	5	7	9	
1989	2	4	6	8	10	
1990	1	3	6	7	9	11

* *Note.* In 1990, for each of the participating schools, an additional class of Grade 1 students was included in the elementary school sample, and a further class of Grade 7 students was added to the secondary school sample. The reason for these additions was to examine the cross-sectional stability of within-school effects on students' reading achievements.

(at each grade level) within each selected school at the second stage, and all students in the selected classes were included at the third stage. On the basis of an estimated intraclass correlation of 0.2 and an average cluster size of 20, the level of sampling precision within each stratum involved the specification of sampling tolerances of ± 5 percent for 95 percent confidence limits (Ross, 1988a, 1988b). To satisfy these sampling error constrains, it was calculated that a designed sample of at least 164 classes, each of ≥ 20 students would be required (i.e., n = 164 x 20 = 3280). However, given the longitudinal nature of the study and the potential sample and data attrition over time, a more generous target sample of 280 classes (i.e., 5,600 students) was drawn.

Procedure and Measures

Following invitations to sampled schools and their parent communities to participate in the project, pre-study briefing sessions for teachers from those schools were held to provide detailed information about the objectives, design, and administrative requirements of the study and to distribute the relevant data-gathering instruments. Two major instruments were used, both in the form of questionnaires. A similar procedure was used prior to each of the three subsequent data-collection stages.

Student Level Variables

On a Student Record form, two sets of indicators of home background factors were recorded. First, with the informed consent and cooperation of parents, family socioeconomic indicators (SES) were obtained which included: the number of years of mother's education, father's education, and mother's and father's occupational classification—as measured on the Australian Bureau of Statistics 8-point scale (Castles, 1986). Second, a measure of students' Reading Activity at Home (READACT) was obtained from self-report responses on three Likert-type items, each measured on 4-point rating scales: (1) "Do you read books, magazines, or newspapers at home?" (2) "Do any of your family or friends read books or stories to you?" (3) "Do you talk about books or stories you have read with your family or friends?" For each item, students were asked to respond in one of the following categories: Never, Not Very Often (defined as: once or twice per month), Often (once or twice per week), Every Day (coded 0 - 3, respectively). Student Gender (SEX) was coded 1 for females and 0 for males. Additional sociodemographic data included: country of birth for student, mother and father; the number of years student has lived in Australia; the number of persons who live in the student's residence; and the extent to which English is spoken at home (five indicators).

Students' Attitudes Towards Reading (ATTITUDES) were indicated on three items: (1) "Do you ENJOY reading?" (2) "Do you find reading USEFUL?," and (3) "How WELL can you read?"— each measured on 5-point ordinal scales: *Not at all, Not very much, Moderately, Quite a lot*, and *Very Much* (coded 0 - 4). In the event that some students had difficulty with reading and/or understanding the self-report items, teachers used the response form as an interview schedule to assist students in making their responses.

Table 2
Items Measuring Attentiveness in the Classroom

1. Cannot concentrate on any particular task; easily distracted	• • • • •	Can concentrate on any task; not easily distracted
2. Perseveres in the face of difficult or challenging work	• • • • •	Lacks perseverance; is impatient with difficult or challenging work
3. Persistent; sustained attention span	• • • • •	Easily frustrated; short attention span
4. Aimless activity	• • • • •	Purposeful activity

On a Teacher Record form, a measure of students' Attentiveness in the classroom (ATTENTIVE) was obtained from four teacher rated items each measured on 5-point ordinal scales following the bipolar format advocated and used by Kysel, Varlaam, Stoll, and Sammons (1983). The psychometric characteristics of this domain and its constituent items for the present sample have been reported by Rowe and Rowe (1989, 1993). On the scale provided for each paired behavioral statement, teachers were asked to mark a category nearest to the statement which best describes typical behavior of the student. The relevant items are shown in Table 1. Scores on each item were coded 1 - 5, from negative to positive behavior.

Reading Achievement (ACHIEVE) was assessed in two ways: (a) scores on a criterion/domain-referenced reading comprehension test and (b) teacher ratings on a criterion-referenced profile of student reading behaviors.[2] For 5-6 year old students, the Primary Reading Survey Test, Level AA (ACER, 1979) was administered. For older students, selected sub-tests from the *Tests of Reading Comprehension* (TORCH) battery (Mossenson, Hill, & Masters, 1987) were administered. The TORCH tests are a set of 14 untimed reading tests for use with students in Grades 3 to 10 that assess the extent to which readers are able to obtain meaning from text. These tests use an item-response modeling (IRM) approach (Masters, 1982) that provides vertically calibrated estimates of reading ability on a common scale that ranges from zero to 100. Such tests have particular advantages in a study of the present kind since they allow

---

[2] In the design of this study a conscious decision was taken to not depend primarily on standardized test results to measure students' reading achievement. Whereas the use of such tests for the measurement of learning outcomes is typically justified on the grounds of maximum reliability, this has often been at the expense of validity. Moreover, there has long been criticism of the utility of such tests as measures of either learning or competence (e.g., Darling-Hammond, 1994; Frederiksen, 1984; Lacey & Lawton, 1981; Linn, 1986; Newmann & Archibald, 1990; Wigdor & Garner, 1982). Such criticism has since gained credence in the areas of standards monitoring and performance assessment, where new approaches to obtaining more curriculum-specific and *authentic* (Wiggins, 1989) measures of assessment are being tried (Lesh & Lamon, 1992; Moss, 1994; Murphy, 1990; Nisbet, 1993; O'Connor, 1992; Resnick & Resnick, 1992; Shavelson, 1994; Taylor, 1994), but it is a criticism that has been largely ignored in almost all studies of factors affecting student learning outcomes.

meaningful comparisons to be made across age groups and over time.

All students were rated by their teachers on the English Profiles—*Reading Bands* (Victoria, 1991)—a developmental, IRM-scaled inventory of nine bands (labeled A-I), each consisting of multiple indicators describing reading behaviors. A full account of the development of the Reading Bands is given by (Griffin, 1990; Griffin & Jones, 1988; Griffin & Nix, 1991; Rowe, Hill, & Holmes-Smith, 1994). For each band of indicators, students were assigned a score of: (0) for no evidence, (1) beginning, (2) partial, and (3) for complete evidence—that the indicators listed are consistently displayed by the student. The ratings for each band were added together to give a total score out of 27.

A key assumption underlying the English Profile Reading Bands is that they form a cumulative scale similar to that described by Guttman (1944). Using the Guttman method of scaling, lower bound estimates of *true reliability* for the Reading Bands were computed for large samples of students at each year level (Preparatory - K to Grade 11) and are summarised in Table A1 of the Appendix. The results indicate that the profiles do function as cumulative scales or growth continua and that teachers are consistent in their use of the scales. Further evidence regarding the reliability of teacher assessments using the Reading Bands of the Victorian English Profiles is available in the form of test/retest reliabilities and interrater reliability estimates. These are summarised in Table A2 of the Appendix. The limited evidence regarding interrater reliability shown in the third column of Table A2 are Pearson product-moment correlations between the ratings of two or more teachers who rated the same student. These data derived from naturally occurring instances (mostly team-teaching situations) in which two or more teachers in the same school were able to provide an assessment of the same student. The results indicate a satisfactory level of interrater reliability among teachers. Prior to administration, pilot versions of all instruments were extensively trialed in schools to check on validity and reliability, the results of which were used to refine item content, nomenclature, and presentation format.

Class/Teacher Level Variables

Teachers were asked to respond to a pre-trialed questionnaire instrument designed to obtain information about: Background Training and Experience; Professional Development, Professional Self-Perception, and several literacy-focused aspects related to Teaching Practices and Resources. Of immediate concern to this report, Teacher Experience (TEXP) was measured in terms of the number of years of full-time service. Information about Professional Development (PD) was gained from three questions:

1. How many professional development inservice programs have you attended in the last three years which have involved language and literacy learning?
2. How many inservice programs, other than those related to literacy, have you attended in the last three years?
3. In general, to what extent has your professional development as a teacher been enhanced by participation in inservice programs?

The third question invited teachers to respond in one category of a five-point Likert-type scale, ranging from *Not at all* to *Very much*.

Measures of teachers' Professional Self-perception were obtained from responses on a semantic differential instrument consisting of 34, seven-point evaluative scales adapted from the Professional Self-Perception Questionnaire developed by Elsworth and Coulter (1977). On the adapted semantic differential instrument used in the present study, teachers were required to provide a self-rating on each scale in terms of *myself as a teacher*. From a five-factor solution of 273 teacher responses on this instrument, Rowe and Sykes (1989) found that the first factor (Energy/Enthusiasm) accounted for 47.2 percent of the total variance, while the remaining four factors accounted for only 20.8 percent of the variance between them. To illustrate the relevant items, Table 3 presents those items specifically related to the Energy/Enthusiasm scale.

Table 3
Self-Report Items Measuring Teacher Energy/Enthusiasm

unenthusiastic	•	•	•	•	•	•	•	enthusiastic
burnt-out	•	•	•	•	•	•	•	energized
indifferent	•	•	•	•	•	•	•	eager
unfulfilled	•	•	•	•	•	•	•	fulfilled

Two further variables at the class/teacher level were considered. First, a dummy variable (LITPRG) was included to indicate whether or not teachers of the intact classes in the sample had been trained in one or more of the common literacy professional development programs (coded 0 for not trained and 1 for trained). Second, a further dummy variable (SCHTYP) was included to indicate *School Type* (coded 0 for government schools and 1 for non-government schools). Although this indicator is strictly a school level variable, it was treated as a class/teacher level variable.

Analyses

In fitting the single-level and multilevel explanatory models as illustrated schematically in Figure 1 and Figure 3, maximally reliable composite scores for multiple-indicator variables at the student level (i.e., SES, READACT, ATTITUDES, ATTENTIVE, and ACHIEVE) and at the class/teacher level (PD, ENERGY) were calculated. These scores and their reliabilities were obtained from fitting one-factor congeneric measurement models to the relevant ordinal-scaled indicator items for each construct. In so doing, use was made of a weighted least squares (WLS) method of parameter estimation, fitted to the appropriate polychoric intercorrelation matrix and an asymptotic covariance matrix of these correlations using PRELIS (Jöreskog & Sörbom, 1988) and LISREL 7 (Jöreskog & Sörbom, 1989). For specific details of these well-established procedures, the reader is referred to Alwin and Jackson (1980), Brown (1989), Fleishman and Benson (1987), Jöreskog (1971), Munck (1979), and Werts, Rock, Linn, and Jöreskog (1978). Further details including the rationale for this approach to computing composite variables and their reliabilities have more recently been outlined and demonstrated by Hill, Holmes-Smith, and Rowe (1993) and by Holmes-Smith and Rowe (1994).

For explanatory models of the kind illustrated by Figure 2, simultaneous estimation of the measurement properties of the observed indicators and the structural relationships among their associated latent variables were undertaken using LISREL 7 (Jöreskog & Sörbom, 1989). In fitting these models, use was also made of the relevant polychoric/polyserial intercorrelation matrices and their asymptotic covariance matrices using PRELIS (Jöreskog & Sörbom, 1988). Specific technical details and results of fitting these models to the present data are given in Rowe (1991b) and Rowe and Rowe (1992a, 1992b, 1992c).

Estimates of the proportion of variance in students' reading achievements due to the clustering of students within class/teachers were obtained from fitting multilevel variance-components models to the data using *ML3* (Prosser, Rasbash, & Goldstein, 1991).

Major Findings and Their Implications

Achieved Sample

Of the 100 schools originally invited to participate in the study in 1988, data were received on 5,092 students from 92 schools (72 elementary; 15 secondary, five P-12), including 64 government schools and 28 non-government schools. Frequency details of the achieved student sample by school type, age group, and gender are shown in Table 4. Thus, from a target sample of 280 classes and 5,600 students, data were received from 256 classes on 5,092 students, representing 91 percent of the target sample. Complete data for the four age groups of students were obtained as follows: 5-6 years (n = 1,368), 7-8 years (n = 1,350), 9-11 years (n = 1,329), and 12-14 years (n = 732). Complete data were also obtained from 273 teachers of these students, with a mean teaching experience of 13.5 years (range = 34, SD = 8.0).

One hundred thirty teachers had been trained in one or more of the literacy, inservice professional development courses of interest. With reference to sampling accuracy, the standard errors of the mean values for each of the response variables of interest for both students and teachers during 1988, and since, have not exceeded ± 3.1 percent, which has been well within the designed five percent limit of the targeted population values for determining the sampling frame.

Table 4
Details of Student Sample by School Type, Age Cohort, and Gender***

School Type	Age Cohort									
	5-6 Years		7-8 Years		9-11 Years		12-14 Years		Totals	
	F	M	F	M	F	M	F	M	F	M
Gov Elem	519	448	497	467	476	496			1492	1401
NG Elem	221	203	304	217	200	222			725	642
Gov Sec							264	310	264	310
NG Sec							133	125	133	123
Totals	740	651	801	684	676	708	397	435	2614	2478
	1391		1485		1384		832		5092	

* Gov = Government School; NG = Non-government school; Elem = Elementary; Sec = Secondary
** F = Female student; M = Male student

Data obtained on student family sociodemographic variables indicated that 94.3 percent of the sample were born in Australia, a further one percent were born in the British Isles, one percent from South East Asia, with the balance being made up of students born in Southern Europe, Middle Eastern, and South American countries. The mean number of equivalent full-time years of parents' education was: for mothers (*mean* = 11.6, *SD* = 2.9) and for fathers (*mean* = 12.0, *SD* = 3.4). The data on parents' occupational classifications indicated that the proportions obtained in each of the eight categories were within 95 percent confidence limits for the Australian adult workforce population (Castles, 1986).

For ease of presentation and interpretation, the major findings from the study are reported at each of the levels of analysis, namely, the student level, the teacher level, the combined student and teacher levels, and at the school level. Further, to assist the reader, the results are reported mostly in summary form using graphs and diagrams rather than in tables, showing overall findings rather than those for each of the four age groups separately—except in those instances where tabulated presentations better illustrate the relevant findings. More comprehensive technical details related to the data and findings are available from the papers published to date (Rowe, 1990a, 1990b, 1991b; Rowe & Rowe, 1992a, 1992b, 1992c; Rowe & Sykes, 1989).

Student Level Results

There was positive growth in reading achievement for each of the age cohorts of students. Figure 4 summarizes this growth on the *Reading Profile Bands* using box-and-whisker plots (Tukey, 1977) to describe the *shape* of the distributions for each grade level. The shaded boxes represent the range of achievement for the middle 50 percent of students, with the bottom of each box indicating the 25th percentile and the top of each box showing the 75th percentile. The asterisk in the middle of each box represents the level of achievement for students at the 50th percentile (median). The bottom whisker shows the level of achievement of the 10th percentile, while the top whisker shows the 90th percentile. Lines of best fit have been drawn on each graph for the 10th, 25th, 75th, and 90th percentile values, respectively.

The distributions indicate a period of rapid growth during the first few years of schooling, coinciding with the period during which young people acquire basic literacy skills and thereafter show a consistent rate of growth up to Grade 9. It is noticeable, however, that the range of reading achievement increases markedly over the years of schooling, with more than four band widths separating Grade 9 students at the 10th and 90th percentiles. Of particular concern is the flattening out of the growth trajectory at the 10th percentile, indicating a trend of less than one band width of growth between Grades 4 to 9.

Figure 4 also provides evidence of a discontinuity between elementary and secondary schooling for reading achievement, with a dip in the rate of progress of students in the first year of secondary school (Grade 7). This pattern has been observed frequently in previous studies using common measures over elementary and secondary schooling. Perhaps the most striking feature of this pattern is its similarity with that shown by pediatric percentile growth charts for height and weight during the prepubertal to early adolescent transition period. It is possible that what has become known as an *educational phenomenon* may also have developmental psycho-physiological correlates.

The findings related to students' progress on the Reading Profile Bands over time have been particularly useful in the development of benchmarks' for the expected range of student achievement in reading. Using the data from the Literacy Programs Study for teachers' assessments of student progress on the *Reading Profile Bands* (from Grade 1 to Grade 11), recording sheets for *Records of Achievement* (see Broadfoot, 1986) and for reporting to parents have been constructed. These recording sheets were constructed using the nutshell statements contained in the *English Profiles Handbook* (Victoria, 1991).

To determine the proportions of unique variance in Reading Achievement (ACHIEVE) accounted for by the home background measures (i.e., SES and READACT),[3] students' Attitudes Towards Reading (ATTITUDES), and Attentiveness in the classroom (ATTENTIVE), the composite scores for students' Reading Achievement (ACHIEVE) were regressed onto each linear combination of the relevant manifest (composite) variables. The results of these analyses for the four age groups are presented graphically in Figure 5.

From the data summarized in Figure 5, it is clear that the family SES variables (i.e., mother's education [MEDUC], father's education [FEDUC], and father's occupation [FOCC]) account for very small proportions of the variance in students' reading achievement, ranging from 0.3 percent (7-8 year group) to 3.2 percent (12-14 year group). The correlations between SES and ACHIEVE were likewise very small (5-6 years, r = 0.096; 7-8 years, r = 0.048; 9-11 years, r = 0.070; 12-14 years, r = 0.053).

The comparative contributions of each SES indicator towards Reading Achievement are shown in Table 5. These findings indicate that the best positive predictors are MEDUC and

---

[3] Since 48 percent of mothers indicated *Home Duties*, mother's occupation was excluded from the estimation of family SES. Further, separate analyses for female and male students in each age group were computed, but are not presented here. While there were significant gender differences in favour of girls on all variables (with the exception of SES variables), the magnitudes of the intercorrelation estimates were very similar.

Figure 4. Students' progress in reading on the Victorian *Reading Profile Bands.*

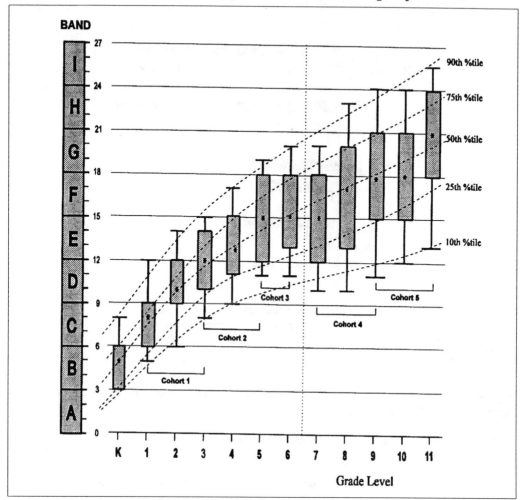

Note. Data for the Preparatory Grade (K) sample (n = 2280) were obtained from a further study reported by Rowe, Hill, and Holmes-Smith (1994). These data have been included here for completeness.

FOCC, but that in general FEDUC is a negative predictor. This result suggests that students' Reading Achievement is positively influenced by mothers' inputs and possibly by family income (from fathers' occupational status), while fathers appear to spend less qualitative time with their children in respect of reading activities. By comparison, the home background variable of Reading Activity at Home (READACT) contributes strongly to the proportion of variance in students' reading achievement, for each of the four age groups (see Figure 5). Although students' Attitudes Towards Reading also contribute positively towards their reading achievement, the strongest influence, regardless of age group, is from Attentiveness, ranging from 13.4 percent (7-8 year group) to 22.9 percent (12-14 year group).

With the student as the *unit of analysis* (for illustrative purposes here), the magnitude of the influences of home background factors (i.e., family SES and Reading Activity at Home) on Reading Achievement, as well as on the mediating variables of students' Attitudes Towards Reading and Attentiveness in the classroom were assessed using structural equation modeling (i.e., Jöreskog & Sörbom, 1989). For simplicity of presentation, the findings are summarized in

Figure 5. Percentage histogram showing proportions of explained variance (unique) in Reading Achievement for four factors by age cohort.

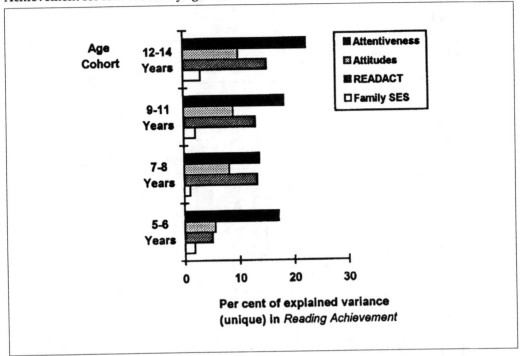

Table 5

Regression of Reading Achievement on Family SES Variables[a] Showing Parameter Estimates (b) and Standard Errors (S.E.) for Four Age Cohorts[b]

Age Cohort	Statistic	MEDUC	FEDUC	FOCC	R^2	% of Variance
5-6 Years (n = 1368)	b	0.083*	-0.024	0.005	0.010	1.0
	S.E.	0.035	0.036	0.029		
	T-value	2.384	-0.068	1.902		
7-8 Years (n = 1350)	b	0.001	0.054	-0.013	0.003	0.3
	S.E.	0.034	0.035	0.029		
	T-value	0.009	1.529	-0.460		
9-11 Years (n = 1329)	b	0.089*	-0.036	0.104*	0.018	1.8
	S.E.	0.035	0.036	0.029		
	T-value	2.518	-1.004	3.625		
12-14 Years (n = 732)	b	0.119*	-0.123	0.156*	0.032	3.2
	S.E.	0.047	0.049	0.039		
	T-valued	2.524	-2.536	3.968		

Note. The multiple R^2 values are adjusted for the degrees of freedom
* Significant beyond the $p < 0.05$ level by univariate 2-tailed test
[a] MEDUC - Number of years of mother's education
FEDUC - Number of years of father's education
FOCC - Occupational classification on 8-point ordinal scale
[b] Age cohorts with complete data

Figure 6.1. Schematic structural equation model showing the effects of home background factors on reading achievement, mediated by attitudes towards Reading and Attentiveness in the classroom.

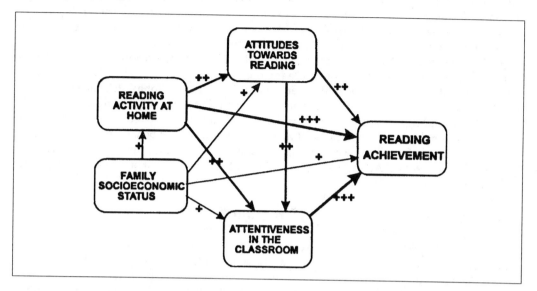

Figure 6.2. Schematic structural equation model showing the reciprocal effects between reading activity at home and reading achievement, mediated by attitudes and attentiveness in the classroom.

Figure 6.3. Schematic structural equation model showing the reciprocal effects between attentiveness in the classroom and reading achievement, mediated by attitudes and reading activity at home.

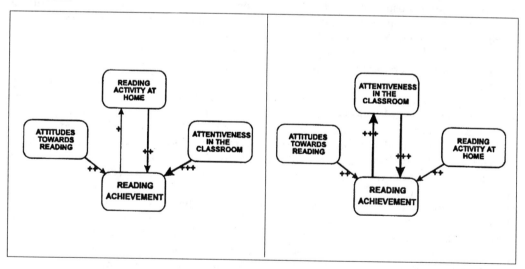

the explanatory model depicted by Figure 6.1. (Note: The plus signs [+] indicate the relative magnitude(s) of the effect(s) among the latent constructs).

These findings indicate that regardless of age and gender, family socioeconomic status has little direct or indirect influence on students' Reading Achievement. However, Reading Activity at Home has significant, positive influences on Achievement, as well as on the mediating variables of Attitudes Towards Reading and Attentiveness in the classroom. In fact, the magnitude of the effects of READACT on ACHIEVE increase across the age groups, suggesting that Reading Activity at Home has an increasing influence on achievement as students progress through elementary and secondary schooling (see Rowe, 1991b). Moreover, there is a strong positive interdependence between students' Attitudes Towards Reading and Reading Activity at Home, both of which have significant positive influences on achievement. The strong positive associations between Attitudes and Attentive behaviors in the classroom underscore the importance of Reading Activity at Home as a powerful influencing variable.

Results related to the magnitude of the reciprocal effects between Reading Activity at Home and achievement, show that the effects are interdependent. That is, while achievement does have significant, positive influences on Reading Activity at Home (for all student age groups), the influence of Reading Activity at Home on achievement is notably stronger (Figure 6.2). Similarly, the findings indicate a strong reciprocal relationship between Attentiveness and reading achievement (Figure 6.3), suggesting that while inattentive behaviors lead to reduced reading achievement, reading achievement—mediated by attitudes and reading activity at home—leads to increased Attentiveness in the classroom, to the benefit of all concerned (Rowe, 1991b; Rowe & Rowe, 1992b).

Literacy Program Effects

A major aim of the present study was to examine the impact of teacher professional development literacy programs (LP) such as ELIC, LaRIC, CLIC, and Reading Recovery on students' reading development over time. The numbers of students whose teachers had been trained in the literacy programs of interest at the outset of the study (1988) indicated that 53 percent of the sample of students in government schools and 41 percent of students in non-government schools were taught by teachers who had been trained in at least one of these programs.

In general, students' reading achievement measures (on the tests of reading comprehension and the Reading Profile Bands) for those taught by LP trained teachers did not differ significantly from those taught by non-LP trained teachers. This finding suggests that, independent of teacher exposure or non-exposure to specific Literacy Programs, students' achievements in reading appear to be relatively uniform. While there was strong evidence of significant improvement in the reading achievement measures for all students over the three data-collection stages of the study, there was greater variability in the range of achievement measures of students taught by LP trained teachers compared with those of students taught by non-LP trained teachers. One exception to this finding was that for those students who had participated in a Reading Recovery (RR) program (147), the variation (range) of RR students' test and profile scores were smaller than those of their non-RR peers. This finding suggests that the Reading Recovery program (Clay, 1985) appears to be meeting its intended purposes for those students involved.

The data summarized in Figure 7 for Reading Recovery and non-Reading Recovery students on the Reading Profile Bands indicate that although the reading achievement distributions of those students who had participated in a Reading Recovery program were generally lower than those of their non-RR-exposed peers, the lower limits of the distributions for the achievement measures are higher. These findings indicate that those students who had been identified as readers at risk and placed in a RR program have benefited notably from participation. In fact, some RR students were achieving beyond the 80th percentile level of their non-RR-exposed peers. Moreover, in spite of the small numbers involved, the earlier gains made by RR students who were in Grades 5 and 6 during 1988 and 1989 appear to have been sustained.

Policy Implications

Above all, the results provide strong empirical support for the benefits of Reading Activity at Home, regardless of family socioeconomic status and the related value of recognising the important contributions which parents can make to the educational development of their

Figure 7. Box plots showing distributions on the Victorian Reading Profile Bands for three age cohorts of Reading Recovery and non-Reading Recovery students.

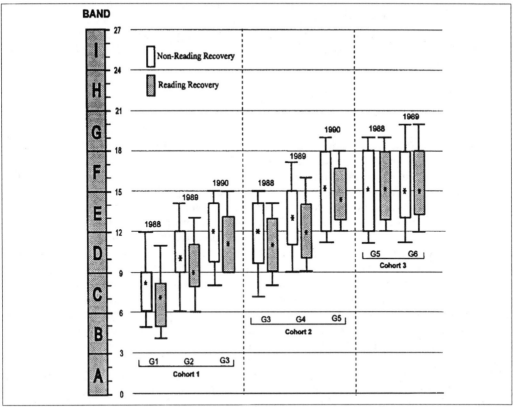

Note. 50 percent of cases lie within the box; the whiskers indicate the 10th and 90th percentiles, respectively; *indicates the 50th percentile (median value).

children. Moreover, these effects have been stable over time (1988-1990). From a more detailed analysis of the READACT items, it is disappointing that so many students in the 5-6 and 7-8 year-old groups indicate that they never or rarely share reading activities with family members or friends. For students in these age groups, high scores on the reading alone item and the shared reading items in particular are strongly associated with positive attitudes towards reading, high levels of attentiveness in the classroom, and high scores on the measures of reading achievement. For older students, related positive associations are mainly with reading alone and discussing reading. This latter finding suggests that, while students may spend less time reading to others and being read to by others as they become independent readers, it is clearly in their interest to participate in activities which encourage discussion of reading materials, both at home and at school.

Given the importance of either direct or indirect parental involvement in students' educational progress, it is clear that the work of schools needs the support of programs designed to assist parents to take an active role in the development of their child's reading skills. The results show that it is important that school based measures to prevent early reading difficulties (such as the Reading Recovery program [Clay, 1985]) should be coupled with an early intervention program designed to encourage and assist parents, where necessary, to take an active role in partnership with teachers. Findings from the study suggest, however, that parental literacy is likely to have a significant impact on such a role. In this context, government policy has a major role to play. Programs of the type which provide opportunities through which both parent and child literacy are enhanced would appear to have particular merit.

In view of the salience of the reciprocal relationship between attentiveness and reading achievement, at least two directions for appropriate classroom management and intervention/ treatment are suggested. First, given the mutuality of learning outcomes and behavior, there is a clear need to focus intervention strategies in both domains simultaneously (Rowe & Rowe, 1992b). Second, there is a clear need to enhance the positive mediating effects of home inputs on students' attitudes, achievement, and attentiveness in the classroom (Rowe, 1991b) or *time on task* (Carroll, 1963, 1984).

Teacher Level Results

A central aim of the project was to examine the nature and impact of teacher inservice literacy programs such as ELIC, LaRIC, and RR on students' reading achievements over time. Following Elsworth and Coulter (1977), it was argued that the notion of change in professional self-perception and level of adjustment holds particular promise as a criterion for judging the effectiveness of teacher inservice training programs. Further, apart from its influence on performance, changes in self-perception (mediated by participation in professional development) may provide useful indicators of teachers' adjustment to professional role demands. Where teachers aspire to be professionally competent and also perceive themselves to be professionally competent, they may then be regarded as *well adjusted* in the sense of being able to realise their professional aspirations, rather than being thwarted or frustrated. What is suggested here is that "if . . . teachers are to self-actualize in their professional roles, they should not only possess that knowledge and skill regarded as necessary for competent role performance; they should also see themselves as competent" (Elsworth & Coulter, 1977, p. 4). That is, on the one hand, inservice training programs should provide teachers with opportunities to develop professional knowledge and skills, and on the other, assist in the development of a positive professional self view.

From factor analyses of the 34-item *Professional Self-Perception Questionnaire* (Elsworth & Coulter, 1977) used in the study, five stable dimensions of teachers' professional self-perceptions have been consistently identified: *Energy/Enthusiasm, Orderliness, Warmth and Supportiveness, Creativity*, and *Clarity*. The first factor (Energy/Enthusiasm) accounted for the largest proportion of the variance by far (47.2 percent), while the remaining four factors accounted for only 20.8 percent of the total variance between them. This finding suggests that Energy/Enthusiasm-related indicators are the most consistent and salient concerns of teachers in terms of professional self-perception. (For specific technical details of these findings, see Rowe & Sykes, 1989).

To examine differences on the five affect dimensions for teachers trained and not trained in literacy inservice programs (i.e., ELIC, LaRIC, CLIC, RR), both univariate and multivariate analyses were computed. The results showed significant positive differences in favour of teachers trained in these programs on all five dimensions, suggesting the efficacy of these professional development programs in terms of teachers' professional self-perceptions.

In terms of teachers' participation rates in inservice programs, as well as their evaluation of personal enhancement due to participation in such programs, there were significant differences between the four education regions (labeled A - D) from which the teacher sample was drawn. The mean ratings on these variables for teachers located in regions A and B were markedly higher than those for their counterparts in regions C and D. Similarly, there were significant differences between the regions on the mean scale scores for the Energy/ Enthusiasm and Clarity dimensions of professional self-perception, with teachers in region B recording notably higher mean ratings on all five affect dimensions than their colleagues in the other three regions. Moreover, it was interesting to observe that teachers in region B also had significantly higher mean participation rates in both literacy and non-literacy professional development programs than their peers in the other three regions. A subsequent check of personnel records for the previous three years revealed that, per capita of teacher population, teachers in region B had less than half the number of absentee days of their nearest regional rival (region A). While this finding may be mere coincidence, it is sufficiently suggestive of a positive impact of professional development on teacher affect to warrant further investigation.

Results from the explanatory modeling indicated strong, positive effects of professional development on teachers' professional self-perceptions, particularly those related to Energy/ Enthusiasm. The reciprocal effects of Professional Development and Energy/Enthusiasm were significantly positive and especially the direct effect of Professional Development on Energy/ Enthusiasm. These findings provided explanatory potency to the observations from the raw data, namely, that those teachers who had frequently participated in inservice programs during the *last three years*, regardless of program type, consistently gave self-perception ratings towards the positive ends of the semantic differential scales. Alternatively, those teachers who had none or minimal inservice participation rates tended to provide ratings at the negative ends of the scales.

Policy Implications

The policy implications of these findings are clear. The results provide overwhelming support for the efficacy of inservice professional development for teachers and suggest that teachers' professional self-perceptions constitute important criteria for evaluating the intended benefits of inservice programs and may also be crucial, not only in monitoring teacher commitment and adjustment to professional role demands, but also in monitoring outcomes for students. Moreover, the results have important implications for the design and adoption of particular models of inservice program delivery for teachers. Consistent with related research (Rowe, 1987), these findings clearly suggest the utility of professional development programs of the ELIC, LaRIC, and RR kind, not just for literacy, but also for other curriculum and school management domains.

Combined Student Level and Teacher Level Results

The data presented in Figure 8 suggested on the one hand, that the student level variables of SEX and SES and the class/teacher level variables of TEXP, LITPRG, and SCHTYP each account for very small proportions of the variance in students' Reading Achievement. On the other hand, Reading Activity at Home (READACT), Attitudes Towards Reading (ATTITUDES), and Attentiveness in the classroom (ATTENTIVE) are strong student level predictors of Reading

Figure 8.1. Percentage histogram showing proportions of explained variance (unique) in reading achievement for five student level variables and five teacher level variables.

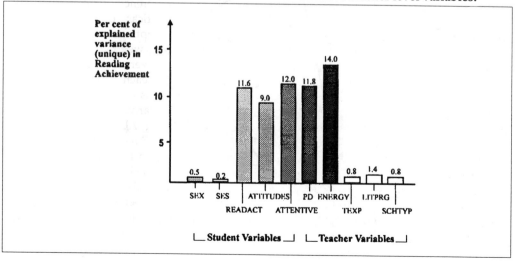

Achievement. Similarly, both Teacher Professional Development (PD) and Teacher Affect (ENERGY) each account for marked proportions of the variance in students' Reading Achievement.

Overall findings from the combined student and teacher level data indicate that teachers' participation in inservice professional development programs have significant, positive effects on their professional self-perceptions (i.e., Energy/Enthusiasm) which in turn, have strong, positive influences on students' attitudes towards reading, attentiveness in the classroom, and reading achievement. The explanatory model shown in Figure 8.2 illustrates the strength of the effect relationships among these factors. For specific technical details, see Rowe (1990b).

All of the findings presented thus far have been based on analyses at a single level. In a study such as the present, teacher and school level effects have crucial implications for analysis, since it is important to account for variation at the student level that may be due to group membership effects. Using multilevel modeling, an important finding was that a large proportion of the variation in students' reading achievement was due to between-class/teacher differences. Much of this variation was accounted for by marked between-class/teacher differences in Teacher Affect (ENERGY) due to participation in professional development, student Attentiveness in the classroom, and levels of Reading Activity at Home—due in the main to the effects of specific school-home literacy programs and home-based activities of students. Figure 9 summarizes the results of fitting two-level variance component models, showing the proportion of explained variation in students' reading achievement due to between-class teacher differences for four grade level cohorts over the three years of the study.

Policy Implications

The finding that teachers' participation in inservice professional development programs has significant positive effects on their affect levels is sufficient justification for the implementation of policies designed to enhance the professional self-perceptions of teachers and their adjustment

Figure 8.2. **Schematic explanatory model showing effects among student level and teacher level factors.**

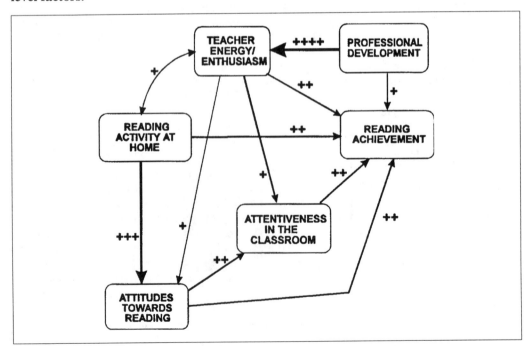

Figure 9. Percentage histogram showing proportion of variation in students' reading achievement due to between-class/teacher differences for four cohorts over three years.

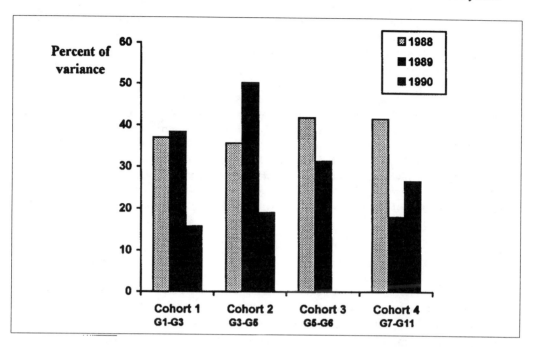

to professional role demands. However, the finding that such teacher level factors have significant positive effects on students' attitudes, behaviors in the classroom, and achievement outcomes is of vital importance.

There is a strong body of research evidence to show that student achievement is mediated by teacher behavior (Ashton & Webb, 1986; Brophy & Good, 1986; Rosenholtz, 1985) and similar evidence that teachers' professional practices are influenced by their self-perceptions (Lee, Dedrick, & Smith, 1991; Levis, 1985; Rowe & Sykes, 1989; Smylie, 1988). In spite of the prevailing emphasis of policymakers on educational outputs in terms of student achievement, the present findings suggest that teachers' professional self-perceptions constitute important criteria for evaluating the intended benefits of inservice programs (inputs) and appear to be crucial for monitoring student outcomes. In any event, the results from the study indicate that professional development does enhance teacher affect and appears to be a powerful means of engendering positive outcomes for students.

The strong evidence from the study for teacher and school effectiveness, in terms of students' achievements in reading, has major policy implications. First, it is important to recognise the high quality work which is being achieved by students, parents, teachers, and schools and to encourage and promote such positive outcomes and their associated *good practices* throughout education systems and the general public. Second, it is essential for any government's public credibility that more than mere lip-service is paid to the identification and promotion of excellence or quality in education. Without evidence of the present kind, claims of *excellence* or *quality* and *good/bad practice* are tenuous at best, as well as being at the mercy of purveyors of popular rumour, anecdote, and faddism. As a basis for policy development, substantive findings of this kind prevent the possibility of irrelevant or unimportant factors being granted greater policy priority than can be justified. Third, and perhaps above all, the value of such findings is that they yield information which enables direct diagnosis of problems (if they exist) and assist parents, teachers, and school administrators to implement positive intervention strategies.

School Level Results

Findings from the multilevel analyses were used to identify those schools in which students consistently attained high levels of reading achievement over the three-year duration of the data collections (1988-1990). The approach adopted involved intensive qualitative investigations in the participating schools during the fourth year of the study (1991), designed to identify and describe the characteristics of schools and classroom programs which are most effective in promoting students' achievements in literacy. This field study component of the project known as *Sharing Strategies for Literacy Improvement* (Holmes-Smith & Charlton, 1992) involved on-site visits to selected schools. The visits included discussions with principals, coordinators, librarians, and teachers; examination of curriculum and school management documents; and observations in classrooms. The outcomes of these investigations have given rise to several propositions that may be used as guiding hypotheses for further investigations.

In those schools in which students had maintained high levels of reading achievement, there was consistent evidence of:

- *Well established procedures for the early detection of non-readers.* There is close monitoring of students' reading achievements in the infant years, together with an intervention program to systematically deal with students having difficulties. While the Reading Recovery program is used in many schools, other schools employ similar strategies of their own design.

- *Quality teachers who are well organised and participate frequently in inservice professional development programs.* Teachers use structured methods, are methodical, reflective, and collaborative, with a well-developed knowledge of theories and practices of language learning—usually acquired through participation in professional development programs. Teachers have high expectations of students and are highly regarded by principals and other staff. They do not necessarily use the latest methods, but are willing to try new ideas and adapt.

- *A whole-school focus on teaching and learning.* Schools have a teaching and learning-focused leadership from the principal and other school leaders. A consistent approach by all teachers in broad curriculum areas is encouraged and there is whole staff involvement in curriculum planning.

- *Well developed school community relationships.* There are close links between the school and community with sustained efforts by schools to involve as many parents as possible, mostly through use of deliberate strategies. All schools have programs for parent participation at the lower grade levels. Some have programs for assisting parents to read with their children, including the well-known School Home and Reading Enjoyment (SHARE) program.

- *Orderly school environments.* The school environments are characterised by stability, routine, and orderliness. Principals are accomplished managers of their schools, although leadership styles differ.

- *Effective use of external consultants.* Either professional school support staff or other experts are used to provide impetus for curriculum development and teaching strategies.

- *The use of strategies that emphasise the importance of reading.* A wide range of reading materials is evident everywhere, especially in classrooms. The materials are readily accessible to students and are obviously used. Emphasis is placed on the importance of reading at upper as well as lower grade levels, and in all curriculum areas. Librarians participate actively in promoting reading in cooperation with classroom teachers.

Since *Reading Activity at Home* has been shown to be important to students' reading achievement, some schools have introduced several initiatives designed to improve school-home-community links. The following two examples illustrate the kinds of strategies being used to improve students' reading achievements.

One such initiative, known as *Readers are Leaders,* was used during the 1991 Education Week program at one of the schools. Well known members of the community, including the local mayor, the regional General Manager, an author, and the local football star were invited to read to students. At another school, storytelling evenings are conducted as part of a comprehensive set of strategies that focus on literacy. In this case, families attend storytelling sessions held on three occasions during the year where community members tell or read a story of their own choice. This program, which includes home visits by teachers and a *Parents in Reading Program* based on ELIC principles, consists of a series of six workshops for parents. The intention is to give parents supportive guidance and encouragement in reading with their children, while working in partnership with teachers.

Discussion and Conclusions

General Summary

In the context of research concerned with factors affecting students' reading achievements, the purpose of the present study was to determine the extent to which students' reading achievements over time are influenced by factors at the student level, at the teacher level, and at the school level. To this end, several explanatory models were proposed and tested using multilevel and covariance-structure modeling. Several outcomes of the study are worth noting.

First, an important conclusion which can be drawn is that in the context of a low-stakes research study, the Profile Reading Bands function as an effective framework for monitoring student progress over Grades K to 11. In addition to providing a broad-based and authentic approach to the assessment of student performance, teacher based Profile assessments of the kind employed here are reliable and appear to be sensitive to student growth and change over the years of schooling (see Figure 4).

Second, in terms of home background factors, the present findings support the argument of Share, Jorm, Maclean, Matthews, and Waterman (1983) that the common practice of using a single index of family socioeconomic status (SES) to measure home background severely underestimates the relationship between the home and students' educational achievement. While SES did have positive effects on measures of students' Attitudes, Attentiveness, and reading Achievement, the effects were small and mostly insignificant. In contrast, both the direct and indirect effects of Reading Activity at Home on students' reading Achievement were significant and positive, as they were on the mediating variables of students' Attitudes towards reading and their Attentiveness in the classroom. Furthermore, the magnitudes of the direct effects of both *Reading Activity at Home* and *Attitudes* on *Achievement* actually increased with student age (Rowe, 1991b). An explanation of this finding is that as students progress through primary and secondary schooling, associated increased curriculum demands require that students spend more time on reading activity for assigned homework tasks, thus increasing both the likelihood of students *reading for pleasure* and *for purpose* and positively influencing achievement and attitudes towards reading (Spiegel, 1981).

Third, the findings related to the magnitude of the effects of Reading Activity at Home on Attentiveness was an especially interesting outcome. This result suggested the presence of a positive carryover effect between activities at home and behavior in the classroom which is clearly in the interests of individual students and other students, as well as teachers. That is, these findings indicate that the opportunity to develop and practice attentiveness-demanding skills at home results in positive transference of similar skills to the classroom. This is underscored by the findings related to the reciprocal effects between attentiveness and reading activity at home which indicated that the effects were strongly interdependent for all student age groups

(Rowe & Rowe, 1992b). At least three directions for appropriate classroom management and intervention are suggested.

First, given the mutuality of learning outcomes and behavior, there is a clear need to focus intervention strategies in both domains simultaneously. While findings from several studies show positive long term effects of remedial programs on literacy skills (Bradley & Bryant, 1983; Limbrick, McNaughton, & Glynn, 1985), there is little evidence for long term gains on behavioral outcomes by remediation of learning difficulties alone. On the basis of findings from a study among hyperactive and learning disabled boys, Merrell (1990) notes: "Perhaps concurrent academic and behavioral intervention would be useful in helping many of these students" (p. 294).

Second, there is a clear need to enhance the positive mediating effects of home inputs on students' attitudes, achievement, and behavior in the classroom. Results from this study have provided strong empirical support for the claimed benefits of Reading Activity at Home and the related value of recognising the important contributions which parents can make to the educational development of their children (Hewison, 1988; Topping & Wolfendale, 1985; Webb, Webb, & Eccles, 1985; Winter, 1988). From a more detailed analysis of the READACT items, it was disappointing that so many students in the 5-6 and 7-8 year-old groups indicated that they never or rarely shared reading activities with family members or friends. For students in these age groups, high scores on the *reading alone* item (READ 1) and the shared reading items in particular, were strongly associated with positive attitudes towards reading, high levels of attentiveness in the classroom, and high scores on the measures of reading achievement. For older students, related positive associations were mainly with reading alone (READ 1) and discussing reading (READ 4). This latter finding suggests that, while students may spend less time reading to others and being read to by others as they become independent readers, it is clearly in their interest to participate in activities designed to encourage discussion of reading materials.

Third, given the importance of either direct or indirect parental involvement in students' educational progress, it is imperative that the work of schools be supported by programs designed to assist parents to take an active role in the development of their child's reading skills. Cox (1987) argued that, "School based measures to prevent early reading failure should be coupled with an early intervention programme designed to encourage and assist parents, where necessary, to take a more active role . . . " (p. 84). Consistent with the work of McGee, Williams, and Silva (1988), findings from this study suggest, however, that parental literacy is likely to have a significant impact on the development of such skills. In this context, government policy has a major role to play. Furthermore, in addition to early intervention strategies of the kind advocated and implemented by Pinnell (1989); Pinnell, Lyons, DeFord, Bryk, and Seltzer (1991); and Wasik and Slavin (1993); programs of the type that provide opportunities through which both parent and child literacy are enhanced would appear to have particular merit (Bushell, Miller, & Robson, 1982, 1985; Dundas & Strong, 1988; Topping, 1986; Turner, 1987).

From the combined student level and teacher level data, the overall findings indicate that teachers' participation in inservice professional development programs had significant, positive effects on their professional self-perceptions (i.e., Energy/Enthusiasm) which, in turn, had strong, positive influences on students' Attitudes towards Reading, Attentiveness in the classroom and on their reading achievement. At the class/teacher level and consistent with the work of Rowe and Sykes (1989) and Smylie (1988), the findings provide strong support for a functional relationship between teacher professional development and their professional self-perceptions. Furthermore, the findings provide substantial support for the claimed benefits of inservice training for teachers made elsewhere (Coulter & Ingvarson, 1985; Ingvarson, 1987; Joyce & Showers, 1988; Rowe, 1987). Herein lies sufficient justification for the implementation of policies designed to enhance the professional self-perceptions of teachers and their adjustment to professional role demands.

Finally, the present study has identified that the large variation in students' reading achievement is due to significant between-class/teacher differences. The fact that such teacher level factors have strong positive effects on students' attitudes, behaviors in the classroom, and achievement outcomes is of vital importance, with profound implications. As Slavin and colleagues' (1994a) evaluations of the *Success for All* program among low SES schools in Baltimore and Philadelphia have shown, students, who regardless of their socioeconomic backgrounds, are taught by well-trained, strategically focused, energetic, and enthusiastic teachers in schools with well-managed and stable environments, and with well-developed school-home-community links, are fortunate indeed (see Slavin, et al., 1994a, 1994b). While it may be impossible to legislate such factors into existence, the fact that students, parents, teachers, and schools make a difference (as shown by the findings of this study) should provide impetus and encouragement to those concerned with the crucial issues of *educational effectiveness.*

Impact of Outcomes

Findings from the *100 Schools Project - Literacy Programs Study* provided considerable impetus and support for the Victorian state government's *Literacy Strategy* between 1988 and 1991 and in particular, for the *Reading Together* policy initiative launched by the then Minister for Education, in April, 1989. In building on findings from the project, the Literacy Strategy stressed the importance of students reading at home and the valuable role which parents play in the educational development of their children. Promotional literature on *Parents as Partners* were produced for use by schools and International Literacy Year (1989) funding was allocated to support schools' home reading schemes. Professional development programs such as ELIC, LaRIC, and CLIC have since become widely available, and Reading Recovery is well established in all state regions.

Outcomes from the study continue to be useful, not only in shaping and supporting policy, but also in meeting accountability requirements. Publications from the research range from articles in local and international scientific journals, conference papers, popular papers, and workshops for school administrators, teachers, and parents. The study has also attracted considerable media interest.

Above all, findings from the present study provided both the impetus and justification for a further four-year longitudinal study of teacher and school effectiveness currently being conducted by the Centre for Applied Educational Research at the University of Melbourne, Australia. Beginning in 1992, this study, known as the *Victorian Quality Schools Project* (VQSP) has been designed to explain variation in students' progress in three literacy domains (*Reading, Writing,* and *Spoken Language*) and two in mathematics (*Number* and *Space*) at the student, class/ teacher, and school levels. The study involves a cluster-designed sample consisting of five entire grade-level cohorts consisting of 13,900 students, including their parents and teachers, drawn from 90 government, Catholic, and independent elementary and secondary schools. To model the complex network of factors affecting student progress, use is made of structural equation modeling and multilevel path analyses to explore structural relationships within the same levels and between different levels. Findings from the VQSP have been reported in various forms by Hill, Holmes-Smith, and Rowe (1993); Hill and Rowe (in press a, b); Hill, Rowe, and Holmes-Smith (1995); and Rowe, Hill, and Holmes-Smith (1994).

Like its predecessor study described in this paper, a feature of the VQSP is the use of teacher profile assessments designed to obtain authentic measures of educational progress, together with standardized test measures of academic ability. The results of fitting multilevel models to the data using different adjustments, indicate that the proportion of total variation in student achievement ranges from as little as three to seven percent at the school level, to as much as 35-54 percent at the class/teacher levels. Moreover, the effect size of teacher participation in literacy inservice professional development programs on students' progress in literacy (adjusted for intake characteristics and initial achievement) has consistently yielded significant estimates of 0.4 of a standard deviation. Similar analyses of the impact of measures of teacher quality (i.e., *teacher responsiveness*) on students' *attitudes to learning* yield standardized effect estimates of 0.6.

The most salient findings from both the *100 Schools Project - Literacy Programs Study* and the *Victorian Quality Schools Project* underscore the fact that learning takes place in classrooms through the interaction of students and their teachers, in partnership with parents. The explanation for the large class/teacher effects and small to insignificant school effects is that they primarily reflect variations in teacher quality. The suggestion here is that (Rowe, Holmes-Smith, & Hill, 1993):

> . . . it is essentially through the quality of teaching and learning that effective schools 'make a difference.' In fact, on the basis of our findings to date it could be argued that effective schools are only 'effective' to the extent that they have 'effective' teachers. (p. 15)

Such findings are entirely consistent with Scheerens (1993) observation that:

> . . . teacher and classroom variables account for more of the variance in pupil achievement than school variables. Also, in general, more powerful classroom level variables are found that account for between-class variance than school level variables in accounting for between-school variance. (p. 20)

The findings also appear to be consistent with Monk's (1992) conclusion based on a comprehensive review of the education productivity research literature, namely: "One of the recurring and most compelling findings within the corpus of production function research is the demonstration that how much a student learns depends on the identity of the classroom to which that student is assigned" (p. 320). Similarly, Reynolds and Packer (1992) observe:

> On the causes of school effects, it seems that early beliefs that school influences were distinct from teacher or classroom influences were misplaced, since a large number of studies utilising multilevel modeling show that the great majority of variation between schools is in fact due to classroom variation and that the unique variance due to the influence of the school, and not the classroom, shrinks to very small levels. (p. 173)

Together with the findings presented here, such observations point to a need for a possible refocus in the *educational effectiveness* research agenda for literacy, numeracy, and other school based curricula, to one that is closer to students' experiences of schooling and reexamines class/teacher influences on student learning outcomes as advocated by Brophy and Good (Brophy, 1981,1986; Brophy & Good, 1986; Good & Brophy, 1984) and more recently by Creemers (1992) and Slavin (1994).

Acknowledgments

By invitation of the editors, this article is adapted from a paper by Rowe (1991a), presented to the Steering Committee of the *100 Schools Project -Literacy Programs Study*, for the State Board of Education and School Programs Division of the Ministry of Education, Victoria, Australia. The frank and willing assistance of the students, parents, teachers, and school principals who contributed to the project is gratefully acknowledged. Special thanks is due to my colleagues: Professors Neil Baumgart, Patrick Griffin, and Peter Hill for their encouragement and support. Financial support for the project was provided under the *Commonwealth Resource Agreement*, administered by the Department of Education, Employment and Training, of the Australian federal government.

Correspondence should be addressed to: Ken Rowe, Centre for Applied Educational Research, Faculty of Education, The University of Melbourne, Parkville, Victoria 3052, Australia [Tel. + 61 3 9344 8741; Fax: + 61 3 9347 0945].

Appendix

Reliability Properties of the Victorian Reading Profile Bands

Using the holistic rating method for each *band* described in the body of the text, the rating pattern for each student formed a qualitative *cumulative* scale similar to that described by Guttman (1944). Reliability analyses have been computed for the *Reading Profile Bands*, by grade level, using the Guttman method to provide *lower bound estimates of true reliability*. The relevant coefficients given in the table below are *standardized item alpha* estimates and refer to data obtained from both the *100 Schools Project - Literacy Programs Study* and the *Victorian Quality Schools Project* (see Hill, Holmes-Smith, & Rowe, 1993). The sample sizes (*ns*) for each grade level cohort are given in parentheses. For the Reading Bands, concurrent validity estimates with the *Test of Reading Comprehension* (TORCH - Mossenson, Hill, & Masters, 1987) are given in brackets under the reliability coefficient estimates for grade levels 3 through 11. These estimates are expressed as Pearson product-moment, zero-order correlation coefficients (r).

Table A1
Guttman Reliability Estimates for the Victorian Reading Profile Bands, by Grade Level

Grade Level	Reading/ (Correlation with TORCH)
Prep (K) (n = 2281	0.791
Grade 1 (n = 1965)	0.754
Grade 2 (n = 2188)	0.769
Grade 3 (n = 1876)	0.800 (r = 0.501)
Grade 4 (n = 2209)	0.843 (r = 0.426)
Grade 5 (n = 2015)	0.831 (r = 0.515)
Grade 6 (n = 5062)	0.845 (r = 0.471)
Grade 7 (n = 3661)	0.902 (r = 0.520)
Grade 8 (n = 2630)	0.876 (r = 0.490)
Grade 9 (n = 3570)	0.926 (r = 0.465)
Grade 10 (n = 2687)	0.876 (r = 0.478)
Grade 11 (n = 730)	0.898 (r = 0.516)

Table A2
Test/Re-Test and Inter-Rater Reliability Estimates* for the Victorian Reading Profile Bands,
by Grade Level

Grade Level	Test/Re-Test Reliability	Inter-Rater Reliability
Grade 1	0.892	0.855
Grade 3	0.908	0.893
Grade 5	0.911	0.871
Grade 7	0.927	0.832
Grade 9	0.929	0.848

*Pearson product-moment correlations

References

Ainley, J., Goldman, J., & Reed, R. (1990). *Primary schooling in Victoria: A study of students' attitudes and achievements in Years 5 and 6 of government primary schools.* (ACER Research Monograph No. 37). Hawthorn, Vic: The Australian Council for Educational Research.

Aitkin, M., & Longford, N. (1986). Statistical modelling issues in school effectiveness studies. *Journal of the Royal Statistical Society, Series A, 149,* 1-43.

Aitkin, M., & Zuzovsky, R. (1991). *A conceptual framework and an indicator system to explain the variability in science outcomes in Israeli elementary schools.* Department of Mathematics & Statistics and School of Education, Tel-Aviv University. Mimeograph.

Alexander, H., & Filler, R. C. (1976). *Attitudes and reading.* Newark, DL: International Reading Association.

Alwin, D. F., & Jackson, D. J. (1980). Measurement models for response errors in surveys: Issues and applications. In D. Schuessler (Ed.), *Sociological methodology.* San Francisco: Jossey-Bass.

American Psychiatric Association. (1987). *DSM-III-R: Diagnostic and statistical manual of mental disorders* (3rd ed. Revised). Washington, DC: Author.

American Psychiatric Association. (1994). *DSM-IV: Diagnostic and statistical manual of mental disorders* (4th ed.). Washington, DC: Author.

Anderson, D. S. (1990, July). *Long term effects of public and private schooling.* Paper presented at XIIth World Congress of Sociology, Madrid. Mimeograph.

Ashton, P., & Webb, R. (1986). *Making a difference: Teachers' sense of efficacy and student achievement.* New York: Longman.

Austin, G., & Reynolds, D. (1990). Managing for improved school effectiveness: An international survey. *School Organisation, 10,* 167-178.

Bank, B. J. (1985). Student sex and classroom behavior. In T. Husen & T. N. Postlethwaite (Eds.), *The international encyclopedia of education,* (Vol. 8, pp. 4878-4881). Oxford: Pergamon.

Banks, D. K. (1992). *Effective schools research: A multilevel analysis of the conceptual framework.* Unpublished doctoral dissertation, The University of Melbourne Institute of Education.

Beach, R. W. (1985). Attitude towards literature. In T. Husen & T. N. Postlethwaite (Eds.), *The international encyclopedia of education,* (Vol. 8, pp. 3115-3117). Oxford: Pergamon.

Beck, I. L., & Carpenter, P. A. (1986). Cognitive approaches to understanding reading: Implications for instructional practice. *American Psychologist, 41,* 1098-1105

Bennett, S. N. (1978). Recent research on teaching: A dream, a belief and a model. *British Journal of Educational Psychology, 48,* 127-147.

Bernstein, B. (1971). *Class, codes and control Vol 1: Theoretical studies towards a sociology of language.* London: Routledge and Kegan Paul.

Bettelheim, B., & Zelan, K. (1982). *On learning to read: The child's fascination with meaning.* New York: Knopf.

Bidwell, C., & Kasarda, J. (1980). Conceptualizing and measuring the effects of school and schooling. *American Journal of Education, 88,* 401-430.

Bloom, B. S. (1976). *Human characteristics and school learning.* New York: McGraw-Hill.

Bloom, B. S. (1980). *The state of research on selected alterable variables in education.* Chicago: Department of Education, University of Chicago.

Bock, R. D. (Ed.) (1989). *Multilevel analysis of educational data.* New York: Academic Press.

Boekaerts, M. (1986). Motivation in theories of learning. *International Journal of Educational Research, 10*(2), 129-141.

Bosker, R. J., Creemers, B. P. M., & Scheerens, J. (Guest Editors) (1994). Conceptual and methodological advances in educational effectiveness research. *International Journal of Educational Research, 21*(2), 121-231.

Bossert, S. T. (1988). School effects. In N. J. Boyan (Ed.), *Handbook of research on educational administration: A project of the American Educational Research Association* (pp. 341-352). New York: Longman.

Bottani, N., & Delfau, I. (1990). Indicators of the quality of educational systems: An international perspectice. *International Journal of Educational Research, 14,* 321-408.

Bradley, L., & Bryant, P. E. (1983). Categorizing sounds and learning to read: A causal connection. *Nature, 301,* 419-421.

Brenner, S. O., Sörbom, D., & Wallius, E. (1985). The stress chain: A longitudinal confirmatory study of teacher stress, coping and social support. *Journal of Occupational Psychology, 58,* 1-13.

Broadfoot, P. M. (Ed.) (1984). *Selection, certification and control.* Sussex, UK: The Falmer Press.

Broadfoot, P. M. (1985). Alternatives to public examinations. In D. Nuttall (Ed.), *Assessing Educational Achievement.* Sussex, UK: The Falmer Press.

Broadfoot, P. M. (Ed.) (1986). *Profiles and Records of Achievement: A review of issues and practice.* London: Holt, Rinehart and Winston.

Broadfoot, P. M. (1987). *Introducing profiling: A practical manual.* London: Macmillan.

Broadfoot, P. M. (1988). The national assessment framework and records of achievement. In H. Torrance (Ed.), *National Assessment and Testing: A Research Response* (pp. 3-14). London: British Educational Research Association.

Brophy, J. (1981). Teacher praise: A functional analysis. *Review of Educational Research, 51,* 5-32.

Brophy, J. (1986). Teacher influences on student achievement. *American Psychologist, 41,* 1069-1077.

Brophy, J., & Good, T. L. (1986). Teacher behavior and student achievement. In M. C. Wittrock (Ed.), *Handbook of research on teaching* (3rd ed., pp. 328-375). New York: Macmillan.

Brown, R. L. (1989). Using covariance modeling for estimating reliability on scales with ordered polytomous variables. *Educational and Psychological Measurement, 49,* 383-398.

Bryk, A. S., & Raudenbush, S. W. (1987). Application of hierarchical linear models to assessing change. *Psychological Bulletin, 101*(1), 147-158.

Bryk, A. S., & Raudenbush, S. W. (1989). Towards a more appropriate conceptualization of research on school effects: A three-level hierarchical linear model. In D. Bock (Ed.), *Multilevel analysis of educational data* (pp. 159-204). New York: Academic Press.

Bryk, A. S., & Raudenbush, S. W. (1992). *Hierarchical linear models: Applications and data analysis methods.* Newbury Park, CA: Sage.

Bryk, A. S., Raudenbush, S. W., & Congdon, R. T. (1992). *HLM-3L: Computer program and users' guide.* Mooresville, IN: Scientific Software.

Burstein, L. (1980). The analysis of multilevel data in educational research and evaluation. In D. C. Berliner (Ed.), *Review of research in education*, Vol. 8 (pp. 158-233). Washington, DC: American Educational Research Association.

Burstein, L. (1988). Units of analysis. In J. P. Keeves (Ed.), *Educational research, methodology, and measurement: An international handbook* (pp. 775-781). Oxford: Pergamon.

Bushell, R., Miller, A., & Robson, D. (1982). Parents as remedial teachers: An account of a paired reading project with junior school failing readers and their parents. *Journal of the Association of Educational Psychologists, 5*, 7-13.

Bushell, R., Miller, A., & Robson, D. (1985). The development of paired reading in Derbyshire. In K. Topping & S. Wolfendale (Eds.), *Parental involvement in children's reading* (Ch. 14). Beckenham: Croom Helm.

Butler, S. R., Marsh, H. W., Sheppard, M., & Sheppard, J. L. (1985). Seven-year longitudinal study of the early prediction of reading achievement. *Journal of Educational Psychology, 77*, 349-361.

Cairns, L. G. (1985). Behavior problems in the classroom. In T. Husen & T. N. Postlethwaite (Eds.), *The international encyclopedia of education*, (Vol. 1, pp. 451-456). Oxford: Pergamon.

Calfee, R., & Drum, P. (1986). Research on teaching reading. In M. C. Wittrock (Ed.), *Handbook of research on teaching* (3rd ed., pp. 804-849). New York: Macmillan.

Cantwell, D. P., & Baker, L. (1991). Association between attention deficit-hyperactive disorder and learning disorders. *Journal of Learning Disabilities, 24*, 88-95

Caplan, N., Choy, M. H., & Whitmore, J. K. (1992). Indochinese refugee families and academic achievement. *Scientific American, 262*(2), 18-24.

Carroll, J. B. (1963). A model of school learning. *Teachers College Record, 64*, 723-733.

Carroll, J. B. (1984). The model of school learning: Progress of an idea. In L. W. Anderson (Ed.), *Time and school learning* (pp. 15-45). Beckenham, Kent: Croom Helm.

Castles, I. (1986). *Australian standard classification of occupations: Statistical classification*. Australian Bureau of Statistics. Canberra: C. J. Thompson Government Printer.

Chapman, J., Angus, L., Burke, G., & Wilkinson, V. (Eds.) (1991). *Improving the quality of Australian schools*. (Australian Education Review No. 33). Hawthorn, Vic: The Australian Council for Educational Research.

Charlton, M., & Holmes-Smith, P. (1987). *An evaluation of the Key Group Project: A professional development program for teachers*. Melbourne, Vic: Curriculum Branch, Ministry of Education (Schools Division).

Cheung, K. C., Keeves, J. P., Sellin, N., & Tsoi, S. C. (Eds.) (1990). The analysis of multilevel data in educational research: Studies of problems and their solutions. *International Journal of Educational Research, 14*, 215-319.

Chubb, J. E. (1988). Why the current wave of school reform will fail. *The Public Interest, 90*, 93-105.

Chubb, J. E., & Moe, T. M. (1990). *Politics, markets and America's schools*. Washington, DC: The Brookings Institute.

Clay, M. M. (1985). Reading Recovery: An early intervention programme. In *The early detection of reading difficulties* (3rd ed., Part two, pp. 47-116). Auckland, NZ: Heinemann.

Coleman, J., Campbell, E., Hobson, C., McPartland, J., Mood, A., Weinfield, F., & York, R. (1966). *Equality of educational opportunity*. Washington, DC: U.S. Government Printing Office.

Coleman, J. S., Hoffer, T., & Kilgore, S. D. (1982). *High School achievement: Public, private and Catholic schools compared*. New York: Basic Books.

Commonwealth Schools Commission (1984). *Commonwealth standards for Australian schools*. Canberra: Australian Government Publishing Service.

Cooley, W. W., & Leinhardt G. (1975). *An application of a model for investigating classroom processes*. Pittsburgh: Learning Research and Development Centre, University of Pittsburgh.

Cooley, W. W., & Lohnes, P. R. (1976). *Evaluation research in education*. New York: Irvington.

Coulter, F., & Ingvarson, L. C. (1985). *Professional development and the improvement of schooling.*

Canberra: Commonwealth Schools Commission.

Cox, T. (1987). Slow starters versus long-term backward readers. *British Journal of Educational Psychology, 57,* 73-86.

Creemers, B. P. M. (1992). School effectiveness, effective instruction and school improvement in the Netherlands. In D. Reynolds & P. Cuttance (Eds.), *School effectiveness: Research policy and practice.* London: Cassell.

Creemers, B. P. M., & Scheerens, J. (Eds.). (1989). Developments in school effectiveness. *International Journal of Educational Research, 13,* 685-826.

Cronbach, L. J., & Webb, N. (1975). Between and within-class effects in a reported aptitude-by-treatment interaction: Reanalysis of a study by G. L. Anderson. *Journal of Educational Psychology, 6,* 717-724.

Cuttance, P. (1992). Evaluating the effectiveness of schools. In D. Reynolds & P. Cuttance (Eds.), *School effectiveness: Research, policy and practice.* London: Cassell.

Darling-Hammond, L. (1994). Performance-based assessment and educational equity. *Harvard Educational Review, 64*(1), 5-29.

Davie, R., Butler, N., & Goldstein, H. (1972*). From birth to seven: A report of the National Child Development Study.* London: Longman/National Children's Bureau.

Dawkins, J. S. (1988). *Strengthening Australia's schools: A consideration of the focus on content of schooling.* Canberra, ACT: Australian Government Publishing Service.

Day, A. M., & Peters, R. DeV. (1989). Assessment of attentional difficulties in underachieving children. *Journal of Educational Research, 82,* 356-361.

Debus, R. L. (1985). Students' cognitive characteristics and classroom behavior. In T. Husen & T. N. Postlethwaite (Eds.), *The international encyclopedia of education,* (Vol. 8, pp. 4886-4890). Oxford: Pergamon.

deJong, P. F. (1993). The relationship between students' behavior at home and attention and achievement in elementary school. *British Journal of Educational Psychology, 63,* 201-213.

Department of Education and Science (1983). *School standards and spending: Statistical analysis.* London: Author.

Department of Education and Science (1984*). School standards and spending: Statistical analysis— a further appreciation.* London: Author.

Douglas, J. W. B. (1964). *The home and the school: A study of ability and attainment in the primary school.* London: MacGibbon and Kee.

Dundas, P., & Strong, T. (1988). *Readers, writers and parents learning together.* Melbourne: ASCCO.

Dunkin, M. J. (Ed.) (1987). *The international encyclopedia of teaching and teacher education.* Oxford: Pergamon.

Dunkin, M. J., & Biddle, B. J. (1974). *The study of teaching.* New York: Holt Rinehart and Winston.

Dunkin, M. J., & Doenau, S. J. (1985). Student ethnicity and classroom behavior. In T. Husen & T. N. Postlethwaite (Eds.), *The International encyclopedia of education,* (Vol. 8, pp. 4841-4845). Oxford: Pergamon.

Dykman, R. A., & Ackerman, P. T. (1991). Attention deficit disorder and specific reading disability: Separate but often overlapping disorders. *Journal of Learning Disabilities, 24,* 96-103.

Ecob, R., Evans, J., Hutchison, D., & Plewis, I. (1982*). Reading between the numbers: A critical guide to educational research.* London: BSSRS Publications Ltd.

Edmonds, R. R. (1979a). Effective schools for the urban poor. *Educational Leadership, 37,* 15-27.

Edmonds, R. R. (1979b). Some schools work and more can. *Social Policy, 9,* 28-32.

Edmonds, R. R. (1981). Making public schools effective. *Social Policy, 12,* 56-60.

Elkins, J., & Izard, J. (Eds.) (1992). *Student behaviour problems: Context, initiatives and programs.* Hawthorn, Vic: The Australian Council for Educational Research.

Elly, W. B. (1992). *How in the world do students read?: IEA Study of Reading Literacy.* The Hague: The International Association for the Evaluation of Educational Achievement.

Elsworth, G. R., & Coulter, F. (1977). *Aspiration and attainment: The measurement of professional self-perception in student teachers* (Occasional Paper, No. 11). Hawthorn, Vic: The Australian

Council for Educational Research.

Eraut, M. (1985). Inservice teacher education. In T. Husen & T. N. Postlethwaite (Eds.), *The international encyclopedia of education*, (Vol. 5, pp. 2511-26). Oxford: Pergamon.

Felton, H. (1986). ELIC in Tasmania: *The implementation of the Early Literacy Inservice Course in Tasmania in 1985*. Hobart: Curriculum Development and Evaluation Section, Education Department, Tasmania.

Fisher, G. W., Berliner, D. C., Filby, N. N., Marliave, R., Cahen, L. S., & Dishaw, M. M. (1980). Teaching behaviors, academic learning time, and student achievement: An overview. In C. Denham & A. Lieberman (Eds.), *Time to learn* (pp 7-32). Washington: The National Institute of Education.

Fleishman, J., & Benson, J. (1987). Using LISREL to evaluate measurement models and scale reliability. *Educational and Psychological Measurement, 47*, 925-939.

Fletcher, J. M., Morris, R. D., & Francis, D. J. (1991). Methodological issues in the classification of attention-related disorders. *Journal of Learning Disabilities, 24*, 72-77.

Floden, R. E. (1994). Reshaping assessment concepts. *Educational Researcher, 23*(2), 4.

Fotheringham, J. B., & Creal, D. (1980). Family socioeconomic and educational-emotional characteristics as predictors of school achievement. *Journal of Education Research, 73*, 311-317.

Fraser, B. J. (1989). Research syntheses on school and instructional effectiveness. *International Journal of Educational Research, 13*(7), 707-719.

Fraser, B. J., Walberg, H. J., Welch, W. W., & Hattie, J. A. (1987). Syntheses of educational productivity research. *International Journal of Educational Research, 11*(2), 145-252.

Frederiksen, N. (1984). The real test bias: Influences of testing on teaching and learning. *American Psychologist, 39*, 193-202.

Freiberg, H. J., Prokosch, N., Treister, E. S., & Stein, T. (1990). Turning around five at-risk elementary schools. *School Effectiveness and School Improvement, 1*(1), 5-25.

Geekie, P. (1988). *Evaluation report on the Reading Recovery field trial in central Victoria 1984*. Centre for Studies in Literacy, Faculty of Education, University of Wollongong.

Glass, G. V., Cahen, L. S., Smith, M. L., & Filby, N. N. (1982). *School class size: Research and policy*. Beverly Hills: Sage.

Glen, M. (1986). *The Early Literacy Inservice Course in Queensland: An evaluation of the 1985 trials and implementation*. Brisbane: Research Services Branch, Department of Education, Queensland.

Goldstein, H. (1979). *The design and analysis of longitudinal studies: Their role in the measurement of change*. London: Academic Press.

Goldstein, H. (1980). The statistical procedures. In B. Tizard (Ed.), *Fifteen thousand hours: A discussion* (Bedford Way Papers, No. 1): University of London Institute of Education.

Goldstein, H. (1986). Multilevel mixed linear model analysis using iterative generalized least squares. *Biometrika, 73*, 43-56.

Goldstein, H. (1987). *Multilevel models in educational and social research*. London: Charles Griffin & Co. Ltd.

Goldstein, H. (1995). *Multilevel statistical models*. London: Edward Arnold.

Goldstein, H., & McDonald, R. P. (1988). A general model for the analysis of multilevel data. *Psychometrika, 53*, 455-467.

Good, T. L., & Brophy, J. (1984). *Looking in classrooms* (3rd ed.). New York: Harper & Row.

Good, T. L., & Brophy, J. (1986). School effects. In M. C. Wittrock (Ed.), *Handbook of research on teaching* (3rd ed., pp. 570-604). New York: Macmillan.

Grant, G. (1988). *The world we created at Hamilton High*. Cambridge: Harvard University Press.

Gray, J., Jesson, D., & Jones, B. (1984). Predicting differences in examination results between local education authorities: Does school organisation matter? *Oxford Review of Education, 10*(1), 45-68.

Griffin, P. E. (1990). Profiling literacy development: Monitoring the accumulation of reading skills. *Australian Journal of Education, 34*, 290-311.

Griffin, P. E., & Jones, C. (1988). *Assessing the development of reading behavior: A Report of the Profiles and Reading Band development*. Melbourne, Vic: Ministry of Education (Schools Division).

Griffin, P. E., & Nix, P. (1991). *Educational assessment and reporting: A new approach*. London: Harcourt Brace Jovanovich.

Grimmett, S., & McCoy, M. (1980). Effects of parental communication on reading performance of third grade children. *The Reading Teacher, 33*, 303-308.

Guskey, T. (1986). Staff development and the process of teacher change. *Educational Researcher, 15*(5), 5-12.

Guttman, L. (1944). A basis for scaling quantitative data. *American Sociological Review, 9*, 139-150.

Hanusheck, E. A. (1981). Throwing money at schools. *Journal of Policy Analysis and Management, 1*, 19-41.

Hanusheck, E. A. (1985). Production functions in education. In T. Husen & T. N. Postlethwaite, (Eds.), *The international encyclopedia of education*, (Vol. 7, pp. 4059-4069). Oxford: Pergamon.

Harris, C. W. (1963). *Problems in the measurement of change*. Madison: University of Wisconsin.

Harris, M., & Fasano, C. (1988). Toward a policy on continuing professional development of teachers: Australian perspectives. *Journal of Education Policy, 3*, 291-300.

Hattie, J. A. (1992). Measuring the effects of schooling. *Australian Journal of Education, 36*(1), 5-13.

Hewison, J. (1988). The long term effectiveness of parental involvement in reading: A follow-up to the Haringey Reading Project. *British Journal of Educational Psychology, 58*, 184-190.

Hewton, J. (Ed.) (1991). *Performance indicators in education: What can they tell us?* Papers from the Third National Conference. Brisbane: Australian Conference of Directors-General of Education.

Hill, P. W. (1992, October 5). Commentary: The National Schools Project. *Schools Bulletin, 2*(18).

Hill, P. W., Holmes-Smith, P., & Rowe, K. J. (1993). *School and teacher effectiveness in Victoria: Key findings from Phase 1 of the Victorian Quality Schools Project*. Melbourne: Centre for Applied Educational Research, The University of Melbourne. (ERIC Clearing House, Document No. ED 367 067)

Hill, P. W., & Rowe, K. J. (in press a). Multilevel modeling in school effectiveness research. *School Effectiveness and School Improvement*.

Hill, P. W., & Rowe, K. J. (in press b). Educational effectiveness: Multilevel modeling of students' educational progress. *American Educational Research Journal*.

Hill, P. W., Rowe, K. J., & Holmes-Smith, P. (1995). *Factors affecting students' educational progress: Multilevel modelling of educational effectiveness*. Paper presented at the eighth annual International Congress for School Effectiveness and Improvement, CHN, Leeuwarden, The Netherlands, January 3-6, 1995.

Hinshaw, S. P. (1992a). Academic underachievement, attention deficits and aggression: Comorbidity and implications for intervention. *Journal of Consulting and Clinical Psychology, 60*, 893-903

Hinshaw, S. P. (1992b). Externalizing behavior problems and academic underachievement in childhood and adolescence: Causal relationships and underlying mechanisms. *Psychological Bulletin, 111*, 127-155.

Hoffman, S. (Guest Editor) (1991). Educational partnerships: Home-school community. *The Elementary School Journal, 91*(3), 191-319.

Holmes-Smith, P., & Charlton, M. (1992). *Sharing strategies for literacy improvement: A report of major findings*. Melbourne, Vic: School Programs Division, Ministry of Education.

Holmes-Smith, P., & Rowe, K. J. (1994). *The development and use of congeneric measurement models in school effectiveness research: Improving the reliability and validity of composite and latent variables for fitting multilevel and structural equation models*. Paper presented at the 7th International Congress for School Effectiveness and Improvement, The World Congress Centre, Melbourne,

January 3-6, 1994.

Hopkins, D. (1991). *Process indicators for school improvement.* Paris: OECD/CERI INES Project.

Ingvarson, L. (1987). Models of inservice education and their implications for professional development policy. *Independent Teacher, 17*(2), 23-32.

Ingvarson, L., & Mackenzie, D. (1988). Factors affecting the impact of inservice courses for teachers: Implications for policy. *Teaching and Teacher Education, 4,* 139-55.

Jencks, C., Smith, M., Acland, H., Bane, M. J., Cohen, D., Gentis, H., Heynes, B., & Michelson, S. (1972). *Inequality: A reassessment of the effect of family and schooling in America.* New York: Basic Books.

Jesson, D., Mayston, D., & Smith, P. (1987). Performance assessment in the education sector: Educational and economic perspectives. *Oxford Review of Education, 13*(3), 249-266.

Joint Review of Teacher Education, Report. (1986). *Improving teacher education.* Canberra: Commonwealth Tertiary Education Commission and Schools Commission.

Jones, M. G. (1989). *Parental participation in children's reading: What really happens?* Unpublished M. Ed. thesis, Monash University.

Jöreskog. K. G. (1971). Statistical analysis of sets of congeneric tests. *Psychometrika, 36,* 109-133.

Jöreskog, K. G., & Sörbom, D. (1989). *LISREL 7: A Guide to the program and applications.* Chicago: SPSS.

Jorm, A. F., Share, D. L., Matthews, R., & Maclean, R. (1986). Behavior problems in specific reading retarded and general reading backward children: A longitudinal study. *Journal of Child Psychology and Psychiatry, 27,* 33-43.

Joyce, B., & Showers, B. (1988). *Student achievement through staff development.* New York: Longman.

Joyce, B., Showers, B., & Rolheiser-Bennett, C. (1987). Staff development and student learning: A synthesis of research on models of teaching. *Educational Leadership, 45*(2), 11-23.

Kahl, T. N. (1985). Students' social background and classroom behavior. In T. Husen & T. N. Postlethwaite (Eds.), *The international encyclopedia of education,* (Vol. 8, pp. 4890-4900). Oxford: Pergamon.

Kazdin, A. E. (1987). Treatment of antisocial behavior in children: Current status and future directions. *Psychological Bulletin, 102,* 187-203.

Keeves, J. P. (1986a). The performance cycle. *International Journal of Educational Research, 10,* 143-157.

Keeves, J. P. (1986b). Motivation and school learning. *International Journal of Educational Research, 10,* 117-127.

Keller, M. B., Lavori, P. W., Beardslee, W. R., Wunder, J., Schwartz, C. E., Roth, J., & Biederman, J. (1992). The disruptive behavioral disorder in children and adolescents: Comorbidity and clinical course. *Journal of the American Academy of Child and Adolescent Psychiatry, 31,* 204-209.

Kinsbourne, M. (1984). Beyond attention deficit: Search for the disorder in ADD. In L. M. Bloomingdale (Ed.), *Attention deficit disorder,* (pp. 133-145). New York: Spectrum.

Kysel, F., Varlaam, A., Stoll, L., & Sammons, P. (1983). *The child at school: A new behavior schedule.* Internal Report RS 907/83. London: Inner London Education Authority, Research and Statistics Branch.

Lacey, C., & Lawton, D. (1981). *Issues in evaluation and accountability.* London: Methuen.

Lahadern, H. M. (1968). Attitudinal and intellectual correlates of attention: A study of four sixth grade classrooms. *Journal of Educational Psychology, 59,* 320-324.

Lanier, J. E., & Little, J. W. (1986). Research on teacher education. In M. C. Wittrock (Ed.), *Handbook of research on teaching* (3rd ed., pp. 527-569). New York: Macmillan.

Larkin, A. I., & Keeves, J. P. (1984). *The class size question: A study at different levels of analysis.* (ACER Research Monograph No. 26). Hawthorn, Vic: The Australian Council for Educational Research.

Lee, V. E., & Bryk, A. S. (1989). A multilevel model of the social distribution of high school achievement. *Sociology of Education, 62,* 172-192.

Lee, V. E., Dedrick, R. F., & Smith, J. B. (1991). The effect of the social organization of schools on teachers' efficacy and satisfaction. *Sociology of Education, 64*, 190-208.

Lesh, R., & Lamon, S. J. (Eds.) (1992). *Assessment of authentic performance in school mathematics.* Washington, DC: American Association for the Advancement of Sciences.

Levine, D. U., & Lezotte, L. W. (1990). *Unusually effective schools: A review and analysis of research and practice.* Madison, WS: National Centre for Effective Schools Research & Development.

Levis, D. S. (1985). Teacher personality and instruction. In T. Husen & T. N. Postlethwaite. (Eds.), *The international encyclopedia of education,* (Vol. 9, pp. 5016-5021). Oxford: Pergamon.

Levy, F., Horn, K., & Dalglish, R. (1987). Relation of attention deficit and conduct disorder to vigilance and reading lag. *Australian and New Zealand Journal of Psychiatry, 21*, 242-252.

Lightfoot, S. L. (1983). *The good high school.* New York: Basic Books.

Limbrick, E., McNaughton, S., & Glynn, T. (1985). Reading gains for underachieving tutors and tutees in a cross-age tutoring programme. *Journal of Child Psychology and Psychiatry, 26,* 939-953.

Linn, R. L. (1981). Measuring pretest-posttest performance changes. In R. Berk (Ed.), *Educational evaluation methodology: The state of the art* (pp. 84-109). Baltimore, MD: Johns Hopkins University Press.

Linn, R. L. (1986). Educational testing and assessment: Research needs and policy issues. *American Psychologist, 41*(10), 1153-1160.

Loeber, R. (1990). Development and risk factors of juvenile antisocial behavior and delinquency. *Clinical Psychology Review, 10*, 1-41.

Longford, N. T. (1986). VARCL: Interactive software for variance component analysis. *The Professional Statistician, 5*, 28-32.

Longford, N. T. (1987). A fast scoring algorithm for maximum likelihood estimation in unbalanced mixed models with nested effects. *Biometrika, 74*, 817-827.

Lunberg, I., & Linnakylä, P. (1993). *Teaching reading around the world: IEA Study of Reading Literacy.* The Hague: The International Association for the Evaluation of Educational Achievement.

Madden, N. A., Slavin, R. E., Karweit, N. L., Dolan, L. J., & Wasik, B. A. (1993). Success for All: Longitudinal effects of a restructuring program for inner-city elementary schools. *American Educational Research Journal, 30*, 123-148.

Mann, V. (1984). Reading skill and language skill. *Developmental Review, 4*, 1-15.

Masters, G. N. (1982). A Rasch model for partial credit scoring. *Psychometrika, 47*, 149-174.

Maughan, B., Gray, G., & Rutter, M. (1985). Reading retardation and antisocial behavior: A follow-up into employment. *Journal of Child Psychology and Psychiatry, 26*, 741-758.

McGaw, B., Long, M. G., Morgan, G., & Rosier, M. J. (1989). *Literacy and numeracy in Victorian schools: 1988–A report of a study commissioned by the Victorian Ministry of Education.* ACER Research Monograph No 34. Hawthorn, Vic: The Australian Council for Educational Research.

McGaw, B., Piper, K., Banks, D., & Evans, B. (1992). *Making schools more effective: A Report of the Effective Schools Project.* Hawthorn, Vic: The Australian Council for Educational Research.

McGee, R., & Share, D. L. (1988). Attention deficit disorder-hyperactivity and academic failure: Which comes first and what should be treated? *Journal of the American Academy of Child and Adolescent Psychiatry, 27*, 318-325.

McGee, R., Share, D. L., Moffitt, T. E., Williams, S., & Silva, P. A. (1988). Reading disability, behavior problems and juvenile delinquency. In D. H. Saklofske & S. B. G. Eysenck (Eds.), *Individual differences in children and adolescents: International perspectives* (pp. 158-172). London: Hodder & Stoughton.

McGee, R., Williams, S., & Silva, P.A. (1985). The factor structure and correlates of ratings of inattention, hyperactivity and antisocial behavior in a large sample of nine year old children from the general population. *Journal of Consulting and Clinical Psychology, 53*, 480-490.

McGee, R., Williams, S., & Silva, P. A. (1987). A comparison of boys and girls with teacher identified problems of inattention. *Journal of the American Academy of Child and Adolescent Psychiatry, 26*, 711-717.

McGee, R., Williams, S., & Silva, P. A. (1988). Slow starters and long-term backward readers: A replication and extension. *British Journal of Educational Psychology, 58*, 330-337.

McGee. R., Williams, S., Share, D. L, Anderson, J., & Silva, P. A. (1986). The relationship between specific reading retardation, general reading backwardness and behavioral problems in a large sample of Dunedin boys: A longitudinal study from five to eleven years. *Journal of Child Psychology and Psychiatry, 27*, 597-610.

McKinney, J. D. (1989). Longitudinal research on the behavioral characteristics of children with learning disabilities. *Journal of Learning Disabilities, 22*, 141-150.

McNeil, L. M. (1986). *Contradictions of control: School structure and school knowledge*. London: Routledge and Kegan Paul.

Merrell, K. W. (1990). Teacher ratings of hyperactivity and self-control in learning disabled boys: A comparison with low-achieving and average peers. *Psychology in the Schools, 27*, 289-296.

Metz, M. H. (1986). *Different by design: The context and character of three magnet schools*. London: Routledge and Kegan Paul.

Morgan, R. T. (1976). 'Paired Reading' tuition: A preliminary report on a technique for cases of reading deficit. *Child Care, Health and Development, 2*, 13-28.

Morgan, R., & Lyon, E. (1979). 'Paired Reading'–A preliminary report on a technique for parental tuition of reading-retarded children. *Journal of Child Psychology and Psychiatry, 20*, 151-160.

Moss, P. A. (1994). Can there be validity without reliability? *Educational Researcher, 23*(2), 5-12.

Mossenson, L., Hill, P., & Masters, G. (1987). *Tests of Reading Comprehension–TORCH: Manual*. Hawthorn, Vic: Australian Council for Educational Research.

Munck, M. E. (1979). *Model building in comparative education: Applications of the LISREL method to cross-national survey data*. International Association for the Evaluation of Educational Achievement Monograph Series No. 10. Stockholm: Almqvist & Wiksell International.

Murnane, R. (1975). *The impact of school resources on inner-city school children*. Cambridge, MA: Ballinger.

Murphy, J. (1990). *The educational reform movement of the 1980s*. Berkeley: McCutchan.

Newmann, F. M., & Archibald, D. A. (1990). Organizational performance of schools. In Reyes, P. (Ed.), *Teachers and their workplace: Commitment, performance and productivity*. Newbury Park, CA: Sage.

Newman, F. M., Rutter, R. A., & Smith, M. S. (1989). Organizational factors affecting school sense of efficacy, community and expectations. *Sociology of Education, 64*, 221-238.

Nisbet, J. (1993). Introduction. In OECD, *Curriculum reform: Assessment in question*. Paris: OECD.

Nuttall, D. L., Goldstein, H., Prosser, R., & Rasbash, J. (1989). Differential school effectiveness. *International Journal of Educational Research, 13*(7), 769-776.

O'Connor, M. C. (1992). Rethinking aptitude, achievement and instruction: Cognitive science research and the framing of assessment policy. In B. R. Gifford, & M. C. O'Connor (Eds.), *Changing assessment: Alternative views of aptitude, achievement and instruction* (pp. 9-35). Boston: Kluwer Academic Publishers.

OECD (1989). *Schools and quality: An international report*. Paris: Author.

OECD (1993). *Curriculum reform: Assessment in question*. Paris: Author.

Otto, R. (1986). *Teachers under stress*. Melbourne: Hill of Content.

Peaker, G. F. (1967). The regression analyses of the national survey. In United Kingdom, Department of Education and Science, *Children and their primary schools* (Vol. 2, App. 4, pp. 179-221). London: HMSO.

Pinnell, G. S. (1989). Reading Recovery: Helping at-risk children learn to read. *Elementary School Journal, 90*, 161-182.

Pinnell, G. S., Lyons, C. A., DeFord, D. E., Bryk, A. S., & Seltzer, M. (1991). *Studying the effectiveness of early intervention approaches for first grade children having difficulty in reading*. Columbus: Martha L. King Language and Literacy Centre, Ohio State University.

Plowden Report (1967). *Children and their primary schools*. United Kingdom Department of Education and Science. London: HMSO.

Postlethwaite, N., & Ross, K. N. (1992). *Effective schools in reading: Implications for educational planners*. The Hague: The International Association for the Evaluation of Educational Achievement.

Prosser, R., Rasbash, J., & Goldstein, H. (1991). *ML3 - Software for three-level analysis*. Institute of Education, The University of London.

Prosser, R., Rasbash, J., & Goldstein, H. (1993). *ML3-E - Software for three-level analysis (Version 2.3)*. Multilevel Models Project, Institute of Education, The University of London.

Purkey, S. C., & Smith, M. S. (1983). Effective schools: A review. *Elementary School Journal, 83*(4), 427-452.

Purves, A. C. (1973). *Literature education in ten countries: An empirical study*. New York: Wiley.

Quality of Education Review Committee, Report. (1985). *Quality of education in Australia*. Canberra: Australian Government Publishing Service.

Ralph, J. H., & Fennessey, J. (1983). Science or reform: Some questions about the effective schools models. *Phi Delta Kappan, 64*(10), 689-695.

Rasbash, J., Goldstein, H., & Woodhouse, G. (1995). *MLn - Software for n-level analysis (version 1)*. Multilevel Models Project, Institute of Education, The University of London.

Raudenbush, S. W. (1989). The analysis of longitudinal, multilevel data. *International Journal of Educational Research, 13*, 721-740.

Raudenbush, S. W., & Bryk, A. S. (1986). A hierarchical model for studying school effects. *Sociology of Education, 59*, 1-17.

Raudenbush, S. W., & Bryk, A. S. (1988). Methodological advances in analyzing the effects of schools and classrooms on student learning. In E. Z. Rothkopf (Ed.), *Review of research in education 1988-1989*, Vol. 15 (pp. 423-475). Washington, DC: American Educational Research Association.

Raudenbush, S. W., & Willms, J. D. (Eds.) (1991). *Schools, classrooms and pupils: International studies of schooling from a multilevel perspective*. New York: Academic Press.

Report of the Inservice Teacher Education Project. (1988). *Teachers' learning: Improving Australian schools through inservice teacher training and development*. Canberra: Department of Employment, Education and Training.

Report of the Quality of Education Review Committee. (1985). *Quality of education in Australia*. Canberra, ACT: Australian Government Publishing Service.

Resnick, L. B., & Resnick, D. P. (1992). Assessing the thinking curriculum. In B. R. Gifford & M. C. O'Connor (Eds.), *Changing assessment: Alternative views of aptitude, achievement and instruction* (pp. 37-75). Boston: Kluwer Academic Publishers.

Reynolds, D. (Ed.) (1985). *Studying school effectiveness*. London: Falmer.

Reynolds, D., Hargreaves, A., & Blackstone, T. (1980). Review symposium of Rutter et al.'s Fifteen Thousand Hours. *British Journal of Sociology of Education, 1*, 207-219.

Reynolds, D., Creemers, B., & Peters, T. (Eds.) (1988). *School effectiveness and improvement: Proceedings of the first international congress*. Cardiff, Wales: School of Education, University of Wales.

Reynolds, D., Creemers, B. P .M., Nesselrodt, P. S., Schaffer, E. C., Stringfield, S., & Teddlie, C. (Eds.) (1994). *Advances in school effectiveness research and practice* (pp. 25-51). Oxford: Pergamon.

Reynolds, D., & Cuttance, P. (Eds.) (1992). *School effectiveness: Research, policy and practice*. London: Cassell.

Robins, L. N. (1991). Conduct disorders. *Journal of Child Psychology and Psychiatry, 32*, 193-212.

Robinson, W. S. (1950). Ecological correlations and the behavior of individuals. *American Sociological Review, 15*, 351-357.

Rogosa, D. R., & Willett, J. B. (1985). Understanding correlates of change by modelling individual differences in growth. *Psychometrika, 90*, 726-748.

Rosenholtz, S. J. (1985). Effective schools: Interpreting the evidence. *American Journal of Education, 94*, 352-358.

Rosenshine, B., & Furst, N. (1971). Research on teacher performance criteria. In B. O. Smith (Ed.), *Research in teacher education: A symposium*. Englewood Cliffs, NJ: Prentice-Hall.

Ross, K. N. (1988a). Sampling. In J. P. Keeves (Ed.), *Educational research, methodology, and measurement: An international handbook* (pp. 527-537). Oxford: Pergamon.

Ross, K. N. (1988b). Sampling errors. In J. P. Keeves (Ed.), *Educational research, methodology, and measurement: An international handbook* (pp. 537-541). Oxford: Pergamon.

Rowe, K. J. (1987). *An evaluation of the Early Literacy Inservice Course in Victorian schools: Summary report on behalf of the Victorian ELIC Steering Committee.* Melbourne, Vic: Research and Development, Curriculum Branch. Ministry of Education, Schools Division.

Rowe, K. J. (1989). The commensurability of the general linear model in the context of educational and psychosocial research. *Australian Journal of Education, 33*, 41-52.

Rowe, K. J. (1990a). *Issues in the application of linear models to the analysis of hierarchically structured educational performance data: A discussion and worked example.* Paper presented at the Fifth Australian Mathematical Psychology Conference, Department of Psychology, The University of Melbourne, 28-29 September, 1990.

Rowe, K. J. (1990b). *The impact of professional development on students' reading achievement: A multilevel and structural equation modelling approach.* Paper presented at the 1990 annual conference of the Australian Association for Research in Education, University of Sydney, NSW, Nov. 27 - Dec 2, 1990.

Rowe, K. J. (1990c). *The importance of reading at home: Research in Victorian education.* Melbourne, Vic: State Board of Education.

Rowe, K. J. (1991a). *Students, parents, teachers and schools make a difference: A summary report of major findings from the "100 Schools Project - Literacy Programs Study."* Melbourne: Vic: State Board of Education and School Programs Division, Ministry of Education and Training.

Rowe, K. J. (1991b). The influence of reading activity at home on students' attitudes towards reading, classroom attentiveness and reading achievement: An application of structural equation modeling. *British Journal of Educational Psychology, 61*(1), 19-35.

Rowe, K. J. (1992a). *Identifying Type I errors in educational and social research: Comparisons of results from fitting OLS and multilevel regression models to hierarchically structured data.* Paper presented at the Third National Social Research Conference, The University of Western Sydney, Hawkesbury, June 29 - July 2, 1992.

Rowe, K. J. (1992b). Research on reading: What makes a difference? *Education Quarterly, 6*, 33-34.

Rowe, K. J., & Griffin, P. E. (1988). *Literacy programs in Victorian schools: Proposal for a longitudinal study.* Melbourne, Vic: Ministry of Education, Schools Division.

Rowe, K. J., & Hill, P. W. (1994). *Multilevel modelling in school effectiveness research: How many levels?* Paper presented at the 7th International Congress for School Effectiveness and Improvement, The World Congress Centre, Melbourne, January 3 - 6, 1994.

Rowe, K. J., & Hill, P. W. (1995). Methodological issues in educational performance and school effectiveness research: A discussion with worked examples. *Australian Journal of Education* (in press).

Rowe, K. J., Hill, P. W., & Holmes-Smith, P. (1994). *The Victorian Quality Schools Project: A report on the first stage of a longitudinal study of school and teacher effectiveness.* Symposium paper presented at the 7th International Congress for School Effectiveness and Improvement, The World Congress Centre, Melbourne, January 3 - 6, 1994.

Rowe, K. J., Holmes-Smith, P. D., & Hill, P. W. (1993). *The link between school effectiveness research, policy and school improvement: Strategies and procedures that make a difference.* Paper presented at the 1993 Annual Conference of the Australian Association for Research in Education, Fremantle, W.A., November 22 - 25, 1993.

Rowe, K. J., & Rowe, K. S. (1989). *Assessing behavioral change: The development and psychometric properties of a parent and teacher administered child behavior inventory for use in educational and epidemiological research.* School Programs Division, Ministry of Education (Victoria), and Department of Pediatrics, The University of Melbourne.

Rowe, K. J., & Rowe, K. S. (1992a). The relationship between inattentiveness in the classroom and reading achievement (Part A): Methodological issues. *Journal of the American Academy of Child and Adolescent Psychiatry, 30*(6), 349-356.

Rowe, K. J., & Rowe, K. S. (1992b). The relationship between inattentiveness in the classroom and reading achievement (Part B): An explanatory study. *Journal of the American Academy of Child and Adolescent Psychiatry, 30*(6), 357-368.

Rowe, K. J., & Rowe, K. S. (1992c). Impact of antisocial, inattentive and restless behaviors on reading. In J. Elkins & J. Izzard. (Eds.), *Student behavior problems: Context initiatives and programs* (pp. 47-76). Hawthorn, Vic: The Australian Council for Educational Research.

Rowe, K. J., & Rowe, K. S. (1993). *Assessing student behavior: The utility and measurement properties of a simple parent and teacher administered behavioural rating instrument for use in educational and epidemiological research.* Paper presented at the 1993 Annual Conference of the Australian Association for Research in Education, Fremantle, W.A., 22 - 25 November, 1993.

Rowe, K. J., & Sykes, J. (1989). The impact of professional development on teachers' self-perceptions. *Teaching and Teacher Education, 5,* 129-141.

Rutter, M. (1983). School effects on pupil progress: Research findings and policy implications. In L. Shulman & G. Sykes (Eds.), *Handbook of teaching and policy* (pp. 3-41). New York: Longman.

Rutter, M. (1985). Family and school influences on behavioral development. *Journal of Child Psychology and Psychiatry, 26,* 349-368.

Rutter, M., Maughan, B., Mortimer, P., Ouston, J., & Smith, A. (1979). *Fifteen thousand hours: Secondary schools and their effects on children.* Somerset: Open Books.

Rutter, M., Tizard, J., & Whitmore, K. (1970). *Education health and behavior.* London: Longman.

Ryans, D. G. (1960). *Characteristics of teachers; their description, comparison, and appraisal: A research study.* Washington, DC: American Council on Education.

Sampson, O. C. (1966). Reading and adjustment: A review of the literature. *Educational Research, 8,* 184-190.

Scarborough, H. S., Dobrich, W., & Hager, M. (1991). Preschool literacy experience and later reading achievement. *Journal of Learning Disabilities, 24*(8), 508-511.

Scheerens, J. (1990). School effectiveness research and the development of process indicators of school functioning. *School Effectiveness and School Improvement, 1*(1), 61-80.

Scheerens, J. (1992). *Effective schooling: Research, theory and practice.* London: Cassell.

Scheerens, J. (1993). Basic school effectiveness research: Items for a research agenda. *School Effectiveness and School Improvement, 4*(1), 17-36.

Scheerens, J., & Creemers, B. P. M. (1989). Conceptualizing school effectiveness. *International Journal of Educational Research, 13*(7), 691-706.

Schools Council. (1991). *Australia's teachers: An agenda for the next decade.* Canberra, ACT: Australian Government Printing Service.

Scott Long, J. (1983). *Covariance structure models: An introduction to LISREL.* Sage University Paper Series on Quantitative Applications in the Social Sciences, series no. 07-034. London: Sage.

Share, D. L., Jorm, A. F., Maclean, R., & Matthews, R. (1984). Sources of individual differences in reading acquisition. *Journal of Educational Psychology, 76,* 1309-1324.

Share, D. L., Jorm, A. F., Maclean, R., Matthews, R., & Waterman, B. (1983). Early reading achievement, oral language ability and a child's home background. *Australian Psychologist, 18,* 75-87.

Share, D. L., Jorm, A. F., Matthews, R., & Maclean, R. (1987). Parental involvement in reading progress. *Australian Psychologist, 22,* 43-51.

Shavelson, R. J. (Guest Editor) (1994). Performance assessment. *International Journal of Educational Research, 21*(3), 233-350.

Silver, L. B. (1990). Attention-deficit hyperactive disorder: Is it a learning disability or a related disorder? *Journal of Learning Disabilities, 23,* 394-397.

Sinclair, K. E. (1985). Students' affective characteristics and classroom behavior. In T. Husen &

T. N. Postlethwaite (Eds.), *The international encyclopedia of education*, (Vol. 8, pp. 4881-4886). Oxford: Pergamon.

Slavin, R. E. (1993). *Success for All in the Philadelphia public schools: 1991-92 evaluation report*. Baltimore: Centre for Research on Effective Schooling for Disadvantaged Students, Johns Hopkins University.

Slavin, R. E. (1994). Quality, appropriateness, incentive, and time: A model of instructional effectiveness. *International Journal of Educational Research, 21*(2), 141-157.

Slavin, R. E., Karweit, N. L., Wasik, B. A., & Madden, N. A. (Eds.) (1994). *Preventing early school failure: Research on effective strategies*. Boston: Allyn & Bacon.

Slavin, R. E., Madden, N. A., Dolan, L. J., Wasik, B. A., Ross, S. M., & Smith, L. J. (1994a*). Success for All: Longitudinal effects of systematic school by-school reform in seven districts*. Paper presented at the annual meeting of the American Educational Research Association, New Orleans, April, 1994.

Slavin, R. E., Madden, N. A., Dolan, L. J., Wasik, B. A., Ross, S. M., & Smith, L. J. (1994b). 'Whenever and wherever we choose': The replication of 'Success for All'. *Phi Delta Kappan, 75*(8), 639-647.

Smith, B. O. (Ed.) (1971). *Research in teacher education: A symposium*. Englewood Cliffs, NJ: Prentice-Hall.

Smylie, M. A. (1988). The enhancement function of staff development: Organizational and psychological antecedents of individual teacher change. *American Educational Research Journal, 25*(1), 1-30.

Spiegel, D. L. (1981). *Reading for pleasure: Guidelines*. Newark, DL: International Reading Association.

Stanovich, K. E. (1986). Matthew effects in reading: Some consequences of individual differences in the acquisition of literacy. *Reading Research Quarterly, 21*, 361-407.

Stanton, W. R., Feehan, M., McGee, R., & Silva, P. A. (1990). The relative value of reading ability and IQ as predictors of teacher reported behavior problems. *Journal of Learning Disabilities, 23*, 514-517.

Steedman, J. (1983). *Progress in secondary schools*. London: National Children's Bureau.

Stevenson, J., Richman, N., & Graham, P. (1985). Behavior problems and language abilities at three years and behavioral deviance at eight years. *Journal of Child Psychology and Psychiatry, 26*, 215-230.

Stipek, D., & Weisz, J. (1981). Perceived personal control and academic achievement. *Review of Educational Research, 52*, 101-137.

Sutton, R. E. (1987). Teacher education and educational self-direction: A conceptual analysis and empirical investigation. *Teaching and Teacher Education, 3*(2), 121-133.

Taylor, C. (1994). Assessment for measurement or standards: The peril and promise of large-scale assessment reform. *American Educational Research Journal, 31*, 231-262.

Thompson, W. W. (1985). Environmental effects on educational performance. *The Alberta Journal of Educational Research, 31*, 11-25.

Tizard, J, Schofield, W., & Hewison, J. (1982). Collaboration between teachers and parents in assisting children's reading. *British Journal of Educational Psychology, 52*, 1-15.

Tomlinson, T. M. (1980). *Student ability, student background and student achievement: Another look at life in effective schools*. Paper presented at Educational Testing Service Conference on Effective Schools, New York, May 27 - 29, 1980.

Topping, K. J. (1986). *Paired reading training pack* (2nd ed.). Huddersfield, UK: Kirklees Psychological Service.

Topping, K., & McKnight, G. (1984). Paired reading—and parent power. *Special Education—Forward Trends, 11*, 12-15.

Topping, K., & Wolfendale, S. (Eds.) (1985). *Parental involvement in children's reading*. Beckenham, UK: Croom Helm.

Torneus, M. (1984). Phonological awareness and reading: A chicken and egg problem? *Journal of Educational Psychology, 70,* 1346-1358.

Tukey, J. W. (1977). *Exploratory data analysis.* Reading, MA: Addison-Wesley.

Tunmer, W. E, & Nesdale, A. R. (1985). Phonemic segmentation skill and beginning reading. *Journal of Educational Psychology, 77,* 417-427.

Turner, R. (1987). *SHARE Project—Doveton Cluster: A case study.* Melbourne: Ministry of Education, Victoria, School Improvement Plan.

Victoria (1989). *Reading together: A major initiative for literacy Prep-Year 3 from the Ministry of Education.* Melbourne: Jean Gordon Government Printer.

Victoria (1991). *English profiles handbook: Assessing and reporting students' progress in English.* Melbourne, Vic: School Programs Division, Ministry of Education and Training.

Walberg, H. (1986). What works in a nation still at risk. *Educational Leadership, 4,* 7-11.

Walberg, H. J., & Tsai, S. (1985). Correlates of reading achievement and attitude: A national assessment study. *Journal of Educational Research, 78,* 159-167.

Wasik, B. A., & Slavin, R. E. (1993). Preventing early reading failure with one-to-one tutoring: A review of five programs. *Reading Research Quarterly, 28,* 178-200.

Wareing, L. (1985). A comparative study of three methods of parental involvement in reading. In K. Topping & S. Wolfendale (Eds.), *Parental involvement in children's reading* (Ch. 26). Beckenham: Croom Helm.

Wearing, A. (1989). *Teacher stress in Victoria: A survey of teachers' views—summary and recommendations.* Applied Psychology Research Group, Department of Psychology, The University of Melbourne. Melbourne: Ministry of Education, Victoria.

Webb, M., Webb, T., & Eccles, G. (1985). Parental participation in the teaching of reading. *Remedial Education, 20,* 86-91.

Weiner, B. (1984). Principles for a theory of student motivation and their application within an attributional framework. In R. E. Ames & C. Ames (Eds.), *Research on motivation in education* (Vol. 1, pp. 15-38). Orlando: Academic Press.

Wells, G. (1985). *Language development in the preschool years.* Cambridge, England: Cambridge University Press.

Wells, G. (1986). Preschool literacy-related activities and success in school. In D. Olson, A. Hildyard, & N. Torrance (Eds.), *Literacy, language and learning* (pp. 229-255). Cambridge, England: Cambridge University Press.

Werts, C. E., Rock, D. R., Linn, R. L., & Jöreskog, K. G. (1978). A general method for estimating the reliability of a composite. *Educational and Psychological Measurement, 38,* 933-938.

Wheeler, H. G. (1986). *Central Victorian field trials of Reading Recovery in 1984.* Bendigo, Vic: Bendigo College of Advanced Education.

Wigdor, A. K., & Garner, W. R. (Eds.) (1982). *Ability testing: Uses consequences and controversies.* Washington, DC: Academy Press.

Wiggins, G. (1989, April). Teaching to the (authentic) test. *Educational Leadership,* 41-47.

Willett, J. B. (1988). Questions and answers in the measurement of change. *Review of Research in Education - 1988* (pp. 345-422). Washington: American Educational Research Association.

Williams, J. (1984). Phonemic analysis and how it relates to reading. *Journal of Learning Disabilities, 17,* 240-245.

Williams, S. M., & Silva, P. A. (1985). Some factors associated with reading ability: A longitudinal study. *Educational Research, 27,* 159-168.

Williams, T., & Carpenter, P. G. (1990). Private schooling and public achievement. *Australian Journal of Education, 34,* 3-24.

Williams, T., & Carpenter, P. G. (1991). Private schooling and public achievement in Australia. *International Journal of Educational Research, 15*(5), 411-431.

Winter, S. (1988). Paired reading: A study of process and outcome. *Educational Psychology, 8,* 135-151.

Wyatt, T, & Ruby, A. (Eds.) (1989). *Education indicators for quality, accountability and better practice.* Sydney: Australian Conference of Directors-General of Education.

THE ROLE OF EARLY LITERACY INTERVENTIONS IN THE TRANSFORMATION OF EDUCATIONAL SYSTEMS

JANET S. GAFFNEY
University of Illinois
SUSAN Y. PAYNTER
Austin, Texas

Literacy interventions, especially those that are successful in bring students to high levels of literacy, cannot be considered isolated phenomena in schools. The promise of an intervention is that it seeks to impact existing conditions in such a dramatic way as to change the subsequent course of events. Whereas conventional instruction is designed to provide continuous service with no goal for accelerated achievement, a literacy intervention is designed to produce accelerated change, moving student achievement rapidly and providing for sustained performance over time by the participants. Interventions are change agents within educational systems extending the principles of change into the existing host structures. Implementing an intervention is a worthwhile but complicated undertaking and the complexity of the endeavor reflects the magnitude of change required of the individuals responsible for implementation.

It is an important paradox that change must be conceived at the level of a system, but change can only be achieved at the level of the individual's performance. "In saying that change occurs at the individual level, it should be recognized that organizational changes are often necessary to provide supportive or stimulating conditions to foster change in practice" (Fullan, 1991, p. 46). A planned approach to the network of structures that promote or constrain the change process is needed within each system (Clay, 1993b; Dalin, 1978; Fullan & Miles, 1992). Thus, adopting a complex intervention is a problem-solving process that requires understanding of the conceptual congruity of all aspects of the theory, intervention, and training underlying the innovation.

For an innovation to be incorporated into a system effectively, the parts of the innovation must be externally congruent and cohesive with the host system (Clay, 1993b). The type of complex change that actually acts as a catalyst for accelerated progress of students and changes their sustained performance requires more effort than simple or superficial change and must be accompanied by ways of addressing this complexity. In this article, we explore some of the elements within Reading Recovery, an early literacy intervention, that address the complexity of implementation and the accompanying structures that support meaningful change.

Change Within Systems

Structures That Foster Sustained Teaching Success

Perhaps the changes in a teacher's knowledge, skills, and behaviors that must be sustained over time best exemplify the complexity of transforming a system; it is at this individual teacher level that change does or does not occur. One prominent literacy intervention, Reading Recovery, is based on a theory of reading acquisition that acknowledges the complexity of *learning* how to read and write continuous text (Clay, 1990) and a comparable professional development model that acknowledges the complexity of *teaching* children how to read and write, especially children who are experiencing the greatest difficulty getting underway. Just as reading is a problem-solving activity, so is teaching reading a problem-solving activity. One way that Reading Recovery meets the demands of complex change for teachers and learners is through a three-tiered staffing scheme in which trainers of teacher leaders (university level) prepare teacher leaders (district-wide leaders) who in turn conduct extended professional development for teachers (school-based instructors).

The delivery of an intervention demands that teachers be trained to teach in such a way that the lowest-achieving children may produce accelerated rates of progress. This is a new and very complex skill for teachers; even highly capable teachers have to learn how to deliver effective literacy intervention instruction. The magnitude of a teacher's personal effort, reflection, and action that are associated with constructing, deconstructing, and reconstructing one's knowledge and beliefs about how children learn, and specifically about how children learn to read and to write, cannot be minimized. While many educational efforts are evaluated on the basis of either teaching performance or student performance, the success of the Reading Recovery intervention is measured by rigorously evaluating both teaching and learning—not just one or the other. The year-long, professional-development model of Reading Recovery reflects the challenge of preparing high-craft teachers who are able to achieve this goal. In Reading Recovery, teachers improve their teaching as well as children's learning (Clay, 1991, p. 69).

The process of changing one's teaching behaviors can be overwhelming. Even very good teachers may be overcome by the expectation that they need to do more than they are already doing. This expectation comes from the basic assumption that *more* time, more activities, more evaluation, more . . . is better. Reading Recovery and teaching for acceleration is not about teaching harder or doing more; it is about teaching differently. The origins of successful progress lie in the teacher-student interactions. When teachers observe changes in the reading and writing behaviors of children that they are certain have been fostered by changes in their teaching, they assume personal and individual responsibility for the results with these children. The teacher perceives a direct relationship between her decisions and the performance of the student and becomes the owner of the job of teaching. The teacher's response is not "this is a good program," but "I can teach anyone to read." This deep ownership of a reform comes through learning, not before (Fullan & Miles, 1992, p. 749).

Leadership Structures for Addressing Complexity

Change initiatives do not run themselves" (Fullan & Miles, 1992, p. 751). By stating the obvious, Fullan and Miles pointed out the need to manage the adoption and institutionalization of interventions promoting substantive change. They describe school improvement as a problem rich process and argue that effective facilitators "embrace problems rather than avoid them" (p. 750). The complexity of Reading Recovery and the challenge of implementation in the context of each school creates openings for communication with a wide array of educators who enter the process with diverse interpretations. Teacher leaders are deliberately tutored in leadership roles during their initial training and are encouraged to accept differing views about the program as opportunities for education (Clay, 1991). The simultaneous roles of the teacher leader as teacher of children, teacher of teachers, and program implementor enable the leader to communicate with various audiences about the rationales underlying the program. The teacher leader learns to be receptive to the issues and concerns raised by colleagues, interprets them in light of the rationales, and participates in joint problem-solving. In responding to these various constituencies, the teacher leader gradually builds a network of informed colleagues with shared understanding to assist in the continuing effort to promote accelerated change.

The teacher leader is described by Clay (1993b) as fulfilling the role of Goodlad's (1977) redirecting system that preserves the integrity of the innovation from alterations that lead to conformity with previous and ineffective conventional practices. Fullan (1990) describes the tendency of an existing host system to make an innovation look more familiar and conventional as a way of simplifying the concept or down-sizing the scale due to the initial challenges of implementation. Smoothing the rough edges may actually sandpaper the project to death. Simple projects have smaller problems and although start-up problems may be eliminated by reduction and oversimplification, the effects of the project are often modest and result in a trivial enterprise (Huberman & Miles, 1984). Supported by these researchers is the truth of the ancient Talmud, "For a great goal every hardship is trivial, for a trivial goal every hardship is great."

Structures for Leading Consensus-Building Communication

Within each system, teachers and administrators construct a set of shared assumptions about their work. These "normative agreements are at the heart of the school enterprise" (Rosenholtz, 1989, p. 30). Change is the result of the transformation of these normative agreements that emanate from communication among school personnel. Clear statements about significant goals remain imperative for engaging others in the change process, but Fullan (1991) cautions that clarity at the outset helps, but does not eliminate problems. "Each and every individual who is necessary for effective implementation will experience some concerns about the meaning of new practices, goals, beliefs, and means of implementation" (p. 45). The role of the Reading Recovery community (teacher, teacher leader, and site coordinator) is to promote communication about what is important and what is possible in terms of student achievement among other educators and community leaders. The skill required to lead such consensus-shifting dialogue is the result of the substantial training, extended modeling, and personal transformation experienced by Reading Recovery personnel.

A particular challenge to most school personnel is to choose not to participate in a "conspiracy of tolerance" (Rosenholtz, 1989, p. 175) in which educators tacitly agree that there will always be a group of children for whom reading and writing at average levels is unattainable. A shift of this normative agreement comes only after the experience of seeing "unexpected" children excel frequently enough to question the conventional consensus model. The layers of experience and communication that lead to such a shift are all steps toward a new consensus.

The results of Rosenholtz's (1989) study of teachers' workplaces indicated that in schools with a high consensus regarding shared goals, teacher talk is predominately about the substance of teaching and student learning, whereas in schools with moderate or low consensus about instructional goals, teachers' talk revolves around student conduct. The function of an informed literacy team within the system is to engage in conversations which help to build a new consensus regarding the universal nature of literacy and the possibility of intervention methods to effectively support and sustain achievement. The new consensus is a shift from a conspiracy of tolerance to a promise of success.

Consensus and shared meaning are developed and reshaped through waves of communication. One teacher leader has described this process as requiring many opportunities for dialogue over time to promote the focus of resources and commitment from administrators, teachers, parents, school board members, and community leaders toward the changing agenda of early literacy success for all children.

Dissemination and Expansion

The Necessity of Networks for Intervention Models

One significant and essential element of systemic change resulting from intervention is the reality of strong networks beyond any single site. An educational intervention, by definition, serves a specific population that is embedded within the general enterprise of schools and is compatible with this enterprise but not central to it (Clay, 1993b). Interventions can provide the system with a potency for change that must be protected even as the intervention begins to affect the rest of the system. The presence of a strong network of support for the broader concepts of an intervention (e. g., the power of intervention to change achievement and literacy for all children) help to build assurances of quality during initial adoption that can then be maintained in subsequent implementations. Without the network of support, quality can wane under the greater weight of conventional practice.

Another essential element for quality is the expectation that the intervention will be structured to work over time. Short-term expectations can impede the change structures of an intervention. "Local educators experience most school reforms as fads" (Fullan & Miles, 1992, p. 747). Adoption of an innovation does not automatically lead to implementation. The fad mentality feeds into decisions to adopt innovations without planning for their maintenance because there is an underlying assumption that the program will not survive. The short-term pattern can result from a number of factors. Administrators and school board members may be attracted to the availability of incentive grants but not be committed to the goals of a selected project (Bernard van Leer Foundation, 1991). Often district leaders want to be perceived as innovative but concern themselves more with associating with symbols of reform rather than its substance (Fullan & Miles, 1992). Initial adoptions may be subject to erosion due to staff mobility, budgetary problems, changing priorities, or other factors. A network of support and common implementation experiences can raise the problem-solving conversation of any given site by adding weight and practical options in an effort to meet local obstacles and setbacks.

Planning for Expansion

There is an evolving emphasis in the dissemination process in the United States which is supporting the importance of long-term change as a result of collaborative implementation procedures. The Department of Education (Farquar, 1993) has outlined a new approach to nationwide dissemination reflecting the influences of systemic-change theories, school-culture research, and a constructivist view of learning. There is new attention to the processes needed to move beyond simple short-term adoption of an innovation to the more desirable endeavor of "institutionalizing change, that is, building and sustaining over time, practices and structures that promote comprehensive school improvement" (Farquar, 1993, p. 2).

Implementation moves into institutionalization as the project evolves in response to the tremendous forces brought to bear on any initial adoption by the unique characteristics of the new host system; this transition is a significant part of the dissemination and implementation process. The community of learners involved in implementation seeks to offer alternatives, actively engage users, and provide them with opportunities to fit innovations to the local setting. The implementation of Reading Recovery in more than 1200 sites has reflected these trends and has been a process of constructing communication networks, analyzing priorities of the host system, and intentionally nurturing the feelings of success for all those involved. The variety of implementation models used for Reading Recovery throughout the United States reflects the flexibility on the part of Reading Recovery providers and implementors to accommodate and maximize the existing vital efforts of the host systems through the complementary acquisition of the innovation (Paynter, 1994).

Significant national educational reform can be shaped by intervention efforts when those efforts represent an intentionally designed structure that not only allows for but promotes wide-scale expansion. "Unless a project can disseminate its ideas and start having an impact on a large scale, it remains a costly experiment, affecting only the lives of a few people" (Bernard van Leer Foundation, 1991, p. 1). For development to be successful, this change of scale must be accomplished while preserving the integrity of the project without sacrificing quality. One prevalent assumption is that if a project is successful, replications will be automatic. Anyone involved in project development and dissemination understands that this is a myth. "Dissemination is not something that a project can do *on the side*" (Bernard van Leer Foundation,

1991, p. 4). The Reading Recovery model uses the role of the university training center as an unconventional but highly effective dissemination network. The three-tiered staffing model in Reading Recovery creates formal and informal collegial networks between and among various implementation sites and the regional university centers.

The strength of a network to help secure adequate financial and personnel support to develop large-scale expansion cannot be overstated. Worthwhile change—substantial and important change—takes effort. Dissemination is a means to change, and like change, dissemination is a process, not an event. The dissemination process needs to be outlined in the initial development of a project so that structures can be incorporated that will increase the likelihood of successful replications.

Some important considerations are essential to wide-scale expansion of a successful project that can promote comprehensive school improvement. The original project must be determined to be stable and the providers need a broad vision of the project that extends beyond their own local site. Fullan and Miles (1992) reiterate that all large-scale change is implemented locally and that no blueprints for change exist. Change is a journey, they suggest, guided by experts who are clear about the purpose, limitations, pitfalls of the innovation, and the rationales underlying quality assurances.

Time between adoption and implementation is needed to attend to matters of quality. Often the time between adoption and implementation is so minimal that adequate preparation has not transpired. In case studies of twelve districts, Huberman and Miles (1984) found that the shorter the time between adoption and implementation, the more problematic the implementation. Similarly, Fullan (1991) notes: "The more complex the change, the more work there is to do on quality" (p. 72).

One aspect of the Reading Recovery network that lends stability to the project as it expands is the constructive nature of the ongoing professional development that promotes continual discourse regarding quality and consistency among a large number of continually expanding project sites. Without on-going inservice for teachers, the results—and therefore the continuation of the project—may be jeopardized. The continuing contact of teachers through participation in four to six inservice sessions, which include observation and evaluation of the teaching of colleagues, represents the sustained assistance required for refinement of teaching expertise of high-craft Reading Recovery teachers and for responding to changes within schools.

The Role of the Provider in the Dissemination Process

For every innovation, a provider guides potential implementors through the decisions that they will use to construct their project. The role of the provider is to nurture additional extensions without allowing new sites to become dependent on the initial provider. The provider functions as a bridge builder for the project to other situations and geographical areas. At the same time, the provider retains a certain detachment in order to promote independent problem-solving by the new local site and prevent overwhelming demands on the existing projects (Bernard van Leer Foundation, 1991). Louis and Miles (1990) report that strong assistance is needed to support local reform including at least thirty days of external assistance annually that is sustained over several years. If adequate resources are not allocated to support a long-term comprehensive implementation plan, the quality is threatened. If providers attempt to rescue local efforts, they may risk the life of the original project or other local project implementations. "Reform fails unless we can demonstrate that pockets of success add up to new structures and school cultures that press for continuous improvement" (Fullan & Miles, 1992, p. 748).

Adoption and continuation are influenced by the degree that the effects of a successful intervention are visible to others. Reading Recovery provides feedback to all participants from the beginning and although there is stress related to being visible in a formative stage, the very visibility of the intervention supports its role as a systemic change agent. Clay (1993a) reported that children are the first to experience success after only a few weeks, followed by parental responses soon thereafter. Classroom teachers notice positive changes at about eight weeks followed by administrators and finally, researchers.

As a provider, Reading Recovery has structured central data and information centers to support expansion efforts. Reading Recovery has a system of quality assurances built into the adoption process that outlines implementation in calibrated stages. Comprehensive annual reports of each Reading Recovery site include data on the progress of all children served at the site and the accomplishments of the teachers and teacher leaders. Results of questionnaires completed by parents, central administrators, principals, classroom teachers, and Reading Recovery teachers are reported. As a National Diffusion Network project, data for all children served by Reading Recovery within the United States are collected and consolidated, site by site, state by state. The documentation of the results of the intervention is a significant factor contributing to the continuation of Reading Recovery and its visibility.

To create opportunities for children to undergo breakthroughs in literacy learning, effective interventions must thrive and contribute to the transformation of their host systems beyond the intervention itself. Indeed, change can only happen at the level of the individual; one child, one teacher, one administrator at a time. The role of interventions, embedded in host systems that provide substantial change for the most needy individuals in the system, is an essential role toward the transformation of American education.

Stakeholders in the education of children must make informed choices about the use of limited financial and personnel resources. Clarity regarding the goals and benefits of an intervention will assist educators in selecting only options that have the greatest leverage for impact on all levels of their system and that use a child's learning time economically (Clay, 1993a). Making an informed decision to implement a powerful intervention may not only transform the system but alter the way the participants in that system view the system, themselves, and others (Bernard van Leer Foundation, 1991) and challenge beliefs about change and the rate at which change is possible.

References

Bernard van Leer Foundation. (1991, April). Dissemination. *Bernard van Leer Foundation Newsletter, 62*, 1-11.

Clay, M. M. (1990, September). *The challenge of the 1990s: International literacy decade.* Invitational address to the 17th New Zealand Reading Association Conference, Palmerston North.

Clay, M. M. (1991). Reading Recovery surprises. In D. E. DeFord, C. A. Lyons, & G. S. Pinnell (Eds.), *Bridges to literacy: Learning from Reading Recovery* (pp. 55-74). Portsmouth, NH: Heinemann.

Clay, M. M. (1993a). *Reading Recovery: A guidebook for teachers in training.* Portsmouth, NH: Heinemann.

Clay, M. M. (1993b). Reading Recovery: The wider implications of an educational innovation. In A. Watson & A. Badenhop (Eds.), *Prevention of reading failure* (pp. 22-47). New York: Ashton Scholastic.

Dalin, P. (1978). *Limits to educational change.* New York: St. Martin's Press.

Farquar, E. (1993, November). *A new approach to nationwide dissemination.* Paper presented at the National Dissemination Association, Phoenix, AZ.

Fullan, M. G. (1990). Staff development, innovation, and institutional development. In B. Joyce (Ed.), *Changing school culture through staff development* (pp. 3-25). Alexandria, VA: Association for Supervision and Curriculum Development.

Fullan, M. G. (1991). *The new meaning of educational change.* New York: Teachers College Press.

Fullan, M. G., & Miles, M. B. (1992). Getting reform right: What works and what doesn't. *Phi Delta Kappan, 7*, 744-752.

Goodlad, J. I. (1977). *Networking and educational improvement: Reflections on a strategy.* Washington, DC: NIE.

Huberman, M., & Miles, M. (1984). *Innovation up close.* New York: Plenum.

Louis, K. S., & Miles, M. B. (1990). *Improving the urban high school: What works and why.* New York: Teachers College Press.

Paynter, S. Y. (1994). Implementing innovation: Integrity and flexibility. *Network News, 6*(2), 6-7.

Rosenholtz, S. J. (1989). *Teachers' workplace: The social organization of schools.* New York: Longman.

Descubriendo La Lectura: An Early Intervention Literacy Program in Spanish

KATHY ESCAMILLA

University of Colorado at Denver

Need and Significance

There are currently 7.5 million school aged children in the United States who enter school speaking languages other than English (Lyons, 1991). About 70 percent of these students speak Spanish as a first language (Lyons, 1991). The number of Spanish-speaking students entering U. S. schools has steadily increased over the past decade. These children constitute the fastest growing group in U. S. public schools (Brown, 1992).

During the past twenty years, bilingual education programs have been widely implemented in the U. S. as a means of providing quality educational experiences to these Spanish-speaking language minority students. Politically, bilingual education has been extremely controversial. However, research studies have established that bilingual programs are pedagogically sound when fully implemented with well qualified staff and administrative support (Cummins, 1989; Hakuta, 1987).

Bilingual programs are implemented in many different ways. However, they generally utilize a child's native language for initial literacy development and gradually add English as a second language. This model has demonstrated that initial success in native language literacy provides a base for subsequent success in English (Escamilla, 1987; Krashen & Biber, 1988; Ramírez, Yuen, & Ramey, 1991).

In spite of these achievements and the overall positive impact of bilingual education programs, there are some language minority students who have not achieved the desired results in native language or second language literacy. These students, like their English-speaking counterparts, may have difficulty at the beginning stages of literacy acquisition, requiring special attention or something extra in the way of instruction to achieve the levels of literacy and biliteracy needed to be academically successful.

Typically, this something extra has taken the form of pullout compensatory programs designed to remediate the student's academic weaknesses. Pullout programs for language minority and majority students, largely funded through Chapter 1 programs in local elementary schools, have been widely criticized during the past few years (Allington & Broikou, 1988; Barrera, 1989; Hornberger, 1992). This criticism asserted that students continue to participate in remedial programs year after year. There is little evidence to suggest that student achievement improves as a result of participation in these programs (Allington & Broikou, 1988; Barrera, 1989). Further, compensatory programs become life sentences for students; once they get in, they never get out.

An additional problem for language minority students in need of some sort of remediation, particularly in literacy, is that the remediation is often offered in English whether or not the child has a sufficient command of it to benefit from such instruction. This approach to remediation often creates a situation where the child may be receiving formal reading instruction in Spanish (or another native language) in the regular classroom, and English reading instruction for remediation, a situation that may well result in further confusion and failure for the child (Barrera, 1989).

Added to this is the overall problem that 95 percent of the bilingual programs for language minority students in the United States are transitional in nature. Their stated purpose is to transfer students from native language to English language programs as quickly as possible (Fradd & Tikunoff, 1987). This transitional policy exacerbates difficulties for language minority students who may be struggling to learn to read in their native language. Teachers often feel pressured to get students into English reading, so they give up trying to help students become literate in their first language and simply teach in English.

Given these factors and the research results establishing the efficacy of native language programs, there is a real need to look at innovative early intervention programs that are offered in the native language of the students. Native language programs may be the best vehicle to assist language minority children struggling with literacy acquisition. At the same time, it is important that such programs not condemn these children to a lifetime of remedial instruction.

One educational intervention that focuses its efforts on helping English-speaking students who are struggling to learn to read is Reading Recovery. Briefly defined, Reading Recovery is a first grade intervention program designed to identify and remediate reading difficulties early in a child's school career. Children in Reading Recovery receive intensive individual instruction by specially trained teachers. The purpose of Reading Recovery is to cycle children as quickly as possible into and out of intervention and back into a basic classroom experience. Reading Recovery was developed and implemented in New Zealand and has recently been implemented throughout the United States and in Australia, Canada, and Great Britain. Reading Recovery has met with great success in areas where it has been implemented (Clay, 1989; Pinnell, 1988; Pinnell, Fried, & Estice, 1990). So great is its success in the U. S., that in 1992 there were Reading Recovery programs in thirty-four states and the District of Columbia (Dyer, 1992). It would seem that Reading Recovery, given its success with English-speaking students, might also be effective when applied in Spanish with Spanish-speaking students. However, there is a need to examine this notion beyond the point of theoretical supposition.

In 1988, bilingual education staff at a large urban school district in Southern Arizona made the commitment to develop and study the application of Reading Recovery in Spanish. This project was given the name Descubriendo La Lectura (DLL) and is an adaptation of Reading Recovery. It is equivalent in all major aspects to the program originated by Marie Clay in New Zealand.

The study reported herein is an examination of one aspect of the DLL program which entails an examination of the notion of acceleration as defined by English Reading Recovery. In English Reading Recovery, acceleration is one of the theoretical underpinnings of the program. The theory of acceleration suggests that it is possible to take students who are struggling in their efforts to become literate, and through a specific, intensive one-to-one instructional program, provide the something extra that the child needs to accelerate from struggling to average. Struggling generally refers to those children who are at the lowest 20 percent in their class with regard to literacy, and average refers to literacy levels of other students in a school. Reading Recovery provides measures to observe student literacy development that can be used, along with teacher judgment, to identify children who are struggling as well as those who are average. These same measures can be used to observe student growth across time.

The study examined the initial impact of DLL on twenty-three students who participated in the program during 1991-92, and examined whether these children accelerated from struggling to average. This study should be viewed as a beginning effort and the reader should note that the data not only provide valuable information about the initial impact of DLL on students, but also will serve as a baseline for future longitudinal studies which will assess the impact of this program across grade levels and examine the extent to which gains made in Spanish literacy subsequently apply to the acquisition of English literacy.

From a theoretical standpoint, this study is significant for several reasons. First, it utilizes the knowledge base and theoretical framework from two important fields (bilingual education and Reading Recovery) for the purpose of addressing a large and growing need in our country. This need is how to assist Spanish-speaking children who are having difficulty learning to read without prematurely submersing them in English and without permanently placing them in classes for slow learners.

The projected growth of Spanish-speaking students in U. S. schools is 35 percent over the next decade (Lyons, 1991). This, coupled with the continued overrepresentation of these students in remedial programs, makes studies such as this one significant for policymakers and practitioners. Moreover, these studies are imperative if the academic potential of Spanish-speaking students in our country is to be realized.

Reading Recovery: An Overview

Reading Recovery (RR) is designed to assist first grade students who are having difficulties learning to read. Students identified as needing Reading Recovery are pulled out of their classrooms for intensive one-to-one instruction for thirty minutes per day. Reading Recovery differs from other remedial programs in several significant ways. First, the intent of the program is to accelerate struggling students so that they can catch up with their peers. The program is not intended to take the place of good classroom instruction but is seen as providing the something extra that is needed to provide struggling readers with the inner control needed to become independent readers. The program is designed to be short-term and to cycle students into and out of the program as quickly as possible. Average student participation in Reading Recovery is twelve to sixteen weeks (Clay, 1989; Pinnell, 1990). Reading Recovery is delivered by a trained teacher and RR teachers undergo an intensive one year training program to learn Reading Recovery theory and procedures. As they learn the theory, they simultaneously apply these procedures with children under the guidance of a teacher leader and the support of a peer training group.

Reading Recovery lessons follow a similar structure. However, there are no prescribed step-by-step kits or consumable materials. Trained teachers select and use a wide range of books. Lessons are designed to actively involve children in their own learning. Children are guided to think and solve problems while reading. Teachers provide support, but the children do the work and solve problems. Daily writing and using children's writing to teach reading are important aspects of RR (Pinnell, DeFord, & Lyons, 1988).

Reading Recovery programs have demonstrated that children can accelerate their reading progress in this program and that their reading progress can sustain itself across grade levels (Clay, 1989; Pinnell, 1990). Thus, once students are successfully discontinued from RR programs, their gains are maintained without the need for further remediation.

Research results on the impact of English RR have been very promising. Results of the original program developed by Marie Clay in New Zealand (Clay, 1979a, 1979b, 1982) indicated that children who had been identified as RR students made accelerated progress while receiving individual tutoring. After an average of 12-14 weeks, almost all children in the initial program had caught up with their peers who were considered to be average readers. Three years later, children who had received RR continued to progress at average rates. Although the initial research group in New Zealand included bilingual Maori children, bilingual Pacific Island children, children whose ancestry was European, and children with special needs, it is important to note that RR, in its inception, was conducted exclusively in English. Since that time, however, RR has also been developed in Maori (M. M. Clay, personal correspondence, May, 1992).

Programs implemented in the United States have reported similar results. During the 1984-85 school year, a U. S. program was piloted in Ohio. The program was implemented in six urban schools with high proportions of low income students. Fifty-five students received RR during the pilot year, with an average of twelve weeks of intensive tutoring. At the end of the pilot year, two-thirds of the children were substantially above comparison group students on standardized tests. Further, students were within the average range of achievement based on national norms of the Stanford Achievement Test (Huck & Pinnell, 1985). Follow-up studies conducted during the years 1985 to 1987 found that RR children maintained their gains over comparison children and continued to perform within the average level two years after discontinuing RR (DeFord, Pinnell, Lyons, & Young, 1987). By 1988, the Ohio project had expanded to serve 3,000 children in 143 school districts. In essence, the RR program helped underachieving students make rapid gains in reading by fostering student independence and enabling them to continue to do well after completing the program.

The success of RR programs in English, particularly with low-income students in Ohio and bilingual Maori students in New Zealand, prompted the development of a program in Spanish. Development began in the 1988-89 school year with funds from an Arizona district's Chapter 1 office. The district's decision to develop a Spanish RR program was influenced by several other factors. First, the district has a large and extensive population of language minority students who are receiving initial literacy instruction in Spanish in Tucson. This population includes first grade students who need extra assistance in initial literacy acquisition.

Second, the district has a formal language policy that establishes maintenance of two languages and development of bilingualism and biliteracy as fundamental educational goals for all district language minority students (District Policy 1110, 1981). Development of a RR program in Spanish was deemed the most theoretically sound approach given the research in bilingual education that had found the use of the child's native language to be the most appropriate medium of instruction (Cummins, 1989; Krashen & Biber, 1988; Ramírez, Yuen, & Ramey, 1991), and the research in RR which emphasized children's competence and not their deficits (Clay, 1989; Pinnell, 1990).

The Development of Descubriendo La Lectura

There are numerous considerations to be addressed when adapting an English language program for students from other cultural and linguistic groups. For Descubriendo La Lectura (DLL), such issues included differences in language and culture between Spanish-speaking students and their English-speaking counterparts, as well as the need to reconstruct all program components into Spanish.

Initial program development included the identification of children's literature books in Spanish for use in the program, the development of a Spanish Observation Survey, and the training of three Spanish-speaking Reading Recovery/Descubriendo La Lectura teachers. Currently, the program has over 300 children's literature books in Spanish which are written at 28 different levels of difficulty. In Spanish, as in English, the inventory of books provides the reading material for DLL, but does not recommend sequence.

The Spanish Observation Survey (*El Instrumento de Observación del Desarrollo Literato Principiante*) was created for use in the DLL program as a reconstruction of the English Observation Survey originated by Clay (1989). Studies conducted by Escamilla and Andrade (1992), and Escamilla, Basurto, Andrade, and Ruíz (1992) found the Spanish reconstruction to be valid and reliable. The Spanish Observation Survey consists of six observational tasks that collectively provide a profile of a student's reading repertoire. These observational tasks include: (a) letter identification, (b) word test, (c) concepts about print, (d) writing vocabulary, (e) dictation, and (f) text reading.

While the Spanish DLL program was being created, it was simultaneously being field tested with students. Case study results of the field testing included 14 students (2 in 1989-90 and 12 in 1990-91). Results of this field testing demonstrated that DLL, like RR, was having a positive impact on students (Escamilla & Andrade, 1992; Escamilla, Basurto, Andrade, & Ruíz, 1992). Positive results from these studies led to the expansion of the DLL program to serve more students, involve more teachers in the training program, and expand the research efforts which resulted in this study.

Research Questions

The purpose of this study was to examine whether the Descubriendo La Lectura Program achieved acceleration with Spanish-speaking first grade students in a manner equivalent to English Reading Recovery programs in New Zealand and Ohio. As stated above, acceleration implies movement from being a struggling reader to being an average reader. Research questions generated for the study were:

1. How do DLL, control, and comparison children compare at the end of first grade on a variety of measures of reading ability?

2. How do DLL, control, and comparison children perform at the end of first grade on a nationally normed, standardized test?

3. How do DLL, control, and comparison children compare with the average progress of the total population of first grade students?

4. What proportion of successfully discontinued DLL students achieved end-of-year scores equivalent to the average band of first grade students who are reading in Spanish?

Methods and Subjects

Subjects for the study were 180 first grade, Spanish dominant students who attended school in a large urban Southern Arizona school district. Subjects included all Spanish-speaking, first grade students from six elementary schools who were receiving their initial literacy instruction in Spanish. Students were identified as being Spanish dominant on the basis of the Home Language Survey administered by the school district in September, 1991, and the Language Assessment Scales (LAS) test which was administered in both Spanish and English in October, 1991. Mean scores for all subjects on the LAS test were 3.9 in Spanish and 1.5 in English (the LAS is scored on a 5-point scale). These results clearly indicated that study subjects were dominant Spanish speakers and very limited in English.

In October, 1991, all 180 students were given the Spanish Observation Survey reconstructed for DLL and the Aprenda Reading Achievement Test (Nivel *Preprimario* – Subtests 2, 3, 4, and total reading). From these data for all six schools in the study, students who were in the bottom 20 percent were identified. Four of the schools had the DLL program and two did not. For the four schools with the DLL program, study subjects were chosen by using the results of the Spanish Observation Survey in combination with teacher recommendations as to which students were most in need of DLL. Teacher recommendations were documented via a procedure known as alternate ranking.

In alternate ranking, a teacher takes a copy of his or her class list and ranks the students according to his or her perceptions of student reading abilities. Teachers begin by identifying the strongest reader and ranking the child #1 and then identifying the weakest reader and ranking that child with the lowest class number. The procedure of alternate ranking (highest/ lowest) continues until all students in the class have received a rank.

DLL subjects were those who received the lowest class ranking by their teachers and had the lowest scores on the Spanish Observation Survey. A total of 50 students were identified as DLL students for 1991-92. Of this total, 23 received the program.

In order to control for treatment effects that might result from having DLL trained teachers in regular classroom situations, control group students were chosen from two schools that had no DLL teachers nor a DLL program. Control group students were also selected on the basis of the results on the Spanish Observation Survey and the Aprenda Spanish Reading Achievement Test and were identified as being in the lowest 20 percent of their class. From this group, 23 control group students were identified. These students were children who could have benefited from the DLL intervention, but did not receive it.

From the six schools in the study, all students not identified as DLL or control group students were assigned to the comparison group (n = 134). All 180 study children (DLL, control, and comparison) were retested in May, 1992, using the Spanish Observation Survey and the Aprenda Spanish Reading Achievement Test (Nivel *Primer Nivel Primario* — Subtests 2, 3, and total reading).

For Research Question 1, all subjects were given the Spanish Observation Survey during October, 1991, and May, 1992. Mean pre and post-observation scores were compared for the three groups.

For Research Question 2, pretest and posttest results for DLL, control, and comparison group students on the Aprenda Spanish Reading Achievement Test were compared. Analyses utilized scores for the total reading. Because different forms of the test were used from the fall to the spring, (fall – Nivel *Preprimario*; spring – Nivel *Primer Nivel Primario*) student raw scores were converted to scaled scores for comparison and analysis. A t test was then used to analyze the significance of the difference between groups. The fall form of the Aprenda has three subtests of reading (*sonidos y letras* – sounds and letters, *lectura de palabras* – word reading, and *lectura de oraciones* – reading sentences). The spring form has only two forms (*lectura de palabras* – word reading and *comprehensión de lectura* – reading comprehension). For purposes of analyses, only total reading achievement test scores for each form were used.

Research Question 3 analyzed the reading progress of DLL, control, and comparison children compared to the average progress of the total group of first grade Spanish-reading students for the 1991-92 school year. Comparisons were made by analyzing October and May gains on tasks on the Spanish Observation Survey and on the Aprenda Spanish Achievement Test (total reading fall and spring). Average progress was considered to be ± .5 standard deviations from the mean of the total group (DLL+control+comparison). Comparisons were made for each of the observation tasks on the Spanish Observation Survey and for the total Aprenda Spanish Reading Achievement Test.

Research Question 4 was analyzed by calculating the percentage of DLL students who met and/or exceeded the end-of-year average band of achievement among all first grade students reading in Spanish. The average band was calculated for all six observation tasks of the Spanish Observation Survey and was calculated using the same method used for Research Question 3. Descubriendo La Lectura students included all students completing at least 60 DLL lessons including successfully discontinued and not-discontinued students.

Results

For Research Question 1, all subjects were given the Spanish Observation Survey during October, 1991, and May, 1992. Mean pre and post-observation scores were compared for the three groups and are presented for each group on Table 1.

All three groups made gains from the pretest to the posttest on all observation tasks. To test the significance of the difference in gains between the three groups, a t test for significance was applied. Results of the t tests are presented in Table 2.

In the fall of 1991, there were significant differences between the DLL group and the comparison group on all six observation tasks ($p < .001$). Further, these differences were statistically significant on all tasks with the comparison group showing significantly higher scores on all six tasks. By May, the DLL group had not only caught up to the comparison group, but had surpassed them. May, 1992 results showed the DLL students outperformed comparison students on all six observation tasks. Further, these differences were statistically significant ($p < .05$) on all observation tasks except text reading.

Differences between the DLL group and the control group were not significant on the Spanish Observation Survey during the fall on three tasks, but were significant on three others. Tasks with significant differences included Word Test ($p < .05$), Concepts about Print ($p < .05$), and

Table 1

Means and Standard Deviations for Descubriendo La Lectura (DLL) Children, Control Group Children, and Comparison Group Children

Observation Task	Month	*DLL Children n=23		Control Group Children n=23		Comparison Group Children n=134	
		mean	SD	mean	SD	mean	SD
Letter Identification (Max=61)	September	18.9	12.9	24.0	11.78	33.4	17.0
	May	54.7	8.8	47.6	13.3	49.1	13.5
Word Test (Max=20)	September	0.0	0.0	0.3	0.69	3.6	5.6
	May	15.9	6.1	10.3	7.56	11.7	8.0
Concepts About Print (Max=24)	September	6.0	2.9	8.3	2.98	10.7	3.7
	May	16.0	3.4	12.7	3.5	14.3	4.1
Writing Vocabulary (10 Minutes)	September	3.0	1.8	4.6	3.49	9.7	10.8
	May	48.5	14.5	25.7	18.8	32.7	20.8
Dictation (Max=39)	September	2.6	4.0	9.3	13.9	16.2	11.5
	May	33.8	6.5	25.6	14.2	29.1	10.4
Text Level Reading (Max=28)	September	1.6	.95	1.6	0.99	3.6	3.8
	May	13.9	8.6	6.2	5.2	11.4	9.6

*Includes both successfully discontinued and not-discontinued program children who received at least 60 DLL lessons.

Dictation ($p < .001$). These differences favored the control group who had started ahead of the DLL group on all measures. Spring results, however, indicated that there were statistically significant differences between the DLL and control group on all six observation tasks. The DLL group significantly outperformed the control group ($p < .05$) on all measures.

Between group comparisons for the control and comparison groups showed that in the fall of 1991, there were statistically significant differences between the two groups on each of the observation tasks ($p < .01$). During the fall, the performance of the comparison group was statistically superior to the control group. However, during the spring of 1992, results indicated that while the mean scores for the comparison group were still above those of the control group for all six observation tasks, these differences were not statistically significant. Both groups made gains. However, the control group did not catch up to the comparison group and the DLL group did.

Research Question 2 examined the differences between the DLL, control, and comparison groups on a standardized test of reading achievement. For this comparison, the Aprenda Spanish Achievement Test was used. All three groups took this test in October, 1991, and May, 1992. Between October, 1991, and May, 1992, comparisons were made on the total reading (*lectura* total) scores.

For this comparison, student raw scores were converted to standard scores and percentiles. Standard scores and percentiles for the DLL, control, and comparison groups are presented on

Table 2
t Values and Levels of Significance for DLL, Control, and Comparison Group Children on Spanish Observation Survey

Observation Task		DLL/ Control	DLL/ Comparison	Control/ Comparison
Letter	Fall	1.40	4.73*	3.29***
Identification	Spring	2.13**	2.69**	0.5
Word	Fall	2.14**	7.5*	6.6*
Test	Spring	2.77**	2.89***	0.81
Concepts	Fall	2.64**	6.81*	3.43***
About Print	Spring	3.27***	2.09**	1.98
Writing	Fall	0.68	6.63*	4.32*
Vocabulary	Spring	4.60*	4.49*	1.62
Dictation	Fall	5.78*	10.54*	5.31*
	Spring	2.52	2.90	1.13
Text	Fall	0.069	5.13*	5.13*
Reading	Spring	3.67***	1.26	0.397

* $p < .001$
** $p < .05$
*** $p < .01$

Table 3
Aprenda Spanish Achievement Test Gain Scores for DLL, Control, and Comparison Groups

Group	Fall 1991 Mean Scaled Score	Percentile	Spring 1992 Mean Scaled Score	Percentile	Gain (In Percentile Points)
DLL Group	455	28th	521	41st	+13
Control Group	453	26th	503	28th	+ 2
Comparison Group	460	35th	508	31st	- 4

Table 3. Standard scores for all three groups were higher in May than October. However, when the standard scores were connected to percentiles, only the DLL group and the control group made gains. The DLL group went from the 28th percentile to the 41st percentile while the control group went from the 26th to the 28th percentile. The comparison group dropped from the 35th to the 31st percentile. If one considers the 50th percentile to be an indicator of a national average, it is important to note that the DLL group is the only group approaching this national average.

Research Question 3 examined how DLL, control, and comparison group children compared to the average progress of all first grade students. This comparison was made using the six

Table 4

Letter Identification Scores of Total DLL Group, Control, and Comparison Groups Compared with Average Band of First Grade Spanish-Speaking Children

	DLL mean	Control mean	Other mean
Fall	18.9	24	33.4
Spring	54.7	47.6	49.1

Average band = ± .5 standard deviations from *mean*
mean = 49.8 (Average band = 43.2 – 56.4)
Letter Identification (61 total)

Table 5

Word Test Scores of Total DLL Group, Control, and Comparison Groups Compared to the Average Band of First Grade Spanish-Speaking Children

	DLL mean	Control mean	Other mean
Fall	0.0	.3	3.6
Spring	15.9	10.3	11.7

Average band = ± .5 standard deviations from *mean*
mean = 12.2 (Average band = 8.2 – 16.2)
Word Test (20 total)

Table 6

Concepts About Print Scores of Total DLL Group, Control, and Comparison Groups Compared to the Average Band of First Grade Spanish-Speaking Children

	DLL mean	Control mean	Other mean
Fall	6.0	8.3	10.7
Spring	16.0	12.7	14.3

Average band = ± .5 standard deviations from *mean*
mean = 14.5 (Average band = 10.4 – 16.6)
Concepts About Print (24 total)

Table 7
Writing Vocabulary Scores of Total DLL Group, Control, and Comparison Groups Compared to the Average Band of First Grade Spanish-Speaking Children

	DLL mean	Control mean	Other mean
Fall	3.0	4.6	9.7
Spring	48.5	25.7	32.7

Average band = ± .5 standard deviations from *mean*
mean = 34.7 (Average band = 24.3 – 45.1)
Writing Vocabulary (10 minute limit)

Table 8
Dictation Scores of Total DLL Group, Control, and Comparison Groups Compared to the Average Band of First Grade Spanish-Speaking Children

	DLL mean	Control mean	Other mean
Fall	2.6	9.3	16.2
Spring	33.6	25.6	29.1

Average band = ± .5 standard deviations from *mean*
mean = 29.1 (Average band = 24.6 – 34.8)
Dictation (39 total)

Table 9
Text Reading Scores of Total DLL Group, Control, and Comparison Groups Compared to the Average Band of First Grade Spanish-Speaking Children

	DLL mean	Control mean	Other mean
Fall	1.6	1.6	3.6
Spring	13.9	6.2	11.4

Average band = ± .5 standard deviations from *mean*
mean = 11.7 (Average band = 6.9 – 16.5)
Text Reading (28 maximum)

observation tasks of the Spanish Observation Survey and the Aprenda Spanish Reading Achievement Test-Total Reading Score. For each of the measures, the average band was calculated from the mean and standard deviation. The average band was considered to be ± .5 standard deviations from the mean. For the six observation tasks on the Spanish Observation Survey student raw scores were used to calculate average. For the Aprenda Spanish Reading Achievement Test scaled scores were used. This procedure for determining whether student progress was average was the same method used at The Ohio State University when studying the impact of reading on English-speaking students (DeFord, Pinnell, Lyons, & Young, 1987).

Tables 4 through 9 illustrate the gains made by each study group for each of the measurement criteria. Gains for each group are compared to the band of what is considered average progress.

By the spring testing dates DLL students had reached the average band on all measurement criteria. On one task (writing vocabulary), the spring mean for DLL students was above the average band. This is interpreted as an indication that DLL students have accelerated to a level of average according to these criteria, and are demonstrating that the theory of student acceleration in DLL programs can work in Spanish as well as in English. As with Research Questions 1 and 2, DLL students surpassed both control and comparison students in May on all criteria.

Control and comparison students, on the other hand, also made progress from fall to spring. Control group students reached the average band of progress on five out of six of the observation tasks and comparison students were in the average band on all observation tasks. However, progress of both groups lagged behind the DLL group at statistically significant levels.

Research Question 4 examined the proportion of DLL students who successfully achieved end-of-year scores on measures of Spanish reading that were equivalent to the average band. In other words, aside from the mean for all students in the DLL group, it was determined how many actually accelerated into the average group on all measures. For this question, the Spanish Observation Survey was once again utilized. For the twenty-three children who participated in the DLL program, each of their scores on the May, 1992, observation tasks was compared to the average band scores used for Research Question 4. The number of students achieving average scores for each observation task was then noted. After all scores were calculated, the percentage of DLL students achieving in the average range was calculated. Scores and percentages are presented in Table 10. Twenty-one of the 23 DLL students (91 percent) achieved end-of-year scores on all six observation tasks that either equaled or exceeded the average. This result is interpreted as another indicator that the DLL program is achieving student acceleration and is positively impacting program students.

Table 10
Numbers and Percentages of Descubriendo La Lectura Children in End-of-Year Average Band

Measure	Average Band	Met or Exceeded Number	%	Met or Exceeded Number	%
Letter Identification (61 total)	43.2 – 56.4	21	91%	2	9%
Word Test (20 total)	8.2 – 16.2	21	91%	2	9%
Concepts about Print (24 total)	10.4 – 16.6	22	96%	1	4%
Writing Vocabulary (10 minutes)	24.3 – 45.1	21	91%	2	9%
Dictation (39 total)	24.6 – 34.8	22	96%	1	4%
Text Reading (28 total)	6.9 – 16.5	17	74%	6	26%

Note. This group includes both successfully discontinued and not-discontinued program children who received at least 60 DLL lessons.

Discussion

The data reported establish that the DLL program achieved acceleration with Spanish-speaking students who were struggling while learning to read in Spanish. Its impact on students could be interpreted to be positive as DLL program students made significant gains in their literacy acquisition during the course of this project. Further, these gains were significant when compared to a control group of children who were also struggling in Spanish literacy, but did not have the DLL program. Fall and spring differences between the DLL and control group students were significant on all measurement criteria. Even more significant was the fact that DLL student learning growth surpassed that of a comparison group of first grade students learning to read in Spanish. The comparison group consisted of students who were not in the lower 20 percent of their class (all were above that level). Fall and spring differences between the DLL and comparison groups were also significant on all measurement criteria. These findings are seen as evidence to support the theory that Descubriendo La Lectura, like Reading Recovery, can help students who are struggling to learn to read in a relatively short period of time (12-16 weeks). Further, the program accelerates the students to the point of being on par with average readers in a class. In fact, on all measurement criteria used in the study, DLL students not only caught up with their average peers, but surpassed them at statistically significant levels. While this finding is greatly encouraging for DLL students, it raises some concerns with regard to the quality of Spanish reading instruction for children in the regular bilingual classrooms. The overall instructional program in Spanish literacy is one that merits further study and consideration.

While the research is positive relating to the potential of the DLL program in Spanish, it must be emphasized that this project involved only twenty-three students. Additional data need to be collected at other sites and with other cohorts of students in order to provide additional evidence as to the initial effectiveness of the program in Spanish. These data, however, provide evidence that the program has been highly effective with the children who were involved.

Of equal importance is the extent to which children involved in this program will be able to sustain the initial benefits of the program as they move on to other grade levels and as they make the transition from reading in Spanish to reading in English. These twenty-three children will become the first data bank for a longitudinal study that will examine the sustaining effects of DLL across grade levels and the transfer of DLL strategies from Spanish to English. It can be concluded, however, that initial results of this study with this group of children demonstrated that the program has a great deal of promise in assisting children who are struggling to become literate.

References

Allington, R., & Broikou, R. (1988, April). Development of shared knowledge: A new role for classroom and specialist teachers. *The Reading Teacher, 41,* 806-821.

Aprenda-Technical Data Report. (1991). The Psychological Corporation. San Antonio: Harcourt Brace Jovanovich.

Barrera, R. (1989, January). *Issues related to pullout and remedial programs and student achievement: A review of the research.* Symposium presented at the University of Arizona (R. Barrera, chair), Tucson.

Brown, A. (1992, April). Building community support through local education funds. *NABE News, 15*(4-5), 11-26.

Clay. M. (1979a, 1985). *The early detection of reading difficulties* (3rd ed.). Auckland, NZ: Heinemann.

Clay, M. (1979b). *Reading: The patterning of complex behavior.* Auckland, NZ: Heinemann.

Clay, M. (1982). Reading Recovery: A follow-up study. In M. Clay (Ed.), *Observing young readers: Selected papers.* Exeter, NH: Heinemann.

Clay, M. (1989). Concepts about print in English and other languages. *The Reading Teacher, 42,*

268-276.

Cummins, J. (1989). *Empowering minority students.* Sacramento: California Association for Bilingual Education.

DeFord, D., Pinnell, G., Lyons, C., & Young, P. (1987). *Report of the follow-up studies: Vol. 7 Columbus, Ohio, Ohio Reading Recovery Project 1985-86 and 1986-87.* Columbus: The Ohio State University.

District Policy 1110: Bilingual/bicultural education. (1981, March). Tucson: Tucson Unified School District.

Dyer, P. (1992). *Reading Recovery: A cost-effectiveness and educational outcomes analysis.* Arlington, VA: Educational Research Service.

Escamilla, K. (1987). *The relationship of native language reading achievement and oral English proficiency to future achievement in reading English as a second language.* Unpublished doctoral dissertation, University of California, Los Angeles.

Escamilla, K., & Andrade, A. (1992). Descubriendo La Lectura: An application of Reading Recovery in Spanish. *Education and Urban Society, 24,* 212-226.

Escamilla, K., Basurto, A., Andrade, A., & Ruíz, O. (1992, January). *Descubriendo La Lectura: A study of methods of assessing and identifying the reading needs of Spanish-speaking first grade students.* Paper presented at the National Association for Bilingual Education Conference (NABE), Albuquerque.

Fradd, S., & Tikunoff, W. (1987). *Bilingual education and bilingual special education: A guide for administrators.* Boston: College Hill.

Hakuta, K. (1987). *Mirror of language.* New York: Basic Books.

Hornberger, N. H. (1992). Bi-literacy contexts, continua, and contrasts: Policy and curriculum for Cambodian and Puerto Rican students in Philadelphia. *Education and Urban Society, 24,* 196-211.

Huck, C., & Pinnell, G. (1985). *The Reading Recovery project in Columbus, Ohio: Pilot year 1984-85* (Technical Report). Columbus: The Ohio State University.

Krashen, S., & Biber, D. (1988). *On course: Bilingual education's success in California.* Sacramento: California Association for Bilingual Education.

Lyons, J. (1991, May). The view from Washington. *NABE News, 14*(5), 1.

Pinnell, G. (1988). Holistic ways to help children at risk of failure. *Teachers Networking – The Whole Language Newsletter, 9*(1), 3.

Pinnell, G. (1990). Success for low achievers through Reading Recovery. *Educational Leadership, 48*(1), 17-21.

Pinnell, G., DeFord, D., & Lyons, C. (1988). *Reading Recovery: Early intervention for at-risk first graders.* Arlington, VA: Educational Research Service.

Pinnell, G., Fried, M., & Estice, R. (1990, January). Reading Recovery: Learning how to make a difference. *The Reading Teacher, 43*(4), 282-295.

Ramírez, D., Yuen, S., & Ramey, D. (1991). *Executive summary, final report: Longitudinal study of structured English immersion strategy, early-exit and late-exit transitional bilingual programs for language minority children* (Contract No. 300-87-0156). San Mateo, CA: Aguirre International.

READING RECOVERY AND LEARNING DISABILITY: ISSUES, CHALLENGES, AND IMPLICATIONS

CAROL A. LYONS

The Ohio State University

For twenty-five years the learning disabilities (LD) field has been driven by three fundamental questions: What is a learning disability? Who are the learning disabled? What kind of instruction will help them? Countless articles have been written and research studies have been conducted to address these questions, which remain unanswered. Why? The educational community, researchers, practitioners, and professional organizations (e. g., Association for Children with Learning Disabilities (ACLD), Council for Exceptional Children (CEC), Orton Dyslexia Society) cannot agree on how to: (a) to define the concept, (b) differentiate among various learning problems to classify students, (c) design effective educational programs for LD students, and (d) design staff development programs that enable teachers to learn how to help low achieving students. According to Adelman (1992), experts in the field are having difficulty reaching consensus because they have not developed a theory-based classification scheme, diagnostic criteria, assessment procedures, and effective programs. While the LD field struggles with the many issues resulting from a concept that is hard to define and describe, the number of students considered learning disabled is skyrocketing. Figures reported by the U. S. Department of Education (1990) indicated that from 1976 to 1986, students labeled LD grew from approximately 800,000 representing 22 percent of the special education population to 1.9 million, or 43 percent of the special education population (Singer & Butler, 1987).

There is, however, a well researched intervention program, Reading Recovery, developed in New Zealand by Marie M. Clay (1985), that has substantially reduced the number of children referred for ongoing services. According to figures from the New Zealand Department of Education (1988), the lowest 21.24 percent of the 6 year-old age cohort were served by Reading Recovery and .8 percent of these children were referred for special needs programs (Clay, 1990). Data collected in Ohio during a five year period revealed that less than one percent of Reading Recovery program students were referred to specialists for LD screening (Table 1). These data suggest that Reading Recovery has the potential to reduce the burgeoning number of students diagnosed as LD in the United States.

The phenomenal success of Reading Recovery may be the result of over thirty years of research and development. Clay's understanding of literacy learning is based on approximately ten years of close observation of children engaged in reading work, careful observation of superb teaching, and the study of seminal and recent research provided by a number of scholars and experts in the profession (Clay, 1991). Clay offered the following explanation of literacy acquisition:

> A theory emerges which hypothesizes that out of early reading and writing experiences the young learner creates a network of competencies which power subsequent independent literacy learning. It is a theory of generic learning, that is, learning that generates further learning. The generic competencies are constructed by the learner as he works on many kinds of information coming from the printed page in reading or going to the printed page in writing. (p. 1)

Table 1

Reading Recovery program Children in Ohio Referred for LD Screening 1988-1993

	88-89	89-90	90-91	91-92	92-93
Reading Recovery program children	3344	3994	4336	4652	5091
Reading Recovery program students referred for LD screening	42 (1.26%)	26 (0.65%)	32 (0.74%)	35 (0.75%)	26 (0.51%)

As the preceding quotation suggests, Clay engaged in the necessary conceptual and empirical work to develop the program; something researchers and experts in the LD field are charged with failing to do (Adelman, 1992; Stanovich, 1991).

Perhaps an examination of the theories and principles that underpin the Reading Recovery program will provide helpful insights into how to respond to the issues and challenges faced by practitioners and researchers in the LD field and enable the field to move forward. The purpose of this article is threefold: first, to address the questions and issues raised by recognized scholars in the LD field (Aram, Morris, & Hall, 1992; Moats & Lyon, 1993; Seigle, 1992) from a Reading Recovery perspective; second, to respond to Adelman's (1992) challenge to provide demonstration projects that encompass a comprehensive approach to learning disability; and third, to make recommendations for the future of Reading Recovery and learning disability in the United States.

Addressing Major Questions and Issues

What is Learning Disability?

After thirty years of debate, there is still no universally accepted definition of a learning disability (LD). Further, there is dissatisfaction with prevailing definitions because practitioners and researchers continue to use a variety of descriptors to define the concept. The main issue is how to differentiate LD from underachievement. A discrepancy formula predicated on mismatches between intelligence and achievement is typically used. Many researchers (Fletcher, 1992; Rispens, Van Yperen, & van Dujin, 1991; Stanovich, 1991) argued that using a discrepancy formula is irrelevant to the definition of learning disabilities. Clay (1987) supported this contention and argued that the term learning disability defies definition. Program evaluation data collected during a two-year period in Ohio confirm that the discrepancy formula does not adequately define LD.

In 1985-86, 66 percent and in 1986-87, 80 percent of the first grade children who prior to receiving Reading Recovery were classified as LD by interdisciplinary teams of school professionals, were released from the program reading with the average of the first grade class (Lyons, 1989) (Table 2). These data suggest that it is not possible to distinguish first grade students who are underachieving from those who are learning disabled in order to define the concept.

An alternative point of view may be that children enter first grade with different profiles of achievement because they have had different and varied preschool experiences. For the majority of first grade students, literacy begins early—long before they encounter formal schooling. They have listened to and discussed thousands of stories. They have had many opportunities to read, respond to, and write their own messages. Family members have provided many literacy lessons every day in response to their early attempts to read and write; experiences that will benefit them greatly before they enter kindergarten.

Table 2

Program Children in Ohio Classified as LD Prior to Receiving Reading Recovery and Discontinued (Released) from the Program Reading with the Average of the Class

	1985-86	1986-87
Program students	110	1130
Program students classified as LD*	35 (32%)	110 (10%)
RR program students classified as LD released from the program reading with average first graders	23 (66%)	88 (80%)
RR program students referred for LD screening	12 (34%)	22 (20%)

Note. *Children classified as learning disabled by interdisciplinary teams of school professionals prior to receiving Reading Recovery.

Other children, for a variety of reasons enter school with limited knowledge about literacy and are behind their classmates in reading and writing ability. These children have experienced few literacy lessons. Nobody read to them or helped them write their names. They have had limited opportunities to read or write because there were few books or paper in their homes. While they could express themselves using language and participate in oral stories, they had few opportunities to respond to written language in the form of stories or poems or draw a picture to express themselves. No one served as a model, provided reading and writing materials, demonstrated their use, or offered support as they attempted to read and write. These children have not had literacy experiences that build school valued skills which are necessary for first grade instruction (Heath, 1983; Taylor, 1991). These children, however, are often targeted to receive Reading Recovery. Do they have a learning disability?

Clay's (1991) research indicated that during formal schooling there is a period of transition that may last a few days for some children but several months for others. During this time, children gradually change from nonreaders to beginning readers each in his or her own way and own time. This concept of a time for transition when preschool behaviors change into new forms of responding suggests that within a first grade classroom there are wide variations in patterns of progress. This transition occurs no matter what the approach to beginning reading instruction (e. g., whole language, phonics, literature based, and/or basal). Children are active learners changing over time within their contexts at home, in school, and in the community. Those who enter school with limited knowledge about literacy have more catching up to do in order to benefit from regular classroom instruction.

In 1992-1993, Reading Recovery teachers in approximately 3,800 schools throughout North America served almost 37,300 children. For all these replications, the success rate remained high, with the average percent released from the program reading with the average of the class ranging from 83 percent to 87 percent (Lyons, Pinnell, & DeFord, 1993). Perhaps Reading Recovery should be designated as a prereferral or first net program for first grade students who are having academic or learning difficulties. Then children, who after an extended time in the program do not make progress, would be referred for a specialist's evaluation. This procedure would reduce the number of children misclassified as LD, while distinguishing students with more difficult learning problems who need specialized long-term programs. This approach would enable researchers and practitioners to differentiate between underachievement caused

Research in Reading Recovery

by neurological dysfunctioning and that caused by environmental factors, and in the process would contribute to a better definition of learning disability.

Who are the Learning Disabled?

Since a wide range of individual definitions have been employed in the identification of LD students, it is little wonder that our nation's school districts vary in the ways of determining which students are learning disabled. Federal regulations developed in accordance with the implementation of P. L. 94-142, the Education for All Handicapped Children Act (EHA), advocated the diagnosis of learning disability in terms of process deficits in the presence of average or above average intelligence along with performance assessments in reading, writing, spelling, and math. The process deficits are measured by a battery of tests adapted from various instruments that assess auditory, visual, perceptual, spatial, and motor coordination. In spite of criticism from experts in the field these tests are still used extensively (Algozzine & Ysseldyke, 1986; Fletcher, 1992).

Government policy (P. L. 94-142) stated that the learning disabled are individuals who have a severe discrepancy between intellectual ability and achievement in one or more specific areas. In the state of Ohio, the term does not apply to "children who have learning problems which are primarily the result of a visual, hearing, or motor handicap, mental retardation, emotional disturbance, or environmental, cultural, or economic disadvantage" (Ohio Department of Education, 1983, p. 3). It is generally agreed that a severe discrepancy occurs when the student's score on the intelligence test is higher than his or her score on the achievement test by some specified amount. In Ohio, a discrepancy score that is equal to or greater than two years is generally accepted as reflecting a severe discrepancy.

A procedure for determining the existence of a severe discrepancy between intellectual ability and achievement has not been specified at the federal level or at most local levels (Gartner & Lipsky, 1987). Consequently, methods for making this determination have varied widely across states and school districts within each state. According to Stanovich (1991), any individual with any learning problem can be diagnosed as learning disabled. Because of this identification problem, many low progress readers who do not have a disability are treated as if they do.

Subtests designed to measure student's processing are not the only measures that have been criticized for diagnosing a learning disability. Developmental and educational psychologists generally agree that IQ test scores do not measure an individual's potential in any sense and are irrelevant to identification and analysis of learning disability (Seigel, 1989) or reading disability (Seigel, 1988). Stanovich (1991) argued that discrepancy definitions of reading disability have led educators astray:

Thus, to the extent that IQ scores were viewed as measures of potential, the practice of diagnosing dyslexia (reading disability) by measuring discrepancies from IQ scores was misconceived from the beginning. In short, we have been basing systems of educational classification in the area of reading disabilities on special claims of unique potential that are neither conceptually nor psychometrically justifiable. (p. 10)

Perhaps it is time to stop relying on process deficit tests, IQ tests, standardized reading tests, scores on reading readiness tests, discrepancy scores, and reading age when selecting students who are in need of specialized help. It would be better to help teachers become careful observers and recorders of young children's early attempts to learn how to read and write. Recent research (Pinnell, Lyons, DeFord, Bryk, & Seltzer, 1994) revealed that the teacher's ability to observe, analyze, and follow the lead of the child while he or she is engaged in reading and writing tasks and be ready to shift as the child extends capacities is a critical context element in helping low achieving first grade students become successful readers and writers. The most effective teachers change their behaviors in response to children's behaviors.

Clay (1985, 1993) developed an Observation Survey that enables teachers to observe how children engage in reading and writing tasks and note their successful and unsuccessful responses. The observation tasks include (a) running records, (b) letter identification, (c) concepts about print, (d) word tests, (e) writing, and (f) hearing sounds in words (dictation). The six subtests, none of which is sufficient on its own to measure a student's abilities, provide a foundation for what the child has already learned and what he or she needs to learn next. "In complex learning, what is already known provides the learner with a useful context within which to embed new learning" (Clay, 1993, p. 20).

The most important question teachers can ask students, regardless of their ages, is, "What do you know about . . . ?" If teachers do not know what students know and can do, how can they expect to help students construct new understandings? Generally speaking, first grade children have difficulty telling adults what they know. The Observation Survey is a tool for enabling children to demonstrate what they understand about the reading and writing process. It is used by teachers to distinguish among a variety of learning problems. While the Observation Survey does not answer the question, "Who are the learning disabled?" directly, it provides a needed framework for specifying the learning needs of individual students. Then, based on this information teachers can design and implement more effective intervention programs.

What Kind of Intervention Will Help the Learning Disabled?

The third question plaguing the LD field has been more illusive and difficult to answer because researchers and practitioners have not been able to define learning disability or describe and explain differences among low achieving students' learning processes. According to Adelman (1992), "The scope of misdiagnosis and misprescriptions in the field has undermined prevention, remediation, research, training, and the policy decisions shaping such activity" (p. 17).

An extensive body of research supported Adelman's (1992) claims. Gartner and Lipsky (1987), Slavin and Madden (1989), and Allington and Walmsley (in press) documented the general ineffectiveness of learning disability and reading disability programs. The research also suggested that once elementary students are placed in instructional support programs, most often remedial (Chapter 1) or special education (learning disability), they generally remain on the remedial track for a lifetime, rarely outgrowing their disability (Allington & McGill-Franzen, 1989). Yet in America we are continuing to identify primary children as LD and place them in LD programs that have no or limited success. There is little expectation that these students will ever be able to keep up with their peers in regular education classrooms in spite of the fact that the U. S. Office of Education encourages general educators and special educators to make a significant effort to find inclusive solutions for children considered to be LD (Rogers, 1993).

Researchers examining special education and remediation programs (McGill-Franzen & Allington, 1991; Moats & Lyon, 1993; Slavin & Madden, 1989) called for comprehensive programs to help low achieving students learn how to read. Adelman (1992) developed a framework representing a continuum of programs beginning with early age prevention to treatment for chronic problems and challenged the field to design comprehensive demonstration projects that have preventative and corrective implications for a wide range of learning and behavior problems. An examination of longitudinal data collected in ten U. S. school districts that have recently implemented Reading Recovery, as well as Reading Recovery program evaluation data collected over a six year period in two Ohio school districts revealed that there is a comprehensive demonstration project that responds to Adelman's challenge.

Meeting the Challenge

The National Study

In a study conducted in ten school districts representing urban, suburban, and rural areas, Schmidt (1993) found that prior to Reading Recovery, 2.3 percent of the first grade population was referred to LD resource rooms. After Reading Recovery was implemented in the ten school districts, 1.3 percent of the first grade students were placed in LD classrooms (Table 3).

The reduction in the number of students placed in LD resource rooms over the two year period is impressive. What is more impressive, however, is the fact that this reduction was evident in spite of the fact that only 10 percent of the first grade students was served by Reading Recovery during year one and 14 percent of the population was served during year two. As more teachers are trained, the percentage of coverage will increase and as a result fewer students should be referred for LD services.

The Suburban Study

Approximately 400 first grade children are enrolled annually in the five elementary schools in a suburban Ohio school district. The majority of those students learn how to read and write easily. However, approximately one out of every eight experiences difficulty in learning how to read in the primary grades. Prior to implementation of the Reading Recovery program in 1986-87, teachers had adopted a wait-and-see attitude. But after several years of waiting and providing children many opportunities to read and write, they realized that the longer they waited, the further the children fell behind. Reading Recovery program evaluation data revealed that waiting was not the answer. In the eight years (1986-1993) the program had been operating in this school district, 70 percent to 86 percent of the lowest achieving first grade readers reached average reading levels and continued to make progress with regular classroom literacy instruction. As reported in Table 4, the percentage of Reading Recovery program students classified as LD and placed in LD resource rooms decreased significantly over the five year period.

Follow-up data (Lyons & Beaver, 1995) revealed that the majority of the students served in LD resource rooms were not receiving additional help in reading. One student was phased out of the LD program at the end of fourth grade. These data suggest that when Reading Recovery is used as a prereferral program, it is possible to target students who are in need of more intensive specialized help.

Table 3

First Grade Students in Ten U. S. School Districts Referred to Learning Disability Services Prior To and After One and Two Years of Reading Recovery Implementation

	Prior to RR	RR Year 1*	RR Year 2
Total number of first grade students	2569	2602	2572
Number of first grade students referred for LD services at the end of first grade	59 (2.3%)	53 (2%)	34 (1.3%)

Note. *Year 1 refers to the year teachers were learning to become RR teachers.

The Urban Study

In an urban school district, nine elementary schools served approximately 700 first grade students every year. General education and special education district administrators decided that Reading Recovery had the potential to reduce the growing number of first grade children referred to learning disability classrooms.

Table 4
Suburban School District: Reading Recovery program 1986-1991

	1986-87	1987-88	1988-89	1989-90	1990-91
Grade 1 enrollment	340	369	404	391	406
Reading Recovery program students*	22	36	41	42	66
Reading Recovery program students classified LD**	8 (36%)	16 (44%)	12 (29%)	8 (19%)	6 (9%)

Note. *Program students are defined as completing 60 lessons or discontinued prior to 60 lessons. The number of program students served increased as more RR teachers were trained. Initially only one RR teacher was assigned per building; in 1991, there were two teachers per building.

**RR students identified using district and state criteria as learning disabled. No student received both programs at the same time. RR was always implemented prior to the LD program except in a few cases. Less than .05 percent of the children from the total population of first grade students over a five year period were identified to receive LD services rather than RR services prior to Kindergarten and/or first grade.

Table 5
Urban School District: Grade One Students Placed in LD Classrooms Prior To and After Reading Recovery

	1984-1987 (3 Years) Prior to RR Implementation**	1987-1991 (4 Years) After Partial Implementation*
Grade 1 enrollment	1781	1573
Number of students placed in LD	32 (1.8%)	10 (.64%)

Note. *Partial implementation (1987-1988): .08 percent of the first grade population served by nine RR teachers (one RR teacher assigned to each of the nine elementary buildings).

**Full implementation (1988-1991): Sixteen percent in 1988-89 and 20 percent from 1989-91 of the first grade population served by 15 RR teachers (one or two RR teachers assigned to each of the nine elementary buildings).

Figures reported by the U. S. Department of Education (1990) revealed that prior to full implementation, 1.8 percent of the first grade enrollment was placed in LD resource rooms (Table 5). Once Reading Recovery became a prereferral program, that is, low achieving first grade children received Reading Recovery before they were referred for LD screening, the percentage of children classified as LD was reduced to .64 percent. A cost-benefit analysis (Lyons & Beaver, in press) revealed that because the number of first grade students referred for LD placement had been reduced by two-thirds, the school district had saved approximately $100,000 annually.

Program evaluation data collected in these suburban and urban school districts demonstrated that district-wide projects did incorporate prevention, early intervention, and more specialized help for first grade students having learning problems. The results of these evaluations constituted a response to Adelman's (1992) challenge:

> The data from the demonstration project could have major cost-benefit and policy implications for decisions about how to reverse the current overemphasis on special education programs so that limited resources available can be reserved for students who manifest severe and pervasive psychoeducational problems. (p. 21)

Conclusion

Today, school districts throughout the U. S. are reexamining policies and procedures that govern the education of children with special needs, specifically the idea of educating these children in the least restrictive environment. The concept of providing services in the least restrictive environment is not new; it was initiated with the Education for All Handicapped Children Act (P. L. 94–142) in the mid 1970s. What is new is that federal regulations are being interpreted by U. S. courts to require schools to include special education children (the majority of whom are classified LD) in regular education classroom settings for all or a substantial part of the day. Inclusion, or inclusive education, generally refers to the selective placement of children with disabilities in general education classes (Rogers, 1993).

The inclusion phenomenon has a major impact on this country's regular education and special education programs. Moreover, policies that result from this phenomenon will challenge educators to rethink and redesign instructional programs for children with learning problems. For one thing, regular education teachers have students with special learning needs in their classrooms, and as more and more students are included, teachers will ask for instructional programs to meet the individual needs of these youngsters. In addition, school district administrators will seek programs that are considered inclusive and effective in teaching students with learning problems. Building administrators, with assistance from special educational administrators, will also look for ways to provide high quality professional development programs that prepare general educators to work effectively with children representing a range of abilities and disabilities. Thus, the inclusion revolution raises concerns for special and regular education teachers, administrators, policymakers, and parents. These challenges, however, provide opportunities for educators to work together to determine how to effectively meet the needs of children with learning problems.

The Reading Recovery program for children and professional development programs for teachers provide the needed direction to meet these challenges in three ways. First, the program enables educators to separate first grade low achieving students from children who have more severe learning problems, thus reducing the number of students who will need to be served by special education teachers. Second, the yearlong professional development program provides teachers with opportunities to understand how children think and learn by observing, recording, and analyzing students' reading and writing behaviors. Based on this information, teachers learn how to tailor and adjust their instructional practice to meet the individual's learning gains. Third, effective Reading Recovery teachers continue to develop more complex understandings of the learning and teaching process and refine their skills while interacting with the most difficult to teach students (Lyons, Pinnell, & DeFord, 1993). Thus, the Reading Recovery professional development program not only helps low achieving students learn how to read with the average of the class, but also helps regular education teachers understand and help students with special learning needs who will be placed in their classrooms, and special education teachers better understand how children become literate and their role in assisting the process.

What will it take to define the concept of learning disability, identify the truly learning disabled, and determine what kind of intervention is most effective in helping low achieving students learn? Reading Recovery program evaluation data have provided some valuable insights. The issues discussed in this article represent a part of the picture. If used in conjunction with approaches that address the needs of students with more severe learning needs, Reading Recovery can represent a real chance to make a difference in the lives of young children who are having learning difficulties. The Reading Recovery program presents the opportunity for the merger of special education and general education programs and policies for teachers and children, and perhaps the funding sources of each.

References

Adelman, H. S. (1992). LD: The next 24 years. *Journal of Learning Disabilities, 25,* 17-22.

Allington, R. L., & McGill-Franzen, A. (1989). School response to reading failure: Instruction for Chapter 1 and special education students in grades two, four and six. *Elementary School Journal, 89,* 529-542.

Allington, R. L., & Walmsley, S. A. (1995). *No quick fix: Redesigning literacy programs in America's elementary schools.* New York: Teachers College Press.

Algozzine, B., & Ysseldyke, J. E. (1986). The future of the LD field: Screening and diagnosis. *Journal of Learning Disabilities, 19,* 394-398.

Aram, D. M., Morris, R. M., & Hall, N. E. (1992). The validity of discrepancy criteria for identifying children with developmental language disorders. *Journal of Learning Disabilities, 25,* 449-554.

Clay, M. M. (1985). *The early detection of reading difficulties.* Auckland, NZ: Heinemann.

Clay, M. M. (1987). Learning to be learning disabled. *New Zealand Journal of Educational Studies, 22,* 155-173.

Clay, M. M. (1990). The Reading Recovery programs, 1984-88: Coverage, outcomes and Education Board district figures. *New Zealand Journal of Educational Studies, 25,* 61-70.

Clay, M. M. (1991). *Becoming literate: The construction of inner control.* Portsmouth, NH: Heinemann.

Clay, M. M. (1993). *An observation survey of early literacy achievement.* Portsmouth, NH: Heinemann.

Fletcher, J. M. (1992). The validity of distinguishing children with language and learning disabilities according to discrepancies with IQ: Introduction to the special series. *Journal of Learning Disabilities, 25,* 546-548.

Gartner, A., & Lipsky, D. (1987). Beyond special education: Toward a quality system for all students. *Harvard Educational Review, 57,* 368-395.

Heath, S. B. (1983). *Ways with words: Language, life and work in communities and classrooms.* New York: Cambridge University Press.

Lyons, C. (1989). Reading recovery: A preventative for mislabeling young "at-risk" learners. *Urban Education, 24,* 125-139.

Lyons, C. A., & Beaver, J. (1995). Reducing retention and learning disability placement through Reading Recovery: An educationally sound, cost-effective choice. In R. L. Allington & S. A. Walmsley (Eds.), *No quick fix: Redesigning literacy programs in America's elementary schools.* New York: Teachers College Press.

Lyons, C. A., Pinnell, G. S., & DeFord, D. E. (1993). *Partners in learning: Teachers and children in Reading Recovery.* New York: Teachers College Press.

McGill-Franzen, A., & Allington, R. (1991). Every child's right: Literacy. *The Reading Teacher, 45,* 86-90.

Moats, L. C., & Lyon, G. R. (1993). Learning disabilities in the United States: Advocacy, science, and the future of the field. *Journal of Learning Disabilities, 26,* 282-294.

New Zealand Department of Education. (1988). *Tomorrow's schools.* Wellington: Government Printer.

Ohio Department of Education. (1983). *Ohio guidelines for the identification of children with specific learning disabilities.* Columbus: State Department of Education.

Pinnell, G. S., Lyons, C. A., DeFord, D. E., Bryk, A. S., & Seltzer, M. (1944). Comparing instructional models for the literacy education of high risk first graders. *Reading Research Quarterly, 29,* 1-42.

Rispens, J., Van Yperen, T., & van Dujin, G. A. (1991). The irrelevance of IQ to the definition of learning disabilities: Some empirical evidence. *Journal of Learning Disabilities, 24,* 434-438.

Rogers, J. (1993). The inclusion revolution. *Phi Delta Kappa Research Bulletin, 11,* 1-6.

Schmidt, D. B. (1993). *The effect of Reading Recovery on special education and Chapter One programs.* Unpublished Master's thesis, Pacific Lutheran University.

Seigel, L. S. (1988). Definitional and theoretical issues and research on learning disabilities. *Journal of Learning Disabilities, 21,* 264-266.

Seigel, L. S. (1989). IQ is irrelevant to the definition of learning disabilities. *Journal of Learning Disabilities, 22,* 469-478.

Seigel, L. S. (1992). An evaluation of the discrepancy definition of dyslexia. *Journal of Learning Disabilities, 25,* 618-629.

Singer, J. D., & Butler, J. A. (1987). The Education for All Handicapped Children Act: Schools as agents of social reform. *Harvard Educational Review, 57,* 125-182.

Slavin, R. E., & Madden, N. A. (1989). What works for students at risk: A research synthesis. *Educational Leadership, 67,* 4-13.

Stanovich, K. E. (1991). Discrepancy definitions of reading disability: Has intelligence led us astray? *Reading Research Quarterly, 26,* 7-29.

Taylor, D. (1991). *Learning denied.* Portsmouth, NH: Heinemann.

U. S. Department of Education. (1990). *U. S. Office of Special Education and Rehabilitative Service, Twelfth annual report to Congress on the implementation of the Education of the Handicapped Act,* Table AA20, pp. A33-34. Washington, DC: Author.

READING RECOVERY IN ENGLAND

ANGELA HOBSBAUM
Institute of Education, University of London

This paper presents findings from the first nationwide collection of Reading Recovery data ever carried out in England. As this is our first national monitoring, there were many issues which we urgently needed to explore to examine the implementation and to see what we could learn about ways to improve. This was our first opportunity to look at the overall effectiveness of the programme, to compare new and experienced teachers, to look at the profile of the children on entry and the levels they achieved at outcome, to look at different language groups, and to examine different measures of effectiveness. The data presented here represent very much a first look at that information to search for clues to some of the answers to these questions.

A Brief History of Reading Recovery in England

Before 1990, Reading Recovery had taken place in England only as a result of the efforts of individuals who had generally been trained in New Zealand and were visiting this country (e.g. Pluck, 1989). However, in 1989, one Head Teacher persuaded her county to send her to New Zealand to train as a tutor (teacher leader) and on her return in 1990, she immediately began to train teachers to implement the programme in Surrey schools. News of this venture spread and even before the professional reports appeared (Wright, 1992), there was considerable interest in the enterprise. As a result of this and with assistance from the Paul Hamlyn Foundation, in 1991, Professor Marie Clay was invited to bring a team of trainers and tutors over from New Zealand for two years to the Institute of Education at London University to lead courses for tutors and teachers there. In 1991, the New Zealand team trained the first cohort of seven tutors (teacher leaders) and 37 teachers while Jean Prance, our first English tutor, trained 12 teachers in Surrey.

This initiative was further consolidated when in 1992, approval was given by the Secretary of State for Education for a national pilot project to run from 1992-95, which the Institute of Education was asked to coordinate and oversee. In the event, the pilot project was funded from the GEST initiative (Grants for Education Support and Training) for which the Local Education Authorities (Boroughs or Counties) contribute 40 percent of the funds, which are then matched by 60 percent from central government. The GEST initiative under whose umbrella Reading Recovery fell was the Raising Standards in Inner Cities scheme designed to raise achievement in inner city schools. This restricted the pilot project to schools which fell within areas already designated as deprived urban areas.

Twenty metropolitan Local Education Authorities (Boroughs) took advantage of this scheme to send tutors to train and to set up their own Reading Recovery sites with training facilities. A further five were persuaded to join the training courses, supporting the programme without additional government funds. The urban areas included Bradford in West Yorkshire in the North, St. Helens on Merseyside in the North West of England, Birmingham and Wolverhampton in the Midlands, and twelve London boroughs. Thus, in the second cohort, 25 tutors and 100 teachers entered courses based at the Institute, with outreach centres in Sheffield to cover the north of England and Birmingham for the Midlands.

By September, 1993, there were 26 Reading Recovery sites around the country, stretching from Jersey in the south to Bradford in the north, running courses to train teachers. Two trainers of tutors were also trained in anticipation of our need to become self-sustaining. Also in 1993, the government sent two of Her Majesty's Inspectors of Schools to New Zealand to examine the scheme there; their report was highly favourable (OFSTED, 1993) and proved influential in persuading the government that since the New Zealand team would be leaving at the end of the academic year, some system needed to be established to monitor and coordinate the national enterprise. The Department for Education agreed to support a national coordination network consisting of the two trainers and two staff from the Institute of Education who had been involved with the training courses there. The National Network received approximately 100,000 pounds per year from the Department for Education which covers a portion of the salaries of the four people involved, the travel costs incurred in making visits to every site, administrative costs, the cost of a one-week professional development course, the production of regular bulletins, national data-collection, and other costs. In 1994, the Department for Education agreed to extend this for one further year to cover the end of the pilot project, whose funding expired in April, 1995. Thus, just as it gets launched, the programme is threatened by uncertainty over its future. A current concern is the future funding for the implementation of Reading Recovery in the United Kingdom after 1995.

In 1993, before she returned to New Zealand (and then came on to Texas) Marie Clay analysed the data collected over the two years of the training programme consisting of the results obtained by the children taught by teachers-in-training, who had been trained by the New Zealand team, and she compiled a report noting the reactions of her team to their experiences of English teachers and schools. These impressions and the findings from these data formed the basis of a report which was presented to the tutors in February, 1994, at Tutor Development Week and which has informed our data collection subsequently.

The programme has thus expanded rapidly in England and from 1991-94 has been implemented by fairly inexperienced personnel. As we embarked on the school year in September, 1994, 26 of our tutors had one year of experience in the field and a minority, six, had two years of experience behind them; three were new to this role. At September, 1994, we had two trainers and 36 tutors in 29 training sites (local education authorities) including newly established centres in Wales and Northern Ireland.

The data to be presented are taken from our first national monitoring exercise which was carried out in July, 1994. We can confidently plan one further national monitoring in July, 1995, and although the future is uncertain we hope to be able to sustain it after that date.

Two cautionary notes:

(1) *Statistical analysis:* Because these data have been collected from a large sample and are based on the Observation Survey tests administered by teachers to children, there are gaps in the data and therefore the numbers included in every analysis vary slightly. While the total sample consisted of 3,131 children; where numbers are given there may be some slight variation across subtests.

(2) *Outcomes:* In our implementation, we recognise two possible outcomes to a Reading Recovery programme: a child may be successfully discontinued or referred. Two other possibilities are also recorded: when a child leaves the school and when a child has an incomplete programme because they have not received 20 weeks of instruction (we include the two weeks *in the known* in our computation of programme length). The definition of *successfully discontinued,* for research purposes, is the same as the operational definition used by the Reading Recovery teacher on the spot: (i) the child should have a secure literacy system, as shown by scores on the Observation Survey, in general a Book Level above 15 and a Writing Vocabulary greater than 30, together with some evidence of active processing and self-correction, and (ii) should be reading at the average level of the class. We have not so far used any other standardised tests to assess the child's reading level or the class average.

There is a widespread concern in England at the present time about levels of literacy achievement and while we cannot throw any light directly on this, we became aware that in many cases the average level of literacy of the class from which the Reading Recovery pupils were drawn was considerably lower than that represented by a Book Level of 15. We have tried to adhere to the first criterion for successful discontinuation, that the child should have a secure literacy system, but it is clear that this has been interpreted in different ways according to the grade of the class. This will be dealt with more fully in Section 2.5.

The Teachers

Teachers for the Reading Recovery training courses were recruited from fully qualified teachers who had sound experience of teaching at Infant (lower elementary) level and who could be released to teach four children every day. In the early years this meant that head teachers (principals) and deputy heads (assistant principals) were often the only members of a school staff who could find this time (or who thought they could). In fact, it became clear that they had many other conflicting demands on their time and we are now reluctant to train teachers who hold senior posts of responsibility.

Table 1
Numbers of Teachers and Children Involved in England 1990–93

	Number of teachers trained	Number included in 1994 survey	Number of children taught
1990	19 (in Surrey)	9 (2%)	63 (2%)
1991	49	24 (5%)	174 (6%)
1992	124	115 (24%)	778 (27%)
1993	330	328 (69%)	1886 (65%)
Total	522	476	2901

It is clear from these data in Table 1 that the majority of our informants are teachers in their year of training for Reading Recovery and they have provided data on the largest group of children. Almost 70 percent of the teachers were in training and they had provided data on 65 percent of our sample of almost 3,000 children.

One of our concerns has been to look for evidence that teachers become more effective with increased experience. We have looked for three kinds of evidence:

(a) pupil outcomes,
(b) length of programme, and
(c) numbers of children taught per year.

Do more experienced teachers achieve more successful outcomes?

Table 2 demonstrates the imbalance in the distribution both of teachers and pupils and the preponderance of inexperienced teachers and children taught by teachers still in training. It also suggests that as teachers become more experienced they become more successful at enabling pupils to achieve successful outcomes. Although the numbers of children and teachers involved are small, over 80 percent of the pupils taught by more experienced teachers achieved success; while less than 70 percent of those taught by teachers in training are successfully discontinued.

These proportions are mirrored by the proportions referred who do not achieve the programme's goals: about 10 percent of those taught by the most experienced teachers are referred while 25-30 percent of those taught by less experienced teachers fail to reach a successful outcome.

Table 2
Pupil Outcome x Year of Teacher Training, For Complete Programmes Only

	Teachers Trained				
Pupil outcome	1990	1991	1992	1993	Total
Successfully discontinued	**37** (88%)	**99** (83%)	**353** (77%)	**883** (68%)	**1372**
Referred	**5** (12%)	**20** (17%)	**130** (27%)	**418** (32%)	**573**
Total	42	119	483	1301	1945

Do experienced teachers get children through the programme at a faster rate?

Reaching an effective outcome is only desirable if it is not at the expense of a prolonged programme. Do experienced teachers manage to achieve these results without any increase in the length of the programme? Table 3 shows the length of programme (in weeks) for successfully discontinued children according to the year of teacher training.

Table 3
Average Length of Programme in Weeks x Year of Teacher Training

	Median	Mean	SD
trained 1990:	21 weeks	20	5
trained 1991:	20 weeks	20	8
trained 1992:	21 weeks	21	6
training 1993:	26 weeks	25	7

Note. In England we include the two weeks *in the known.*

This indicates that as teachers gain experience they also take less time to complete a child's programme. Although the trend is in the right direction, it is nevertheless worrying that the mean never falls below 20 weeks and the range, although it too narrows, remains high, especially in the training year.

How many children are reached by teachers as they get more experienced?

This decrease in length of programme with increased experience is reflected in the number of children reached, although this may also be affected by the number of programme places permitted. It is not always possible for schools to release teachers to offer four places on the programme at any one time; some schools have only been able to provide two or three places. Unfortunately, we omitted to collect information on the number of places available that year.

This demonstrates that as teachers become more experienced and move children faster through the programme, this enables them to get a faster throughput, so that more children can

Table 4
Average Number of Children Receiving the Programme per Teacher x Year of Training

	Mode	Mean
trained 1990	6	7.00
trained 1991	8	7.25
trained 1992	8	6.70
training 1993	4	5.75

receive the programme. Thus, on three measures of teacher effectiveness our data show that as teachers get more experienced they become able to implement the programme more effectively. This is reassuring; the challenge now is to ensure that we can retain teachers in the programme so that more children can benefit from their improved performance.

The Children

Characteristics of the Sample

The data collected in 1994 provide the most extensive information yet available in England on the characteristics of pupils having difficulty with literacy and selected on that basis for Reading Recovery. Our sample of 3,131 children was made up of 1,955 boys (62 percent) and 1,176 girls (38 percent). Their mean age at entry to programme was 6 years, 1 month (SD = 3 months).

When the programme was first trialled in England, from 1990-1992, the target group of children was drawn from those aged 6:0 to 6:6 who were in what are called Year 2 classes. However, because of different policies on admission to school, children may enter school at any time between four and five and thus by six, some children will have had more than one year at school. The criteria for admission to the programme, that the child should have received one year at school and be aged over six years, identified two separate and only partially overlapping groups: those who had been in school for one year and those aged six. During their time in England, the New Zealand training team became aware of many demands that children in Year 1 should be admitted to Reading Recovery. From September, 1993, it was decided to lower the age of selection to 5:9 in order to include children in Year 1 classes who had already received one full year of schooling. Our age group for selection to the programme is now 5:9 through 6:3 and thus the sample children are drawn from two year groups:

Year 1 children (aged 5:9 – 5:11 in September)
Year 2 children (aged 6:0 – 6:11 in September)

Our Year 1 children are aged between 5:9 and 6:1 at entry to the programme and the Year 2 children are aged between 6:1 and 6:7. Year 2 children are usually selected at the start of the school year and the children who are selected later in the year after the first group have completed their programme are more likely to be Year 1 children. It is interesting that the lowering of the age of entry to 5:9 appears to have had a marked effect on the sample selected to receive the programme since over half of them are drawn from Year 1 classes this year:

Year 1: 1,823 children *(59 percent)*   mean age 5:11   *(SD 2 mo)*
Year 2: 1,121 children *(41 percent)*   mean age 6:4   *(SD 3 mo)*

The significance of grade level is that the early literacy experiences and the school curriculum in the two years differ considerably. The teachers' expectations about the children's literacy achievements will also be very different. The recently introduced National Tests are also taken by children at the end of Year 2. These provide a benchmark for literacy attainments and schools are generally concerned that their pupils should achieve at least average levels on these tests.

This has made schools more receptive to the idea of early identification and intervention and may underlie the targeting of Year 1 children.

Because of different admissions policies, children will have had different lengths of school experience when they enter the programme. In England, the first class in school is called the Reception class; children may, depending on their term of entry which is affected by their date of birth and the school's admission policy, spend from one to three terms in Reception before moving into Year 1. Children selected for Reading Recovery will have had different amounts of schooling. For our sample this ranged from two to eight terms (Table 5).

Table 5
Number of Terms Completed at Start of Programme x Grade Level

	Number of terms of school completed at start of programme						
	2	3	4	5	6	7	8
Y1	41 *(2 %)*	1070 *(60 %)*	424 *(24 %)*	240 *(13 %)*	19 *(1 %)*	1	0
Y2	12 *(1 %)*	176 *(14 %)*	532 *(44 %)*	261 *(21 %)*	210 *(17%)*	14 *(1 %)*	16 *(1%)*

Over half the Year 1 children have had three terms in school at the start of the programme and a further quarter have had four terms. Over 40 percent of Year 2 children have had four terms in school (which is probably made up of three terms in Year 1 plus one term in the Reception class). But about 20 percent have had five and six terms schooling before they enter the programme, so many children in Year 2 have had well over a year at school and 20 percent have had two years of school experience when they start Reading Recovery.

Preschool Experience and Language Background

About ten percent of the sample had no preschool experience, about ten percent were in play groups, and about 80 percent were in nursery schools or nursery classes. This is higher than average for England but probably reflects the fact that the programme was running in inner city areas which generally have better preschool provision than suburban or rural areas or counties.

Given the areas in which the programme was sited, it is not surprising that the children were drawn from a range of ethnic backgrounds and 20 percent were bilingual, having a first language other than English. It is not possible without further investigation to be sure whether this proportion of bilingual speakers is fairly representative of the proportion of such children in the classes from which our sample was drawn. In some boroughs there were no bilingual children in the Reading Recovery programme whereas in others they constituted over half the sample.

Special Needs

Eighty-two children (2.6 percent of the whole sample) were noted as having a Statement of Special Educational Needs at the start of the programme, i.e. before the programme commenced. Since the process of issuing a statement of special needs is usually very protracted and can take up to a year, this suggests that these children had a significant learning disability which had been noticed early in their school (or even their preschool) career.

Entry and Exit Profiles of Children on the Observation Survey

This pattern of very low entry scores together with quite a wide variation seems to be typical of most of the populations of low achievers who have received Reading Recovery (Table 6); it is similar to the Australian and the Ohio samples. The entry scores are slightly lower than those of the first Surrey cohorts, reported in Wright (1992), who are our only other English reference point.

Table 6
Observation Survey Profiles for the Whole Sample

	Book Level	Concepts About Print	Hearing Sounds	Letter Identification	Word Test	Writing Vocabulary
Entry level (n = 2,900)						
mean	1.17	9.5	8.4	27.3	1.6	4.8
SD	1.6	3.7	8.1	15.7	2.2	5.2
Exit level (n = 1,900)						
mean	13.6	18.2	30.4	49.0	10.8	37.0
SD	4.5	3.5	7.3	7.3	3.7	15.0

However, the levels reached at the end of the programme for the whole sample, including those not successfully discontinued, while encouraging, are of limited value. More informative is the level reached for the successfully discontinued children, and here we need to examine the levels reached for different groups: those in Year 1 and Year 2, the bilingual speakers, and girls and boys.

The Effect of Year Group on Progress in Reading Recovery

Table 7
Outcome Scores on the Observation Survey for Successfully Discontinued Children in Year 1 and Year 2

	Book Level	Concepts About Print	Hearing Sounds	Letter Identification	Word Test	Writing Vocabulary
Year 1 (n = 645)						
mean	15.3	19.2	32.9	51.5	12.2	41.9
SD	2.0	2.6	3.9	2.6	2.2	11.8
Year 2 (n = 815) *	*	*		*	*
mean	16.5	19.7	33.6	51.7	12.6	44.6
SD	2.3	2.5	3.5	3.4	2.2	12.6

(* indicates a statistically significant difference between scores for Year 1 and Year 2 children)

There are significant differences between children in Year 1 and Year 2, with children in Year 1 having lower entry scores on all measures and lower outcome scores on all measures *except* letter identification. This demonstrates that for Year 1 children to be regarded as successfully completing the programme they do not have to have achieved as high a level of text reading or other literacy achievements as Year 2 children. The only measure where this does not apply is letter identification. The literacy demands on these children will be less exacting as they are in Year 1 and after leaving the programme they will have a whole year before they take the National Tests at seven.

Are the children in Year 1 any less likely to succeed than their Year 2 counterparts?

Table 8
Outcomes for Children in Year 1 and Year 2 Classes

Year (Grade) in school									
	successfully discontinued		referred		left school		incomplete programme		
	n	%	n	%	n	%	n	%	total
Year 1	652	35	298	16	79	4	822	45	1851
Year 2	824	64	321	25	77	6	58	5	1280

The children with incomplete programmes are those who are mid-programme at the end of the school year. In the case of Year 1 children, it is expected that their programme will be resumed after the six-week summer vacation. For Year 2 children, it may be less easy to continue their programmes because they will enter the Junior department of the Primary school, or in some cases, a completely separate school, and liaison between Infant and Junior departments becomes more difficult. It is notable that a far higher proportion of Year 1 children have incomplete programmes. This is a by-product of the rolling programme since these children are more likely to be selected after the first children to be selected have completed their programmes. It appears from this that children in Year 1 are less likely to be successfully discontinued. But if we look at the distribution excluding those children who are still mid-programme at the end-of-year data collection point, the figures look slightly different. From these figures, there is no significant difference in the likelihood of being referred or successfully discontinued for children in Year 1 and Year 2.

Table 9
Outcomes for Children with Complete Programmes in Year 1 and 2 Classes

	successfully discontinued		referred		left school	
	n	%	n	%	n	%
Year 1	652	63	298	29	79	7
Year 2	824	68	321	26	77	6

The Effect of Gender on Progress in Reading Recovery

As two thirds of the children who enter the programme are boys, are there gender differences in the effectiveness of the programme?

The only measure on which girls are superior at entry and retain their superiority at outcome is Writing Vocabulary (Table 10). In terms of outcome, there are no gender differences in the likelihood of being successfully discontinued. Thus, whatever factors in the classroom and the world outside conspire to produce a disproportionate number of low-achieving boys, once they are in Reading Recovery they are as successful as girls. Table 11 shows this; the children with incomplete programmes have been excluded.

Table 10
Scores of Boys and Girls on the Observation Survey for the Whole Sample

	Book Level	Concepts About Print	Hearing Sounds	Letter Identification	Word Test	Writing Vocabulary
At Entry						
BOYS (n = 1850)						
mean	1.2	9.6	8.1	27.0	1.6	4.6
SD	1.7	3.7	7.9	15.7	2.2	4.8 *
GIRLS (n = 1127)						
mean	1.2	9.5	8.8	27.6	1.7	5.4
SD	1.6	3.6	8.4	15.7	2.2	5.8
At Exit						
BOYS (n = 1157)						
mean	13.5	18.1	30.2	48.9	10.7	35.9
SD	4.5	3.4	7.3	7.3	3.6	15.4 *
GIRLS (n = 750)						
mean	13.6	18.2	30.8	49.2	10.9	38.8
SD	4.6	3.6	7.1	7.3	3.8	16.5

(*indicates a statistically significant difference between boys' and girls' scores)

Table 11
Outcomes of Boys and Girls

	boys		girls	
	n	%	n	%
successfully discontinued	893	65	583	67
referred	388	28	231	27
left school	103	7	53	6
total	1384		867	

The Effect of Bilingualism on Progress in Reading Recovery

Although only 20 percent of the children receiving the programme are bilingual, we need to know whether they benefit from it to the same extent as children who only speak English.

Table 12
Outcomes of Monolingual and Bilingual Children

	successfully discontinued		referred		left school		total
	n	%	n	%	n	%	
monolingual	1172	66	480	27	113	6	1765
bilingual	294	63	134	29	39	8	467
total	1466	65	614	28	152	7	2232

This shows that there is no evidence that bilingual children's outcomes differ from those of the children who only speak English.

Table 13
Scores on the Observation Survey for Monolingual and Bilingual Children

	Book Level	Concepts About Print	Hearing Sounds in Words	Letter Identification	Word Test	Writing Vocabulary
At Entry						
MONOLINGUAL CHILDREN						
mean	1.2	9.8	8.7	27.9	1.7	5.1
SD	1.7	3.6	8.1	15.2	2.2	5.3
BILINGUAL CHILDREN						
	*	*	*	*	*	*
mean	0.9	8.4	7.1	24.5	1.4	4.1
SD	1.5	3.9	7.7	17.1	2.1	4.8
At Exit						
MONOLINGUAL CHILDREN						
mean	13.6	18.2	30.4	49.0	10.7	36.9
SD	4.4	3.4	7.3	7.1	3.6	15.4
BILINGUAL CHILDREN						
mean	13.4	17.9	30.7	49.0	11.1	37.3
SD	4.9	3.9	7.0	8.0	3.8	17.5

(* indicates a statistically significant difference between the two language groups)

It is clear from this that on entry to the programme bilingual children are scoring lower on all the subtests of the Observation Profile, but by the end of the programme there are no differences between them. Multiple regressions carried out on the Observation Survey outcomes shows that the only one for which language exerts a significant effect is the Word Test ($p > = .05$).

Table 14
Outcomes for Bilingual and Monolingual Children in Years 1 and 2: The Effect of Year Group and Bilingualism

		successfully discontinued		referred		left school	
		n	%	n	%	n	%
Year 1	monolingual	548	65	233	28	57	7
	bilingual	99	55	61	34	20	11
Year 2	monolingual	624	67	247	27	56	6
	bilingual	195	68	73	25	19	7

This suggests that bilingual children in Year 1 are less likely to have a successful programme outcome than those in Year 2. By Year 2, bilingual children are as successful as monolingual children. What may account for this?

The Effect of Fluency

The term *bilingual* covers children whose fluency in English differs widely. We asked the Reading Recovery teachers to rate the bilingual children's fluency in English on a four-point scale (fairly widely adopted in the UK) which rates a newcomer to English as 1 and someone with near-perfect fluency as 4. While such a rating is admittedly crude, it may enable us to see whether a certain level of English is necessary in order to benefit from the programme. However, the stages of fluency appear to be evenly distributed across both Year groups.

Table 15
Teachers' Ratings of Fluency for Bilingual Children in Years 1 and 2

	Year 1		Year 2	
	n	%	n	%
stage 1 beginner	41	25	63	24
stage 2	86	52	140	53
stage 3	32	18	48	18
stage 4, fluent	6	5	12	5
total	165		263	

Teachers rate about a quarter of the bilingual children in both years as beginners and half the bilingual children, in both Year 1 and Year 2, at Stage 2 (gaining familiarity). We have unfortunately no other independent measure of the fluency of these children; however it may be that our teachers were not using the fluency ratings accurately and that, rather than using it as a criterion-referenced rating scale according to the descriptions given, they were norm-referencing and tended to have higher expectations of bilingual children in Year 2. The similar distributions across the fluency bands are thus an artifact of teachers' expectations.

The relationship between level of fluency and outcome is affected by Year group. A child who is new to English in Year 1 has a 50 percent chance of being successfully discontinued, while a similar child in Year 2 has a 60 percent chance. The likelihood of being successfully discontinued is greater for Year 2 children at each stage of fluency.

Table 16
Relationship Between Level of Fluency in English and Outcome for Year 1 and Year 2 Children

	Year 1				Year 2			
	successfully discontinued		referred		successfully discontinued		referred	
	n	%	n	%	n	%	n	%
beginner, 1	17	50	17	50	34	59	24	41
stage 2	47	60	31	40	96	74	34	26
stage 3	24	80	6	20	40	83	8	17
fluent, 4	5	83	1	17	12	100	0	0
total	93		55		182		66	

The Contributions of Grade, Gender, Bilingualism, and Entry Scores to Outcome Measures

Multiple regressions were carried out on all the Observation Survey measures to explore the relative contributions of these factors to outcome. Initial test level is significantly related to outcome level on all the Observation Survey measures, as is year in school. Gender is only related to writing vocabulary and bilingualism to performance on the Word Test. Age at entry to the programme is negatively related to Concepts About Print, Hearing and Recording the Sounds in Words, Letter Identification, and Writing Vocabulary.

How Well is the Programme Working in England?

The data presented so far show that in many respects the programme works in England as it has elsewhere: it takes in low-achieving children and raises their levels of literacy achievement. If the criterion of success is taken to be the proportion of children who are classified as *successfully discontinued* on leaving the programme, then we may feel reassured. Of more concern is the large proportion who do not achieve a successful outcome. If we consider only the children for whom programme outcomes are available, the proportions for each outcome are shown in Table 17.

Given that nearly 70 percent of our teachers are in training and that they provided the data on 65 percent of our children, the fact that two-thirds of the children are successfully discontinued is explicable. However, our referral rates still seem higher than those reported elsewhere. This may be associated with our inexperienced group of teachers and tutors and provided that we can increase the proportion of the teaching work force who are more experienced, we should see the programme become more successful year by year.

Table 17
Outcomes for Children with Completed Programmes

successfully discontinued	1476	70 percent
referred	619	30 percent
total	2095	

How long does the programme take?

Reading Recovery teachers are a highly trained resource and the programme strives to ensure that they enable children to progress as quickly as possible to reach the average level of their classmates. From the point of view of cost-effectiveness and efficiency, a prime concern must be the length of the programme.

Table 18
Mean Number of Weeks for Each Year Group (+ Standard Deviation)

	successfully discontinued			referred			left school			incomplete programme		
	n	mean	(SD)	n	mean	(SD)	n	mean	(SD)	n	mean	(SD)
Year 1	652	23	(7)	298	26	(7)	79	10	(8)	822	9	(5)
Year 2	824	24	(7)	321	27	(6)	76	15	(8)	58	13	(7)

This makes it clear that we are not achieving a maximum of 20 weeks in the programme. We are taking on average three or four weeks longer than that. But most of these children are being taught by teachers in training who, as we have seen, take longer to complete a child's programme. However, another interesting aspect is that children who are eventually referred receive on average three weeks more time in the programme than their successful counterparts. Is this caution on the part of fairly inexperienced teachers to reach a decision or does it represent the reluctance of teachers to withdraw the programme's support; or may it be that it is harder for teachers to work effectively with children who are especially slow to accelerate? Table 18 also shows the pressure on teachers to complete the programme for children in Year 2, who will be less likely to be able to receive the programme in the following year. This is reflected in the very few unfinished programmes for this year group, which may also affect the teachers' desire to hang on until the child can be successfully discontinued (or not).

A school year in England lasts 190 days, or 38 weeks. Thus, given the time taken to select children, we shall be unlikely to get two cohorts through in a year unless we can reduce the length of the programme to 17 weeks. At present we are clearly some way from achieving this. This must be a cause for concern for those striving to achieve effective implementation.

Interruptions to Teaching

Earlier indications from the New Zealand team who provided the training in 1991-93 had been that teachers were often unable to teach their children regularly every day. We therefore collected information on teacher absence for illness and other reasons.

Table 19
Average Number of Lessons Lost, By Child Outcome

Reason for teacher missing lesson:			
Child:	teacher off sick	teacher absent for other reason	total
successfully discontinued	4	8	12
referred	5	10	15
left school	3	4	7
incomplete programme	1	4	5

Thus, teacher absence may prolong the programme by two to three weeks. But while teachers' absence through ill-health is unavoidable, teachers missing Reading Recovery lessons because they have been asked to carry out other duties (covering classes for absent colleagues, attending courses, and assisting with National Testing) is a factor which doubles their absence rate and which must be tackled by the school. It is intriguing that children who are eventually referred miss twice as many lessons because the teacher is absent for reasons other than ill-health. It may well be that children whose programmes are intermittently interrupted are less likely to have a successful outcome than those with fewer interruptions. The children, too, missed lessons.

Table 20
Average Number of Lessons Missed by Children

Child missed lesson because:			
Child	off sick	absent for other reason	total
successfully discontinued	9	3	12
referred	15	3	18
left school	10	2	12
incomplete programme	4	1	5

Of interest here is that children's absence through ill-health adds two weeks to a programme and children who do not achieve success in the programme tend to have more absence. It is easy to speculate on the relation between absence through ill-health and poor progress in school. Other reasons which cause children to miss lessons are such things as sports day, swimming galas, trips, and visits.

Issues for Implementation

Whenever Reading Recovery is transplanted from its native soil in New Zealand to other terrains, some adjustments are necessary to align the programme with the educational system of the new country while not jeopardising those features which ensure its success.

Age of Entry

We have already made one adaptation to the programme by accepting children on to the programme at 5:9. This has introduced a group with lower literacy levels at entry and also at outcome. It may be that since these children will have longer to make use of the mainstream programme before national testing at seven this will be beneficial in the longer term. Schools are now able to offer an early intervention programme to those falling behind in Year 1. We shall have to wait until the follow-up next year to see whether there is any difference between Year 1 and Year 2 children in their ability to maintain the progress they have made on the programme.

Bilingualism

We need to be aware that younger and less fluent bilingual children, in effect, those who are struggling at the early stages of learning English, have difficulties with the programme. We shall be addressing the problem of how to find ways to match the early texts we offer them to their style and level of English. At present it may be premature to use lack of fluency with English as a reason for excluding young bilingual learners from the programme.

Withdrawal

For the past ten years there has been a movement towards mainstreaming children with learning difficulties which has produced an ideological resistance to any programme which involves an element of withdrawal from the classroom. We have encountered resistance to this aspect of Reading Recovery.

The New Zealand team who trained our tutors and teachers from 1991-93 commented that while they found English teachers to be very sensitive and caring to the children they taught, they felt that they had very low expectations about what could be achieved especially by children from disadvantaged backgrounds. A possible disadvantage of the widespread ideology of child-centredness is that teachers become reluctant to demand high academic achievements from pupils who appear to be struggling.

Classroom Literacy Programmes

There is great diversity in the approaches to literacy used by class teachers in England and a general eclecticism which makes their practices hard to categorise. We know that the relation between the Reading Recovery programme and the mainstream curriculum is important, but we have not so far been able to explore this further. The GEST funded projects have been monitored by a member of the Schools Inspectorate who has been impressed by the benefits which the programme offers to the literacy practices of the whole school. The National Network will now be disseminating the principles of Reading Recovery more widely and seeking ways to incorporate them into the mainstream literacy programme. The implications for initial teacher training must also be explored.

Expense

Education authorities are always concerned to know how much the programme will cost and we have found it helpful to be realistic in our costings which show how the initial outlay, in terms of setting up the training site and training a tutor (teacher leader), are offset over a number of years to produce a less expensive programme over time. The largest element in cost is the salary of the teacher but we have been able to show that the cost per child is halved over a five year period as the initial outlay is offset and more children receive the benefit. The costs of the programme must of course be offset against the cost of special educational provision for children whose persistent literacy problems require further long-term specialist help. There are also incalculable benefits for the school as a whole.

National Coordination

As a relatively inexperienced group, we have found it essential to establish networks of communication and to have a national coordination team to ensure uniformity and quality control of all aspects of the programme. So many problems were new to us that it was crucial that decisions were reached after full consultation and were applied nationwide. Our current concern is how to maintain some national coordination after the end of 1995.

Funding

The biggest single problem will be how to continue to implement the programme when the special funding provided by the government ceases in April, 1995. Twenty projects have submitted bids to a new government funding body and in January, 1995, it was announced that 12 of them had been successful in securing funds for a further five to seven year period. That leaves a number of tutors understandably anxious about their futures and makes expansion of the implementation hard to anticipate. Thus, just as it begins to operate on a scale large enough to show results, the whole project is threatened with strangulation by financial restriction.

Conclusion

This is both the first and the last report of the *English* national monitoring of Reading Recovery as next year's cohort will include groups from Wales and Northern Ireland.

References

OFSTED. (1993). *Reading Recovery in New Zealand*. London: HMSO.

Pluck, M. L. (1989). Reading Recovery in a British Infant School. *Educational Psychology, 39*(4), 347–358.

Wright, A. (1992). Evaluation of the First British Reading Recovery Programme. *British Educational Research Journal, 18*(4), 351–367.

EARLY WRITING:
TEACHERS AND CHILDREN IN READING RECOVERY

DIANE E. DeFORD
The Ohio State University

When a child first attempts to communicate and to act upon his or her world, the child embarks upon a lifelong journey upon a literacy highway. Is there a destination at the end of the journey? Probably not. For the child is merely learning to communicate, learning about culture, and how to use the adult, or others, to help make sense of the world (Clay, 1991, p. 26). The centrality of language, culture, and meaning to this ongoing endeavor is illustrated best by Halliday (1975) when he stated that language learning involves the construction of social systems, or an interpretative model of the environment and reality. This occurs as the learner learns language, learns through language, and learns about language within complex communicative acts.

As Rogoff (1990) discussed children's cognitive development, she drew the analogy of an apprenticeship. She characterized this apprenticeship as occurring through guided participation in social activities with companions who support and stretch the learner's understanding of and skill in using the tools of culture. Speech, action, and symbols (reading, writing, and mathematics) are tools for learning in our literate world. The most significant moment in the course of intellectual development was described by Vygotsky (1978) as occurring "when speech and practical activity, two previously completely independent lines of development, converge" (p. 24).

Vygotsky (1978) discussed children's speech and action as helping to attain goals. "Children not only speak about what they are doing; their speech and action are part of one and the same complex psychological function, directed toward the solution of the problem at hand" (p. 25). He found that the more complex the task, the more important talk was. "Sometimes speech becomes of such vital importance that, if not permitted to use it, young children cannot accomplish the given task" (p. 26). These two observations led him to conclude that "children solve practical tasks with the help of their speech, as well as their eyes and hands" (p. 26). He posed a unified theory of learning that involves perception, speech, and action that is unique to human behavior.

In this constructive view of the child as literacy learner, the development of literacy and language are intertwined with purposeful action and problem-solving. As a young child learns to read and write, the first goal is learning itself; to communicate as other adults do through written language. "When language splits from an exclusively verbal stream to form a written branch as well, certain profound changes occur in the relationship between speaking and thinking" (Tharp & Gallimore, 1988, p. 104).

The majority of children make the transition from verbal interactions into written interactions within the context provided by formal schooling. Schooling, as suggested by Vygotsky's theory (in Tharp & Gallimore, 1988) "frees the symbol systems of reading, writing, mathematics and science for use as tools, thus allowing forms of thinking different from those of everyday life" (p. 108). Schooled language requires that the child manipulate language and the products of written language in *decontextualized* ways, emphasizing sign-sign relationships over sign-object relationships (Wertsch, 1985). This shift in the child's attention is what sets schooling apart from literacy or language-learning events in the home and community. As Tharp and Gallimore (1988) argued, "the instructional task of the school is to facilitate that developmental process by teaching the schooled language of reading and writing, and facilitating the constant conjunction of these systems with those of every day concepts" (p. 108). The practical activity of the first few years of school for the young child is understanding the symbolic acts of reading and writing, their purposes, interrelationships, and uses in the contexts of school and the world at large.

The purpose of this article is to explore the evolution of writing and its relationship to reading and teaching with first grade children who have been identified as being within the lowest twenty percent of their class at the beginning of the school year. Specifically, through a detailed analysis of videotaped lessons, teacher records, and student writing samples, writing progress and teacher decisions will be described within an instructional program offered to these children in Reading Recovery. The children and teachers were part of a larger study (Lyons, Pinnell, & DeFord, 1993) of early literacy interventions. The children were selected as those making the highest and lowest progress in Reading Recovery. It is hoped that the examination of children just learning about written language will offer insights into two areas: (a) the conjunction of reading and writing, or the reciprocal nature of writing and reading; and (b) the nature of effective teacher decisions that support children's literacy learning in Reading Recovery.

The Research Context on Initial Reading and Writing

In a review of research into reading and writing connections (Irwin & Doyle, 1992), the first research was documented as early as 1929 with most of the research conducted on the relationships between reading and writing occurring between 1970 and the present. While some of the research is interdisciplinary (psychology, linguistics, rhetoric, or foreign language), the majority of studies were published in the field of education. Within the body of research on reading/writing connections, some key insights about the nature of reading and writing and shared knowledge structures within the two processes are evident.

Both reading and writing involve subroutines, or subprocesses (Irwin & Doyle, 1992), as well as networks of related information (Clay, 1991). Knowledge of the subroutines, such as letter formation, directionality, planning, and phonological relationships, and the overarching ability of putting the subroutines into fluent action in reading and writing are influenced by attention and memory (LaBerge & Samuels, 1974), task demands, and processing demands (Bruner, 1974). Readers and writers operate on many levels simultaneously, on information that is organized on serial order principles (print), and those that are organized on hierarchical levels (discourse, sentences, words). Learning how to attend to and act upon serial order information while maintaining simultaneous hierarchical processing can create difficulties for the emergent reader and writer (Clay, 1991).

Bruner (1974), in describing how an infant orchestrates separate activities into controlled, sequenced movement, outlined six stages that involve feedback, intention, repetition, and modification in the development of subroutines and skilled performance. In terms of reading and writing, the intention to use the process in a meaningful way, purposes, monitoring the processes in action, searching for useful information, rehearsal strategies, and self-correction have all been discussed as important to the outcomes of both reading and writing (Butler & Turbill, 1984; Clay, 1991; Dyson, 1989; Goodman & Goodman, 1979; Harste, Woodward, & Burke, 1984).

The proficient reader uses knowledge about the topic at hand, the linguistic system, and the symbol system, and uses these cues to establish expectations and to monitor the reading process and comprehend messages. The proficient writer brings the same knowledge base to writing, and utilizes these sources of information for specific purposes to form meaningful messages for others and self. In characterizing the strategies used by good readers and writers during the process, common terms such as searching, predicting, rereading, redrafting, and revising, monitoring, and rethinking are used (Butler & Turbill, 1984; Clay, 1991; Goodman & Goodman, 1979).

One consistent finding is that better writers tend to be better readers and that better readers tend to produce more syntactically complex writing than poorer readers (Stotsky, 1983). The texts that make up the reader's and writer's worlds, whether from the classroom or experiences in other settings, also have an influence on their writing, in both form and content (DeFord, 1986; Eckhoff, 1983; Spivey & King, 1989).

One area that has received a great deal of attention across reading and writing research is the child's development of phonological awareness (Goswami & Bryant, 1990; Perfetti, Beck, Bell, & Hughes, 1987; Read, 1986; Rohl & Tunmer, 1988). The phonological skill that children bring to both reading and writing is the ability to divide a word into its onset and its rime, and also to categorize words which have the same onset or the same rime. With very little instruction, children quickly learn to associate onsets and rimes with strings of letters, making inferences about new words on these bases (Goswami & Bryant, 1990). In fact, Read (1986) found that young children invented spellings which revealed that they were attending to phonological features that adults no longer distinguish. He further suggested that adults may be influenced by their greater knowledge of spelling conventions, and therefore may not notice some features the young child is still exploring. In the examples of children's invented spellings of *chrac* for the word truck or *aschray* for ashtray, the adult knows that while they articulate a sound similar to *ch* at the beginning of the word *truck*, their knowledge of the spelling convention of *tr* overrides their attention to the sounds they are actually making. Children, however, are more dependent on the sounds they articulate because they have not begun to develop a system of grapheme to phoneme matches. There is little evidence, however, children use grapheme-phoneme information when they begin to read (Goswami & Bryant, 1990). Rather, the research would suggest that children begin to adopt a phonemic code through writing, and eventually apply this knowledge to their reading. So, the research would suggest that there is an initial discrepancy or separation between children's reading and writing in terms of phonological development (Goswami & Bryant, 1990). This would explain why young children can read some words which they cannot write and also write some words they cannot read.

In studies of children who are just learning about writing, Scardamalia and Bereiter (1982) found that so little of their writing process is automatic and they have difficulty maintaining idea generation with other aspects of the process such as executive routines and print conventions, that they may not be able to engage in sustained, independent writing events. In one study of 6- to 8-year-olds from low income families, McLane (1990) found that children in an after school program were unable to sustain writing when teachers who were knowledgeable about the writing process were not present. However, in guided settings, such as the instructional context of Reading Recovery, observations of what the child writes "is a rough indicator of what he is attending to in print, and demonstrates the programmes of action he is using for word production" (Clay, 1991, p. 109).

The transition into the world of written language offers some unique opportunities for analysis of the reading/writing connection, as well as some particular difficulties. Writing slows down the child's processing so that the observer can more easily describe actions and possible links made during reading and writing. The texts the reader is engaged with are relatively simple. Consequently, it is a point in time when it may be easier to describe what the child is attending to and how thoughts, actions, and new learning become integrated. However, as Clay indicated (1991):

. . . at this time, it is well to remember that writing is only a rough guide to what the child's visual analysis skills are because he may well be able to see what his hand is not able to execute. On the other hand, in reading what he says is often a very misleading guide to what his eye is really perceiving. What he says is, at this time, more likely to be driven by his language experiences, what he has heard and what he typically produces. (p. 109)

In order to carefully describe young children's emergence into the use of written language, Clay (1991, 1993a) recommended a longitudinal research strategy based on individual progress across standard tasks to limit the possibility of error or being misled by our observations. This is in keeping with recommendations of Irwin and Doyle (1992) who suggested, "It is important to consider the way individuals interact with the environment in which their abilities develop" (p. 9). Toward this end, this article examines the progress of twelve young literacy learners within daily writing lessons in Reading Recovery across their instructional program.

The Research Context on Teaching in Initial Literacy

The constructivist perspective reflected in the descriptions of children's literacy learning requires a concomitant view of teaching: as knowledge is constructed through social interaction, teaching is the active assistance and guidance of learning processes within socially dynamic activity settings. A metaphor commonly used to describe teaching within this framework is one of a scaffold (Wood, Bruner, & Ross, 1976). This temporary, adjustable scaffold as a metaphor suggests that the teacher enters into joint participation in activity settings to allow the child the greatest level of independent action. Cazden (1988) described the interaction as "a very special kind of scaffold that self-destructs gradually as the need lessens and the child's competence grows" (p. 104). The teacher structures the instructional setting so that the learner grows into increasingly more complex actions.

A key point related to the nature of the activity setting is that the tasks established for learning within this instructional context are not simplified; the difficulty of the task is held constant while the role of the child is varied (Greenfield, 1984). While the dominant use of the term scaffolding "suggests that the principle variations in adult actions are matters of quantity, how high the scaffold stands, how many levels it supports, how long it is kept in place" (Tharp & Gallimore, 1988, p. 34), many adult actions are also qualitatively different. "Sometimes, the adult directs attention. At other times, the adult holds important information in memory. At still other times, the adult offers simple encouragement" (Griffin & Cole, 1984, p. 47).

This form of teaching has also been termed an instructional conversation. Behind this term is a belief that through the conscious use of dialogue by the teacher, students will internalize the dialogue and gradually assume control of the processes involved within the activity setting (Irwin & Doyle, 1992). This is a perspective strongly influenced by Vygotsky (1978) wherein the learner progresses from interpersonal functioning (guided through social interactions) into an intrapersonal functioning (guided by self) through a series of transformations. Speech forms the link within these interactions, so that the conversations, the guiding comments, the questions, the demonstrations, and actions that were all part of the interpersonal interactions become internalized into the self-regulating speech within the learner. The learner, as Wertsch (1979) indicated:

> . . . has taken over the rules and responsibilities of both participants in the language game. These responsibilities were formerly divided between the adult and child, but they have now been taken over completely by the child. The definitions of situation and the patterns of activity which formerly allowed the child to participate in the problem-solving effort on the interpsychological plane now allow him/her to carry out the task on the intrapsychological plane. (p. 18)

This social-constructivist perspective emphasizes both the child's personal construction of literacy and the activeness of adults within the joint activity in contributing to that learning (Cochran-Smith, 1984; Heath, 1983; Wells, 1986; Pinnell, 1989). Clay and Cazden (1990) stated that "as children engage in reading and writing, they are working with theories of the world and theories about written language, testing them and changing them" (p. 207). Within the context of reading and writing instruction the teacher observes, assesses the nature of the child's current level of operation, offers encouragement, asks questions, and provides necessary guidance. The scaffold that assists the learner in this setting changes continually in terms of support, but always at the cutting edge of the child's competencies (Clay & Cazden, 1990). The cutting edge as defined by Clay and Cazden is compared to Vygotsky's (1978) term, the zone of proximal development, the difference between the child's ability to solve problems independently and with adult guidance or in collaboration with more capable peers.

As noted by Clay and Cazden (1990), the term scaffold was never used by Vygotsky, but it has come to be used to describe the interactional support, often in the form of adult-child dialogue, that maximizes the growth of the individual child's independent functioning. "For one child, the Reading Recovery program as a whole is such a scaffold" (Clay & Cazden, 1990, p. 219). The definition of instruction that emerges from this brief review suggests that teaching involves "adult guidance that takes into account the nature of what a child knows, the problem-solving processes used, and an understanding of what needs to be learned in order to strive for the potentials available to the child" (Lyons, Pinnell, & DeFord, 1993, p. 132). Research conducted by Lyons (1993) suggested that teachers involved in the yearlong instructional program in Reading Recovery articulated six key understandings about teaching they had learned as a result of their interactions with children. They learned how to:

1. Become astute observers of student behaviors,
2. Follow the student,
3. Assist students' performance through clear demonstrations and use of explicit language,
4. Question effectively or prompt students based on available information,
5. Observe behaviors to make informed decisions, and
6. Examine the student's way of making sense (Lyons, Pinnell, & DeFord, 1993, pp. 149-162).

In the one-to-one tutorials in Reading Recovery, the teacher guides the child though reading and writing activities that include the reading of familiar materials, a running record of yesterday's new book, writing, and a new book introduction and first reading. Across these lesson components, the teacher prompts, questions, offers information when necessary, and provides demonstrations based upon the observations made of the student's actions and responses. The writing portion is placed within this lesson to facilitate the child's attention to print in a different way from that which must occur in reading. Yet, many of the operations needed in reading are practiced in another form in writing. Writing is a resource for reading and vice versa (Clay, 1985):

> Children's written texts are a good source of information about a child's visual discrimination of print for as the child learns to print words, hand and eye support and supplement each other to organize the first visual discriminations. When writing a message, the child must be able to analyze the word he hears or says and to find some way to record the sounds he hears as letters. (p. 35)

The writing component is surrounded by reading so that the child has the greatest opportunity to create important conceptual links between reading and writing (Lyons, Pinnell, & DeFord, 1993). The teacher and the child work together to generate a topic, then construct the message together with the teacher writing only what the child is unable to write to facilitate pacing of the ten-minute segment (an approximate time). The teacher observes how the child operates, making notes on the lesson record about the child's contributions, important signs in the child's development, and approximations made. This lesson record also includes instructional techniques utilized such as words taken to fluency, new instances of known written vocabulary that might emerge, known words that might be used to help the child problem-solve on new words, and what words were used for Elkonin (1973) boxes, a technique adapted in Reading Recovery to facilitate hearing sounds in words (Clay, 1985). The research study described focused on the interactions that occurred during this component of the Reading Recovery lesson.

The Research Study

The current study involved a subset of teachers who participated in a statewide study of early literacy initiatives in Ohio (Lyons, Pinnell, & DeFord, 1993; Pinnell, Lyons, DeFord, Bryk, & Seltzer, 1994). The original sample of randomly assigned children consisted of 238 male and 165 female students taught by 40 teachers. A series of outcome measures were administered pre and posttreatment. These assessment instruments were also administered to an in-school control group. Each treatment was then compared to its control group, providing a comparison of how each treatment compared with the school's traditional compensatory program. Out of this pool, teachers ($n = 4$) whose children consistently achieved higher and lower outcomes in Reading Recovery were selected for further study. Out of a possible 16 students (four for each teacher), complete instructional records were obtained for 12 students. Pre and posttest Observation Survey (Clay, 1993b) scores can be found in Tables 1 and 2 for the Letter Identification, Word Identification, Concepts about Print (CAP), Writing Vocabulary, Dictation, and Text Reading tasks for each of the students available for study of writing development and teacher decision-making. These data are presented with stanine comparisons, including where the score falls in relation to a normal curve distribution of nine equal intervals.

While all but five of the children scored within stanines one and two on the Observation Survey at the beginning of their instructional program, there was a trend in text reading scores for the lower outcome students to score up to the third stanine. Three students in both groups achieved in the third or fourth stanine on the Concepts about Print task, indicating stronger book handling abilities at the beginning of first grade. Otherwise, the students were fairly well matched at entry to the program.

Table 1
Entry and Exit Scores with Stanine Data for Higher Outcome Students

Teacher	Student	Letter Identification/ Stanine		Word Test/ Stanine		CAP/ Stanine		Writing Vocabulary/ Stanine		Dictation/ Stanine		Text Reading/ Stanine	
						Observation Survey							
						Entry Scores							
1	1	46	1	2	1	12	2	5	1	7	1	A	1
	2	48	2	1	1	15	4	4	1	7	1	1	1
	3	49	2	0	1	6	1	4	1	12	1	A	1
	4	47	2	0	1	10	1	2	1	1	1	A	1
2	5	47	2	0	1	15	4	6	1	11	1	A	1
						Exit Scores							
1	1	53	6	20	9	22	9	40	8	35	8	18	8
	2	53	6	20	9	23	9	54	9	37	9	30	9
	3	53	6	20	9	20	8	54	9	33	7	18	8
	4	54	8	19	9	21	9	50	9	34	7	16	8
2	5	54	8	20	9	23	9	63	9	37	9	22	9

Table 2
Entry and Exit Scores and Stanine Data for Lower Outcome Students

Observation Survey

Teacher	Student	Letter Identification/	Stanine	Word Test/	Stanine	CAP/	Stanine	Writing Vocabulary/	Stanine	Dictation/	Stanine	Text Reading/	Stanine
Entry Scores													
3	6	22	1	0	1	6	1	3	1	3	1	A	1
	7	47	2	0	1	11	2	4	1	11	1	2	2
	8	8	1	0	1	11	2	1	1	2	1	A	1
4	9	49	2	3	1	6	1	1	1	6	1	A	1
	10	47	2	2	1	12	2	8	2	12	1	2	2
	11	48	2	5	2	10	1	4	1	18	2	3	3
	12	43	1	3	1	13	3	2	1	10	1	3	3
Exit Scores													
3	6	50	3	2	1	15	4	20	5	20	3	A	1
	7	52	5	7	3	16	5	24	5	27	5	4	4
	8	20	1	1	1	15	4	7	1	9	1	2	2
4	9	53	6	12	6	18	6	21	5	29	5	6	5
	10	48	2	15	7	19	7	24	5	31	6	6	5
	11	54	8	20	9	20	8	29	6	36	9	20	9
	12	50	3	11	5	19	7	22	5	33	7	6	5

At the end of the program, the higher outcome students scored in the eighth and ninth stanines, except for three students who scored in the sixth stanine and two students who scored in the seventh stanine (see Table 1). These scores were well above average across the tasks of the Observation Survey. There was one student in the lower outcome group who matched these scores (see Table 2). The other six students in this group scored between the first through the sixth stanines, while two students scored in the seventh stanine on selected tasks. The most marked areas of concern for these students was in the area of text reading. The majority of lower outcome students scored at or below the fifth stanine at the end of their program as compared to the eighth and ninth stanines for the higher outcome students.

Research Questions

The major goal of the instructional program in Reading Recovery is to aid the child in constructing a self-extending system, a network of strategies for operating on or with text (Clay, 1991). Some of what a child must weave into this network of strategies is included in the following:

(a) The aspects of print to which they must attend,

(b) The aspects of oral language that can be related to print,

(c) The kinds of strategies that maintain fluent reading and writing,

(d) The kinds of strategies that explore detail,

(e) The kinds of strategies that increase understanding,

(f) The kinds of strategies that detect and correct errors,

(g) The feedback control mechanisms that keep their reading and writing productions on track,

(h) The feed-forward mechanisms (like anticipation or prediction) that keep their information processing behaviors efficient, and

(i) Most important, how to go beyond the limits of the system and how to learn from relating new information to what is already known. (p. 326)

In order to explore the nature of children's development of networks of information in writing and teacher decisions that interacted with children's learning during the writing portion of Reading Recovery lessons to support the child's construction of a self-extending system, three questions were posed:

1. What is the nature of shared responsibility in writing as indicated by the child's independent writing, jointly constructed text, and text written by the teacher for higher and lower progress children at three points in time?

2. After the sentence is generated, what teacher decisions are made about words taken to fluency, use of Elkonin boxes, generating or copying for higher and lower progress children at three points in time?

3. What is the relationship between the texts read and student's independent writing early in the child's program?

It was argued that by detailing the progress of higher and lower outcome students within their Reading Recovery program, it would be possible to see what aspects of the network of information might have been constructed in the higher outcome children and those that might be missing from the written responses of the lower outcome children. It was further argued that from an analysis of written products, lesson records, testing data, and the early books and written texts that were a part of the child's instructional program, the early conjunction of reading and writing could be explored. This analysis is limited, however, to the corpus of decisions made by these particular teachers working with these particular students. There may be other decisions that could be equally effective that cannot be described due to the repertoire of actions and decisions observed in the teachers.

Procedures

Outcome data from a quasi-experimental research design were used to select students ($n = 12$) and teachers ($n = 4$) for this descriptive study: two teachers and their students who achieved higher outcomes in Reading Recovery and two teachers and their students who achieved lower outcomes. All students taught by each teacher were used as a means of exploring and controlling for the impact of the teacher's decisions on student progress. The analysis utilized videotapes of actual lessons, student writing books, Observation Survey (Clay, 1993b) tasks for pre and posttest measures, teacher records of student progress, and lesson records.

To assess shared responsibility, the writing books (see Figure 1) and lesson records were divided into three sections to represent the beginning of the child's program, the middle of the child's program, and the end of the child's program to determine differences in patterns of interaction that might occur at different times within the instructional program. The relationship that existed between independent, joint construction, and teacher-produced text within each writing segment was compared. Students were randomly selected from each teacher to do qualitative analyses within the larger study (Pinnell, Lyons, DeFord, Bryk, & Seltzer, 1994).

Figure 1. Sample Pages in Writing Book.

Time samples of the writing segments were analyzed at two points in time on the video records, the beginning of program (October), and the end of program (February).

Teachers' notes on their lesson records and an analysis of the students' writing on the top and bottom of the writing book (see Figure 1) provided a means of examining teacher decisions. The top page, referred to as the practice page, indicates the joint problem-solving or directions for student practice that resulted from the child's generated story. The bottom page contains the final results of the problem-solving engaged in by the teacher and child characterized by conventional spelling. Consequently, the practice page and observations noted in lesson records indicate the nature of decisions made about any one child at a particular point in time.

Finally, the books that each student read during the first ten lessons and the vocabulary content were itemized and compared to the corpus of words the students wrote during the construction of the story. The texts produced were divided into words that were written independently, or those that were jointly constructed, or those written by the teacher. In each of the previous analyses, patterns of student progress and teacher decisions were contrasted between higher and lower progress children as a means of highlighting the effectiveness of teachers' decisions in guiding students' literacy learning.

Findings

Question 1. What is the nature of time use and shared responsibility in writing as indicated by the child's independent writing, jointly constructed text, and text written by the teacher for higher and lower progress children at three points in time in their Reading Recovery program?

An analysis of the amount of time allocated to the writing component across the first and last videotapes of randomly selected students within teacher groups instructing higher and lower outcome students indicated a variation in time across student outcomes (Table 3). Teachers of higher outcome students allocated more time to writing in general (*mean*, higher outcome = 9.8 minutes, range 7-12 minutes; *mean*, lower outcome = 6.6 minutes, range 3-12 minutes). A comparison of time at the beginning and end of the students' program indicated that teachers of higher outcome students also spent a greater portion of lesson time on writing early in a child's program (*mean*, time 1, 44 percent; time 2, 29 percent) than did teachers working with lower outcome students (*mean*, 28 percent, 31 percent respectively).

Table 3

Analysis of Time Spent on Writing During Videotaped Sessions

	Higher Outcome		Lower Outcome	
	Range	mean	Range	mean
Minutes Across Lessons	7-12	9.8	3-12	6.6
Time 1 — Percent on Writing		44.0 %		28.0 %
Time 2 — Percent on Writing		29.0 %		31.0 %

The results of the analysis of shared writing in written lessons of higher and lower outcome students can be found in Tables 4 and 5. There were marked patterns of interactions among higher and lower outcome students and teachers across the beginning, middle, and end of program designations. The percentages of independent writing by the children differed, with the higher outcome children participating more actively in writing complete words within lessons (*mean* = 56-66 percent, range 50-79 percent). Even during the beginning portion of students' programs, the higher outcome students wrote from 51-59 percent of the texts generated. This compared to 4-51 percent of the text contributed solely by the lower outcome students.

Table 4

Student Writing Book Analysis of Shared Responsibility in Writing for Higher Outcome Children

Teacher	Student	Responsibility	Time in Program			mean
			Beginning % Weeks 1-5	Middle % Weeks 6-10	End % Weeks 11-15	
1	1	Child	58	68	72	66
	2		55	71	71	65
	3		51	63	66	61
	4		54	50	62	56
2	5		59	76	79	71
	1	Joint	33	32	28	31
	2		32	26	21	27
	3		40	27	24	29
	4		38	31	24	31
	5		38	22	15	26
	1	Teacher	9	0	0	3
	2		13	3	9	8
	3		9	10	10	10
	4		8	19	14	14
	5		4	2	6	4

Texts were jointly produced by the higher outcome students and teachers approximately one-third of the time (*mean* = 26-31 percent, range 21-40 percent). This compared to a much higher percentage of words jointly constructed by the lower outcome students under the direction of their teachers (*mean* = 26-31 percent, range 23-56 percent).

The teachers elected to write words for the students to a lesser degree in the higher outcome group than they did for the lower outcome group. The teachers of higher outcome students wrote for them from 0-19 percent of the time, with teacher means of 3-14 percent of the time. The range of words written by teachers of lower outcome students was 8-71 percent, with teacher means of 9-49 percent across children.

The higher outcome students took progressively more responsibility for writing across their instructional program, writing a little more than half of the text by themselves during the early portion of lessons, increasing this participation to 62-79 percent of the time by the end of lessons.

Consequently, there was also a reduction in joint problem-solving as the students grew in competence. This indicated that students were also able to do more of the problem-solving on new words independently as well as gaining in the number of words they could write independently. The one teacher whose students made better progress yet achieved lower outcomes overall indicated some of these tendencies as well (Teacher 4). Patterns of shared responsibility suggested that all teachers and children acted independently and shared problem-solving to accomplish the task of writing in Reading Recovery lessons. However, children were led to greater independent action and problem-solving on new words when their teachers supported their efforts consistently across lessons. The teachers aided the students in forming messages that allowed students to operate as independently as possible. The teachers allocated sufficient time based upon students' needs at different times in their instructional programs, and supported their efforts at independent problem-solving. By these means, increases in independent action were obtained.

Table 5
Student Writing Book Analysis of Shared Responsibility in Writing for Lower Outcome Children

Teacher	Student	Responsibility	Time in Program			
			Beginning % Weeks 1-5	Middle % Weeks 6-10	End % Weeks 11-15	mean
3	6	Child	27	25	37	29
	7		25	28	37	29
	8		4	10	22	12
4	9		33	53	56	48
	10		59	76	79	71
	11		51	65	66	60
	12		41	56	52	50
3	6	Joint	23	54	56	45
	7		52	56	55	55
	8		25	51	37	38
4	9		26	32	38	32
	10		56	39	36	43
	11		38	23	25	29
	12		47	33	34	37
3	6	Teacher	51	22	7	26
	7		23	16	8	16
	8		71	39	41	49
4	9		33	14	12	20
	10		11	8	9	9
	11		11	12	9	11
	12		12	11	14	12

Question 2. After the sentence is generated, what teacher decisions are made about words taken to fluency, use of boxes, generating, or copying for higher and lower progress children at three points in time?

In order to address this question, entries written on the practice page were identified by purpose: fluency practice, hearing sounds in words (phonological analysis), and generating from known to problem-solving new words through analogy and copying. There were different patterns in teacher decisions between higher and lower outcome groups about words taken to fluency, use of the hearing sounds in word boxes, generating from known words to problem-solving new items, or copying across teachers of higher and lower outcome students (see Table 5). In general, there were great differences in the number of entries on the practice page, with the total number of entries varying from 103-268 for higher outcome students, and 25-151 entries for the lower outcome students. One of the teachers directed students to problem-solve or practice very little across lessons (25-47 total number of entries) and her students made the least progress

Table 6

Analysis of Practice Page Entries for Higher and Lower Outcome Children

Teacher	Student	L#	Total Entries	Beginning				Middle				End			
				F	B	G	C	F	B	G	C	F	B	G	C
1	1	62	171	18	15	2	13	23	34	8	0	23	26	9	0
	2	27	103	15	16	0	0	29	8	3	0	19	7	6	0
	3	62	197	41	37	2	0	32	19	9	0	31	17	9	0
	4	98	268	46	41	0	0	45	39	9	0	24	35	29	0
2	5	63	182	47	22	0	6	27	8	2	22	21	10	2	15
3	6	53	40	7	3	0	1	9	0	0	2	14	0	0	4
	7	59	47	13	2	0	5	12	0	0	6	9	0	0	0
	8	48	25	4	2	0	0	7	1	0	3	5	2	0	1
4	9	68	119	34	6	0	0	48	9	3	0	17	2	0	0
	10	64	151	43	6	1	0	51	11	5	0	28	1	5	0
	11	64	116	48	16	1	0	25	4	12	0	10	0	0	0
	12	62	149	51	8	0	0	39	10	6	0	31	1	3	0

F = Fluency
B = Boxes
G = Generating
C = Copying

of any of the four teachers. The second teacher whose students achieved lower outcomes tended to utilize the practice page more often (116-151 total entries) and her students tended to do better in the final testing (see Table 1).

Most of the teachers directed students to take high frequency words to written fluency on the practice page across lessons, even the teacher whose students tested the lowest overall at the end of the year. However, the use of boxes for hearing sounds in words, a tool used by the teacher for problem-solving new words and the selection of known vocabulary from which to help students problem-solve new words through analogy (generating) were used consistently by the teachers whose students achieved higher outcomes. These data suggest that fluent practice of known words, the child's analysis of hearing sounds in words, and using known words to problem-solve new words through analogy support the young child's ability to organize and act upon the world of print (Table 6).

The teachers called upon known vocabulary to help students problem-solve new words through analogy (generating) less during the beginning of their programs, but used it relatively consistently throughout the rest of the students' programs. The consistent use of boxes and generating new words from a known core were used to facilitate the higher outcome children's ability to problem-solve independently. Copying was used very little and only by two teachers. One teacher in the higher outcome group and one in the lower outcome group tended to write words for the child on the practice page for the student to copy.

The data suggest that fluent practice of known words, the child's analysis of hearing sounds in words, and using known words to problem-solve new words through analogy support the young child's ability to organize and act upon the world of print. The teacher's decisions about how to apply these tools to scaffold and extend children's writing and spelling development across their instructional program are related to growth and accelerative progress. Students made rapid progress when teachers guided their growth through practicing, fluent word writing, encouraging independent phonological analysis, generating new words from known exemplars, and flexible use of time. Copying appeared to offer very little power for students in supporting their developing concepts of print and phonological awareness.

Question 3. What is the relationship between the texts read and independent writing early in the child's program for higher and lower outcome students within the first ten lessons of their Reading Recovery instructional program?

In order to address this question, the story texts that were read by each of four children, two higher progress and two lower progress, were compared to the written stories they produced. This analysis produced a comparison of texts read, numbers of different vocabulary encountered across multiple readings of texts, and the writing that children did in lessons (see Table 7).

In terms of storybook reading during the first ten lessons, the children read a little more than five books in each lesson (*mean* = 5.42) with a range of four to seven texts read and an average of 18 different texts read across the four students. These texts were early level

Table 7
Nature of Vocabulary Explored in Reading and Writing Across the First Ten Lessons

	Higher Outcome		Lower Outcome	
Student	1	5	9	7
Number of texts read per lesson	6.7	4.7	5.4	4.9
Number of different texts read	9	18	17	18
Number of different words encountered	118	190	109	142
Total number of words across multiple readings	1572	1871	1264	1637
Written words from texts read	22	19	11	8
Written words not in text read	7	23	23	29
Number of different words written independently	11	12	6	3
Total of independently written words	37	20	12	12
Jointly constructed	14	26	11	20
Elkonin boxes	5	11	2	1
Written by teacher	4	6	0	15

instructional books ranging from text levels one through four. The higher progress children read 118 and 190 different vocabulary items across the ten lessons with multiple readings of texts bringing their total of vocabulary encountered through text reading to 1572 and 1871 respectively. The general indicators were similar for the lower progress students who encountered 109 and 142 different vocabulary items totaling 1264 and 1637 total vocabulary read across the ten lessons analyzed.

There were marked differences, however, in how the higher and lower outcome teachers integrated the texts students read into the writing students accomplished. The higher outcome students generated sentences that included vocabulary also in the texts they read to a greater degree, although they also wrote vocabulary that was different from that found in the storybooks they read. The higher outcome students wrote more independently than the lower outcome students. The joint problem-solving that occurred within the ten lessons was similar across

Table 8
Attention to Print in Initial Lessons of Higher Outcome Students

Student	Vocabulary	Print Setting in Reading		Print Setting in Writing		Teacher support
		Repeated readings	Number of different texts	Independent writing or joint constructions*		
#1	the	233	10	the	8	
	up	121	4	up	1	
	to	96	4	to	6	
	go	81	3	go	3	
	I	80	6	I	7	
	like	74	3	like	2	4
	my	46	3	my: m		1
	can	20	2	can	4	1
	is	14	1	is: s		1
	home	14	1	home: m		1
	at	12	1	at: t; at	1	1
	tree	8	2	tree: t; te		3
	mom	7	3	mom	2	
	cat	6	2	cat	1	
	pool	6	1	pool: p		1
	zoo	6	1	zoo	1	
	climbing	4	1	climb: m		2
	ride	3	2	ride: rd		1
	swimming	3	1	swim: sm		1
	bear	2	1	(bear)		1
	car	2	1	car: r		1
	house	2	1	house: h		1
				work: wk		1
				with: w		2
				eat: et		2
				in	1	
				(salad)		1
				(chocolate)		1
				(cake)		1
#5	the	160	11	the	2	
	a	91	4	a	5	
	I	68	7	I	1	
	to	56	2	to	1	
	said	34	2	said	1	
	and	25	5	and	1	
	little	16	3	little: lt		1
	big	15	2	big: bg; big		2
	wolf	14	1	(wolf)		1
	fish	14	2	(fish)		1
	cat	12	3	cat: ct		1
	pig	10	1	pig		1
	school	9	2	school: shol		1
	bird	9	3	birds: bds		1
	got	7	1	got		1
	frog	6	1	frog: frg		1
	flowers	6	1	flowers: frs		1
	out	4	1	out: ot		1
	all	4	1	all	3	
				some: sm		1
				windy: win		1
				tried: td		1
				kinds: kds; kinds		2
				very: ve		1
				outside: ot		1
				animals: as; anls		2
				nice: ni		1
				bikes: is		1
				things: ths; things		2
				numbers: nmbrs		1
				(think)		1
				there: thr		1
				(bubble)		1
				(named)		1
				of: of		3
				after: aftr		1
				kids: kds; kids		2
				saw: s		1
				fence: f		1
				having: hav		1
				fun: fun		1
				(were)		1

*Note. Use of parentheses indicates the teacher wrote item for the child.

Table 9

Attention to Print in Initial Lessons of Lower Outcome Students

Student	Print Setting in Reading			Print Setting in Writing		
	Vocabulary	Repeated readings	Number of different texts	Independent writing or joint constructions*		Teacher support
#9	the	114	3	the	4	2
	I	63	3	I	3	
	in	26	2	in	1	
	my	17	3	my	1	3
	and	10	2	(and)	4	1
	mom	9	2	(mom)	2	
	tree	8	1	tree: te		1
	cat	6	1	cat	1	
	birthday	4	1	(birthday)		
	teacher	3	1	(teacher)		
	like	3	1	like	1	1
				name	1	
				chunky: c		1
				trouble: t		1
				corect: ct		1
				lunch: l		1
				leaves: l		1
				it: t		1
				cold: c		1
				eating: e		1
				dog: d		1
				food: f		1
				(good)		
				(likes)		
				(me)		
				(wrote)		
				(thing)		
				(on)		
				(chalkboard)		
				(with)		
				(she)		
				(nice)		
				(weather)		
#7	the	174	7	the	2	
	is	7	3	is	1	
	I	77	3	I	8	
	my	37	2	my: m	1	5
	in	36	2	(in)		
	up	27	1	(up)		
	and	16	3	(and)		
	to	2	1	to: t		2
				fire: f		1
				station: t		1
				ate: t		1
				toast: tst		1
				for: fr		1
				breakfast: t		1
				stayed: st		1
				slept: s		1
				brother: e		1
				Bubby's: B		1
				room: rm		1
				till: tl		1
				bedtime: b		1
				bikes: s		1
				been: be		1
				(at): t		4
				(have): h		2
				(house): h		1
				(paste)		
				(this)		
				(morning)		
				(stayed)		
				(friends)		
				(kids)		
				(went)		
				(grandpa)		
				(grandpa's)		
				(practicing)		
				(new)		

*Note. Use of parentheses indicates the teacher wrote item for the child.

teachers, however, the higher outcome students did more joint analysis through the teachers' use of the Elkonin boxes ($n = 5, 11$) while the teachers of lower outcome students did what is referred to as sharing a pen rather than utilizing the tool of Elkonin boxes ($n = 2, 1$). The teachers of lower outcome students also tended to write more of the text for the students.

The written text that students wrote independently and in conjunction with their teacher's support are aligned together in Tables 8 and 9. A consistent pattern that arose from the comparison of text read and text written across the first ten lessons indicates how the interrelationships children construct across reading and writing emerge. A consistent pattern across these four children suggested that the children were more likely to write words independently that they encountered across multiple texts and extend the corpus of sound relationships to other like cases with opportunities to read and write. The teachers of higher outcome children were able to orchestrate links between reading and writing more effectively between the books read and texts written, as suggested by the fact that there were more common words across reading and writing by higher outcome children than with the lower outcome students. All children generated stories that included words not part of their reading, however, the overlap between text reading and the composed sentences was greater for higher outcome students and this may have been a facilitating factor in aiding children's conjunction of sources of information from both reading and writing. Table 10 includes a complete listing of the sentences written by higher and lower outcome students across the first ten lessons of their Reading Recovery program. These data suggest that when the teachers seek to make links across reading and writing events being sensitive to students' strengths in writing and reading, the students are aided in the construction of analogies. This resulting network of analogies feed into the students' ongoing theory development of how print works.

The result of this conscious effort on the teachers' part to aid children in confirming these emerging theories against the print they explored in their environment can be seen from data presented in Table 11 on growth in vocabulary across the instructional program. There were consistently greater numbers of words written independently in the extended evaluation period referred to as *roaming around the known* across the first ten lessons and throughout the total program as indicated by the numbers of words written on the final assessment (higher outcome, $n = 40, 63$; Lower outcome, $n = 24, 21$), with a total of different vocabulary items written independently across lessons and assessments of 57, 80, 30, and 40, even though the students entered the program with similar strengths.

The character of the independently written vocabulary also suggested that the higher outcome students formed sets of sets (Tharp & Gallimore, 1988) or used analogy more strongly to organize their world of print. In the final test setting, the higher outcome students were more likely to group *cook, book, look*, and *took* together, forming chains of associations (Goswami & Bryant, 1990), categorizing what they wrote and read based upon analogies each learner constructed.

Discussion

For the emergent reader and writer, research suggests that a key factor in their literacy development is in understanding the symbolic uses of written language (Vygotsky, 1978; Luria, 1983) and more specifically, in their understandings of the phonological features (Goswami & Bryant, 1990; Read, 1986) within oral language and how these were represented by written symbols. It was proposed that this study would offer insights into two areas of literacy learning and instruction: (a) the conjunction of reading and writing or the reciprocal nature of reading and writing, and (b) the nature of effective teacher decisions that support children's literacy learning in Reading Recovery lessons.

Within this study of twelve students, there was clear evidence that the children were able to develop conceptual links from the varying print settings that occurred across reading and writing events. In Reading Recovery lessons, there are planned experiences that are juxtaposed to facilitate the development of a self-extending system in learning to read and write. Across lessons, these reading and writing events support children's theories of how print works in both

Table 10
Sentence Writing Across Ten Lessons for Higher and Lower Outcome Students

Student	Lesson	Sentence
1	1	I like to eat salad.
	2	I can climb a tree.
	3	The bear is at home.
	4	I like to go to the zoo.
	5	I like to eat chocolate cake.
	6	The cat can climb the tree.
	7	I can ride in the car.
	8	I can go up the tree house.
	9	I like to go to the work with Mom.
	10	I can swim in the pool with my mom.
5	1	A cat tried to get all kinds of animals.
	2	A little frog saw a big flowers and big birds.
	3	I think there was nice bikes.
	4	It was very windy outside.
	5	Kids played all kinds of things after school.
	6	All kinds of animals wear all kinds of things.
	7	A fish said, "Bubble, bubble, bubble."
	8	The wolf named some numbers.
	9	A little pig got out of the fence.
	10	The kids were having fun.
7	1	I cut and paste this morning.
	2	I stayed at my friends house.
	3	The kids went to the fire station.
	4	My grandpa is at my house.
	5	I ate toast for breakfast.
	6	I stayed at my grandpa's.
	7	I slept in my brother Bubby's room.
	8	I stayed up till bedtime.
	9	I have two bikes.
	10	I have been practicing at my new house.
9	1	Janet is good.
	2	The teacher likes me.
	3	I wrote the correct thing on the chalkboard.
	4	My mom is eating lunch with me.
	5	I like my teacher. She is nice.
	6	I like the trees and the leaves.
	7	It is my birthday.
	8	The weather is cold.
	9	My cat is eating dog food.
	10	The books are easy.

Table 11
Growth in Written Vocabulary Across Lessons

Student	Higher Outcome		Lower Outcome	
	#1	#5	#7	#9
Observation				
Pretest	I see the cat m,t,o,p	i a go no to B,k,c,t,s,p,h	name red girl the b,s,m.g,s,h,r	name 8 attempts teh (the) le (l) bet (blue) tet (the) cahe (cat) pen (pig) i,e,s,o,p
Roaming	to a	I the we put red in a	name red girl	name
First week	at go zoo	get all it was and play think kinds	I the is	in is good the on
Second week	in can up	said were some got pig		I
Different vocabulary posttest, end-of-year testing and lesson records	cook book look took looks go going good be we he she like ride side made is in into to and can cans	I is in it to on do into a at an am and ran can has cat cats dog dogs am has ran	I I'm is in it my me we went to go on off big for had name the a at and are red	cat dog mom dad on in is I him a and at am sad had to the they me my bus vow you

Table 11. *Growth in Written Vocabulary Across Lessons* (continued)

Student	High Outcome		Low Outcome	
	#1	#5	#7	#9
Different vocabulary posttest, end-of-year testing and lesson records (continued)	cat	the	bed	they
	cats	then	have	today
	the	they	had	go
	then	this	today	do
	them	go	Mom	coke
	out	going	dad	have
	made	good	not	move
	I	we		time
	Mom	me		red
	Dad	he		eat
	name	she		stop
	down	see		toast
	up	like		seed
	my	live		back
	me	ride		good
	come	made		out
	comes	have		
	some	look		
	play	little		
	playing	find		
	pig	play		
	big	may		
	at	way		
	bat	say		
	car	day		
	cars	here		
	see	were		
	bee	her		
	zoo	him		
	zoos	you		
	stop	dig		
	boy	big		
		no		
		now		
		stop		
		car		
		red		
		black		
		blue		
		green		
		one		
		two		
		three		
		five		
		six		
		yes		
		what		
		are		
		over		
		did		
		up		
		for		
		mom		
		dad		
		love		
Total	**57**	**80**	**30**	**40**

processes. The current study suggested there were some key ideas that facilitate the conjunction of reading and writing: (a) constant analysis of what children know, how children engage in problem-solving, and strategies they are developing; (b) drawing consistent links from a known corpus of information to use in new settings; (c) an emphasis on independent action and problem-solving; and (d) the importance of challenging learning settings.

As a result of opportunities to read, talk with their teachers about books, and write messages about their world of books and life experiences, the twelve children negotiated their understanding of print, conventions, story, and how to utilize their own theories of how print works in reading and writing text. They began with a few words, their names, and a few sound-letter relationships. In the early testing through the Observation Survey (Clay, 1993b), Student #1 was able to write *I, see, the,* and *cat* and represent the sounds of *m, t,* and *o* in writing. In the initial *roaming around the known* period, he added *to* and *at* to his corpus of fluently written words. As he jointly constructed text or wrote independently in the first ten lessons, he gained flexibility in utilizing this information and extended his learning to write *go, like, can,* and *in* and wrote the letters, *m, s, t, o, p, r, d, h, w, k,* and *e,* as contributions during joint problem-solving on new words.

This early corpus of knowledge was critical to how Student #1 read texts as well. The teacher's records indicated how early in the lessons the written vocabulary provided anchors for the student in text reading. Student #1 used *like, the, at,* and *can* as anchors to help monitor his reading and began to attend to words that had known letter-sound relationships within them such as the letters, *m , r,* and *p,* in *my, car,* and *pool.* Comments like "Soup ends with p," "There's an *r* at the end of that word" (builder), and self-correcting the spoken word *rug* for the text item *mat* because he saw the *m,* were all noted in the teacher's records. The data indicate that what the students in this study could write and aspects of phonological features they could use to problem-solve in writing began to aid their problem-solving as readers. What they could read eventually began to inform their problem-solving in writing. By placing an emphasis across lessons on what the child knows or can use in problem-solving, the teacher supports the child's construction of a network of information to use in both reading and writing.

In early lessons, the most effective teachers allocated more time to writing and selected books so that the sources of knowledge the children had as writers and readers could be capitalized upon and extended. Because Student #1 had a particular set of words and special cues within text available to him as resources, his teacher selected books that would allow him to operate independently as a reader of text as well. Vocabulary such as *I, the, cat, Mom, see, up, can, to, go,* and *am* were part of the texts she chose for him to read to capitalize on his strengths. As opportunities arose in reading and writing, she drew attention to how these known features could be used to help him locate where he was in the text, matching spoken and written words.

In helping Student #1 generate sentences for the day's writing, the conversation the higher outcome student and his teacher had about the world of narrative from the stories they read and the experiences they talked about were the basis of composing the sentences (see Table 9). For example, two familiar books were read that dealt with eating or foods on day one of lessons. He then generated the sentence, "I like to eat salad." There was a conscious effort from the higher outcome teachers to build on the stories children read during writing in addition to the personal experiences they wrote about, to help them integrate, confirm, and extend the theories they developed about print across multiple texts and language opportunities. The teachers' conversations drew consistent links from the known corpus of information to encourage the children to use it in new settings. In this way, the teachers were able to provide multiple ways for the children to learn two important aspects about literacy: (a) the aspects of print to which they must attend, and (b) the aspects of oral language that can be related to print (Clay, 1991, p. 326).

Writing allows children to explore a narrow corpus of written language. Children articulate each word slowly and analyze the phonological features of the message to be written. The task of hearing sounds in words helped the higher outcome children in this study assign a place value, so to speak, for the phonemes they articulated within words. In this way, they learned how to manipulate language at the phonemic level, an ability that must be taught to the majority of first grade children (Goswami & Bryant, 1990). By learning to represent the sounds they heard in words and the other features that also applied, each child began to construct a system of categories that eventually lead them to make such statements as, ". . . cave, it either starts with a *c* or a *k*." Through the use of techniques of hearing sounds in words and going from known to problem-solving on new, the higher outcome students operated at high levels of problem-solving and were encouraged to independently apply their growing systems of knowledge in more complex ways.

The teacher's role in this process is to support this concept development and extend this growing network of analogies. For example, Student #1 wrote the sentence, "The bear is coming home," and his teacher drew on the fact that he was attending to words with *s* in them. The story he had read the day before and his running record that day had the vocabulary item *is* in it (7 times). She asked him to try to write *is* on the practice page. He wrote "si," drawing on visual information. She then asked him to "Check to see if you are right." By running his finger under the word to check on his writing, he noticed that the letter *s* was in the wrong place. She pointed out how good it was that he noticed how *is* looked, that he also knew when it was not quite right. Then she showed him how it looked and had him practice it a few times. The higher outcome teacher consistently placed an emphasis on independent action and problem-solving. This may have been one factor in the student's rapid progress.

This emphasis on independent action and problem-solving could also be seen in the types of challenge the higher outcome teachers placed before their children. By week five of the instructional program, the higher outcome students (#1 and #5) read at text level four and six, respectively. The lower outcome students (#7 and #9) read at four and two. At week ten, the higher outcome students were at levels eight and nine, while the lower outcome students were at seven and three. By week fifteen, the higher outcome students read at sixteen and nine. The lower outcome students were at ten and five. Student #1 ended up making the most consistent accelerative progress, although he had started out testing the lowest of the four students highlighted in this portion of the analysis. One key factor was his teacher's ability to keep the level of challenge in both reading and writing at the cutting edge of his new learning, as well as her ability to support that learning with all the tools she had available to her as a teacher. Intuitively, she understood that eventually a child learns more rapidly about complex orthography through text reading (Clay, 1991; Goswami & Bryant, 1990). Consequently, the flexible use of reading and writing across the child's program, keeping the child operating independently, drawing links from known sources of information to problem-solve new elements, and maintaining sufficient challenge to maintain a forward direction in learning were all key components to effective instruction to support the convergence of reading and writing.

Figure 2 presents a model of the reciprocity between reading and writing; how children move from early learning where reading and writing are almost separate systems of knowledge to fully reciprocal processes, each contributing to the development of the other. Each portion of the Reading Recovery lesson framework allows students to negotiate and test their developing theories of print, how stories are constructed, how written language works; confirming or disconfirming hypotheses of print, story, and the world of written language.

As this model suggests by the ever converging and diverging lines, the child's attention to print focuses and expands within the different reading and writing experiences encountered in Reading Recovery. In text reading, Clay (1993a) suggested there are twin aims:

• One is to allow the child scope for practicing the orchestration of all the complex range of behaviors he or she must use (and this is best achieved on easy or familiar texts).

• The other is to encourage him to use his reading strategies on novel texts and to support his or her tentative efforts. (p. 36)

In familiar reading, the child's familiarity with the meaning and language of the story frees his or her attention to explore new aspects of story and text. In the reading of yesterday's new book, while the teacher takes a running record the child is working on text read only once before, testing out some newly acquired strategies and attending to print more closely. In reading the new book, the child encounters a volume of print and the teacher works to draw the reader's attention to the different sources of information across text that will support the child's reading for meaning.

In the writing portion of the lesson, the child attends to the details of print, exploring sound-letter relationships within a narrow corpus of printed information. The child's innate abilities to be sensitive to the sounds of many different language phonemes and to categorize through the use of analogy (Goswami & Bryant, 1990) are key to the development of reciprocity in writing and reading. In writing, the child categorizes the sound and visual aspects of print ("This begins like my name!") through analogy. As she or he encounters the same information in new texts, the knowledge about print is expanded, and the child works to fill out and extend the categories being built, hypothesizing new relationships about print, language, and meaning. As the child continues to read and write, what he or she knows as a reader and writer begins to expand and become integrated.

Figure 2. **Reciprocity Between Writing and Reading.**

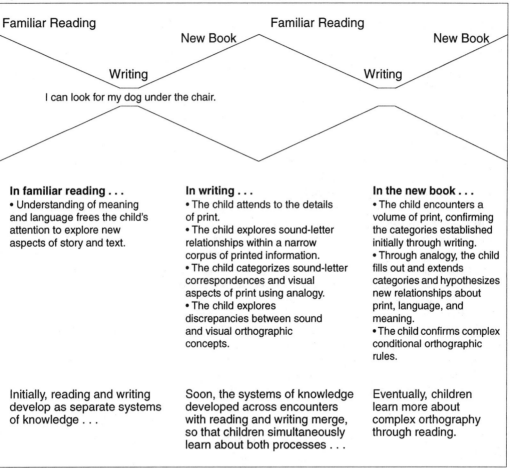

In familiar reading . . .
• Understanding of meaning and language frees the child's attention to explore new aspects of story and text.

In writing . . .
• The child attends to the details of print.
• The child explores sound-letter relationships within a narrow corpus of printed information.
• The child categorizes sound-letter correspondences and visual aspects of print using analogy.
• The child explores discrepancies between sound and visual orthographic concepts.

In the new book . . .
• The child encounters a volume of print, confirming the categories established initially through writing.
• Through analogy, the child fills out and extends categories and hypothesizes new relationships about print, language, and meaning.
• The child confirms complex conditional orthographic rules.

Initially, reading and writing develop as separate systems of knowledge . . .

Soon, the systems of knowledge developed across encounters with reading and writing merge, so that children simultaneously learn about both processes . . .

Eventually, children learn more about complex orthography through reading.

At this early point in children's learning, the teaching is critical, as are the patterns within the symbol system that naturally occur across written language events. Teachers note what information comprises the separate systems of knowledge for children in reading and writing and links what children know through analogies across reading and writing events. Teachers *dig ditches* connecting the separate pools of knowledge so that information begins to be applied from one to the other, back and forth, until the systems of knowledge held in reading and writing converge. Eventually, children learn more about complex orthography through reading (Goswami & Bryant, 1990).

In the metaphor of ditch digging, the teacher must reflect on possible strategies, or in-the-head processes the reader and writer are orchestrating or need to draw upon. As Clay (1991) suggested:

> By means of a network of unobservable in-the-head strategies the reader is able to attend to information from different sources (e. g., reading and writing, oral language and visual learning, meaning and phonology). The good reader can work with both internal and external information and make decisions about matches and mismatches in his or her responses. A dynamic network of interactive strategies allows the reader to change direction at any point of the processing path. (p. 328)

Consistently, the teachers within this study acted upon the notion that children's developing control grows through sequences of behaviors as can be observed when infants meet novel situations (Bruner, 1974):

- There is increased anticipatory behaviour (such as random excited movement of the hands);
- Some behaviours occur but not necessarily in an order that works;
- The behaviour is less variable, uses less effort; and
- The behaviour pattern becomes efficient. (p. 329)

When these behavior patterns and sequences of events recur over time, learners establish new ways of operating (Clay, 1991):

- Some subroutines can be practised without carrying out the whole act and they may become efficient before others;
- A subroutine may be dropped from the act because it is no longer a necessary part; and
- An initial first pattern of action may be displaced by a new routine, a drastic change over the earlier pattern, yet still allowing the old pattern to recur. In this case a higher order pattern has taken over. (p. 330)

The information networks that students began to utilize through lessons in Reading Recovery were powerful sources of personal knowledge for their continued learning in classroom settings. As Clay (1991) indicated from her review of Bruner's (1974) account of infants learning to organize skilled action, "we increase our powers by converting bodies of knowledge into generative rules for thinking about the world and about ourselves" (p. 330). Within this study, the data presented suggested that what children learned through writing in lessons was how to construct generative rules to aid them in learning through text, both reading and writing. The items of knowledge children drew upon at first were later fed into more powerful strategies. As Clay stated, "Only the child can develop strategic control over the experiences and information coded somehow in his brain and governing many of his behaviours" (p. 342).

The teacher supports, asks questions to extend, and works to keep the child's theory development on track. The goal of literacy instruction is to aid the literacy system to become self-extending and for the child to become self-managed and able to learn independently in the complex world that surrounds him or her.

References

Bruner, J. S. (1974). Organization of early skilled action. In M. P. M. Richard, *The integration of a child into a social world* (pp. 167-184). London: Cambridge University Press.

Butler, A., & Turbill, J. (1984). *Towards a reading-writing classroom*. Rozelle, NSW: Primary English Teaching Association.

Cazden, C. B. (1988). *Classroom discourse: The language of teaching and learning*. Portsmouth, NH: Heinemann.

Clay, M. M. (1985). *The early detection of reading difficulties*. Portsmouth, NH: Heinemann.

Clay, M. M. (1991). *Becoming literate: The construction of inner control*. Portsmouth, NH: Heinemann.

Clay, M. M. (1993a). *Reading Recovery: A guidebook for teachers in training*. Portsmouth, NH: Heinemann.

Clay, M. M. (1993b). *An observation survey of early literacy achievement*. Portsmouth, NH: Heinemann.

Clay, M. M., & Cazden, C. (1990). A Vygotskian interpretation of Reading Recovery tutoring. In L. Moll (Ed.), *Vygotsky and education: Instructional implications and applications of sociohistorical psychology* (pp. 206-222). Cambridge, UK: Cambridge University Press.

Cochran-Smith, M. (1984). *The making of a reader*. Norwood, NJ: Ablex.

DeFord, D. E. (1986). Classroom contexts for literacy learning. In T. E. Raphael (Ed.), *Contexts of school-based literacy* (pp. 163-180). New York: Random House.

Dyson, A. H. (1989). *Multiple worlds of child writers: Friends learning to write*. New York: Teachers College Press.

Eckhoff, B. (1983). How reading affects children's writing. *Language Arts, 60*, 607-616.

Elkonin, D. B. (1973). U.S.S.R. In J. Downing (Ed.), *Comparative reading* (pp. 551-580). New York: Macmillan.

Goodman, K. S., & Goodman, Y. (1979). Learning to read is natural. In L. B. Resnick & P. B. Weaver (Eds.), *Theory and practice of early reading: Vol. 1* (pp. 137-154). Hillsdale, NJ: Lawrence Erlbaum.

Goswami, U., & Bryant, P. (1990). *Phonological skills and learning to read*. East Sussex, UK: Lawrence Erlbaum.

Greenfield, P. M. (1984). A theory of the teacher in the learning activities of everyday life. In B. Rogoff & J. Love (Eds.), *Everyday cognition: Its development in social context*. Cambridge: Harvard University Press.

Griffin, P., & Cole, M. (1984). Current activity for the future: The zoped. In B. Rogoff & J. V. Wertsch (Eds.), *Children's learning in the "zone of proximal development" (New Directions for Child Development, No. 23)* (pp. 45-64). San Francisco: Jossey-Bass.

Halliday, M. A. K. (1975). *Learning how to mean: Explorations in the development of language*. London: Edward Arnold.

Harste, J. C., Woodward, V. A., & Burke, C. L. (1984). *Language stories and literacy lessons*. Portsmouth, NH: Heinemann.

Heath, S. B. (1983). *Ways with words: Language, life and work in communities and classrooms*. New York: Cambridge University Press.

Irwin, J. W., & Doyle, M. A. (1992). *Reading/writing connections: Learning from research*. Newark, DE: International Reading Association.

LaBerge, D., & Samuels, S. J. (1974). Toward a theory of automatic information processing in reading. *Cognitive Psychology, 6*, 293-323.

Luria, A. R. (1983). The development of writing in the child. In M. Martlew (Ed.), *The psychology of written language: Developmental and educational perspectives* (pp. 237-277). New York: Wiley.

Lyons, C. A. (1993). The use of questions in the teaching of high risk readers: A profile of a developing Reading Recovery teacher. *Reading and Writing Quarterly, 9*, 317-327.

Lyons, C. A., Pinnell, G. S., & DeFord, D. E. (1993). *Partners in learning: Teachers and children in Reading Recovery*. New York: Teachers College Press.

McLane, J. B. (1990). Writing as a social process. In L. Moll (Ed.), *Vygotsky and education: Instructional implications and applications of sociohistorical psychology* (pp. 304-318). Cambridge, UK: Cambridge University Press.

Perfetti, C. A., Beck, I., Bell, L. C., & Hughes, C. (1987). Phonemic knowledge and learning to read are reciprocal: A longitudinal study of first grade children. *Merrill-Palmer Quarterly, 33*, 283-319.

Pinnell, G. S. (1989). Reading Recovery: Helping at-risk children learn to read. *The Elementary School Journal, 90*, 161-183.

Pinnell, G. S., Lyons, C. A., DeFord, D. E., Bryk, A. S., & Seltzer, M. (1994). Comparing instructional models for the literacy education of high risk first graders. *Reading Research Quarterly, 29*(1), 9-38.

Read, C. (1986). *Children's creative spellings*. London: Routledge and Kegan Paul.

Rogoff, B. (1990). *Apprenticeship in thinking: Cognitive development in social context*. New York: Oxford University Press.

Rohl, M., & Tunmer, W. E. (1988). Phonemic segmentation skill and spelling acquisition. *Applied Psycholinguistics, 9*, 335-350.

Scardamalia, M., & Bereiter, C. (1982). Assimilative processes in composition planning. *Educational Psychologist, 17*, 165-171.

Spivey, N. N., & King, J. R. (1989). Readers and writers. *Reading Research Quarterly, 24*, 9-26.

Stotsky, S. (1983). Research on reading/writing relationships: A synthesis and suggested directions. *Language Arts, 60*, 627-643.

Tharp, T. G., & Gallimore, R. (1988). *Rousing minds to life: Teaching, learning, and schooling in social context*. Cambridge: Cambridge University Press.

Vygotsky, L. S. (1978). *Mind in society*. Cambridge: Harvard University Press.

Wells, G. (1986). *The meaning makers: Children learning language and using language to learn*. Portsmouth, NH: Heinemann.

Wertsch, J. V. (1979). From social interaction to higher psychological processes: A clarification and application of Vygotsky's theory. *Human Development, 22*, 1-22.

Wertsch, J. V. (1985). *Vygotsky and the social formation of mind*. Cambridge: Harvard University Press.

Wood, D., Bruner, J. S., & Ross, G. (1976). The role of tutoring in problem-solving. *Journal of Child Psychology and Psychiatry, 17*, 89-100.

LEARNING TO READ: INSIGHTS FROM READING RECOVERY

NOEL K. JONES

The University of North Carolina at Wilmington

The expression "Learning the ABCs" has come to represent the simplest, most basic kind of learning. Yet, first grade teachers know and young children know, that learning about print and learning to read and write are not simple at all. Although many children seem to acquire literacy almost miraculously on their own, that does not mean that the task has been easy for them; their efforts perhaps extending over several years. Other children find reading and writing very difficult, even with the help of excellent teaching.

Even though it is a significant and sometimes arduous accomplishment, most people succeed in learning to read and write when they are still very young. Understanding how literacy develops, however, is extraordinarily more complex. The mental processes involved in literacy and literacy learning are topics that continue to intrigue and perplex the best human minds. Although remarkable advances in knowledge have been achieved, research still does not reveal all we need and want to know about how children learn and why learning is more difficult for some than for others.

Even though our collective understanding is tentative and incomplete, both theorists and teachers form operational theories based on their interpretations of evidence. In the areas of reading and learning to read, theories as well as curriculum recommendations tend to be sharply divided, clustering toward one or the other of two camps.

One group emphasizes meaning, language context, prediction, anticipation, and parsimonious visual sampling in their theories of reading processing, both for children and adults. In terms of teaching practices, these theorists (including whole language advocates) stress immersion in literacy activities pursued for authentic purposes; reading and writing of complete texts; integration of reading and writing; and the importance for teachers of allowing students choice, accepting approximations, and encouraging risk-taking so that children continue to be active discoverers and meaning-makers (Altwerger, Edelsky, & Flores, 1987; Cambourne, 1988; K. Goodman, 1986, 1989; Y. Goodman, 1989; Goodman & Goodman, 1979; Harste, Woodward, & Burke, 1984; Smith, 1985; Watson, 1989; Weaver, 1990).

Another group of theorists stress research evidence suggesting (a) that readers process almost all of the visual information on the page; (b) that fast, automatic word recognition and thorough knowledge of sound-symbol relations separate good from poor readers; and (c) that phonemic awareness plays a significant, causal role in learning to read. These code-emphasis advocates believe that beginning reading instruction should stress development of phonemic awareness, letter knowledge, sound-symbol associations, and rapid word identification (Chall, 1983; Ehri, 1987, 1989; Ehri & Wilce, 1985; Gough & Hillinger, 1980; Juel, Griffith, & Gough, 1986; Just & Carpenter, 1987; Liberman & Liberman, 1990; Stanovich, 1980, 1986). Many of them advocate direct instruction as the most efficient way of fostering these learnings (Chall, 1983; Ehri & Wilce, 1985; Gough & Hillinger, 1980; Liberman & Liberman, 1990).

These controversies over theory and practice of beginning reading produce serious dilemmas for educators. Increasing numbers of teachers are drawn to recommendations for whole language activities and the establishment of classroom literacy environments. Other teachers and many administrators are influenced by the evidence and arguments from code-emphasis writers. Pressed for objective evidence of reading progress, they push for early acquisition of *the code* and frequently for direct instruction on component skills. Policymakers and educators at all levels often feel that almost any curriculum choice they make will subject them to often quite irrational criticism from one or the other of these positions.

In this article, ideas are offered about beginning reading that may be helpful in moving beyond these entrenched positions. These ideas have become personal insights through my experiences in Reading Recovery, a short-term literacy intervention that accelerates the learning of the lowest achieving first grade children so that they progress as successful readers and writers within the classroom (Clay, 1993b; Pinnell, 1990). Working with Reading Recovery increases understanding of early reading and writing and helps develop new perspectives on both theoretical and practical issues.

Reading Recovery offers a rich source of information concerning the emergence of literacy and literacy processes in young children. This program was based upon and has generated significant longitudinal studies of beginning readers and writers (Clay, 1982, 1991, 1993b; DeFord, Pinnell, Lyons, & Place, 1990). Reading Recovery teachers keep extensive documentation of each child's performance and progress and of their teaching actions and decisions. Standardized report forms are completed for each child for easy generation of local, state, and national reports. Moreover, as teachers work to make their teaching moves contingent upon each child's performance and concepts, they have the opportunity to observe and reflect intently upon each child's functioning and progress in daily, individual lessons. Since everyone involved in Reading Recovery continues to teach children at least some of the time, a vast reservoir of shared understanding of early literacy has developed (Clay, 1993a, 1993b; DeFord, Lyons, & Pinnell, 1991; Lyons, Pinnell, & DeFord, 1993; Pinnell, 1990).

Reading Recovery develops children's abilities in both reading and writing. The aim is to foster strategies in both areas so that the child develops a self-extending system that allows him or her to learn more about reading and writing with every engagement in literacy (Clay, 1991, 1993b; DeFord, 1991). These daily, 30-minute, individual tutoring sessions are short term and supplemental. It is expected that the long term development of literacy, language, and communication processes will occur through classroom programs and other school experiences.

Although reading and writing are integrated in Reading Recovery, the focus of this article is reading. The principles underlying the theory and practice of Reading Recovery are particularly relevant toward understanding the roles of meaning and of print knowledge in early reading. These principles may be useful in moving beyond the meaning-emphasis versus code-emphasis polarization that has plagued both reading theory and reading education. As each principle or insight is discussed, comparisons will be made to key tenets of meaning emphasis (whole language) as well as code-emphasis researchers and educators.

However, a caveat is immediately in order. Treating meaning-emphasis and code-emphasis as distinct, homogeneous, and contrasting belief systems is admittedly an oversimplification in two ways. First, it suggests that all people who tend, for example, to give greater emphasis to meaning think alike and hold similar views on all issues relevant to beginning reading. Second, it may be unfair to the knowledge and beliefs of individuals who may be well aware of the complexity and range of factors influencing early literacy, but whose research has focused on one or the other end of the spectrum from meaning to decoding. These positions, however, exist and are influential far beyond the academic community. The categorizations used here reflect the beliefs of educational practitioners and the lay public, which tend to cast these views in stark and contrasting colors, as well as researchers and scholars of early literacy.

The ideas presented draw heavily on the work of Marie Clay and others in Reading Recovery. However, treating the beliefs of Reading Recovery practitioners as if they were homogeneous is also an oversimplification. The author takes full responsibility for their expression and development of Clay's theories and the *Reading Recovery position* in this article, including any omissions, gaps of logic, or other distortions.

Reading Is a Complex Socio-Psycholinguistic Process

Reading is an extremely complex psycholinguistic, socio-communicative, and cognitive process. Because of the complexity of the mental processing and the number of factors (in the text, the reader's experience, and the context) that may influence the processing, it is almost impossible to study the reading process in entirety. Theorists and researchers have tended to take a particular stance for their investigations, sacrificing breadth of view to obtain depth of understanding. Many researchers, typically cognitive psychologists, have tended to study reading *synchronically*, motivated by interest in what is going on in the mind of the reader at particular points in time. Other theorists and researchers have investigated reading *diachronically*, interested in the changing concerns and processes of the reader as he or she initiates a reading activity; becomes absorbed in the text and in thoughts engendered by the text and prior knowledge; rereads to problem-solve; reflects about meanings; and assimilates, communicates, and acts upon ideas stimulated from the experience.

Viewed *synchronically* (at particular points in time), reading is a high-speed, automatic, simultaneous operation of complex linguistic and cognitive processes. At any moment, a reader of any level of proficiency must keep in mind story meaning, sentence meaning, sentence syntax, and some metacognitive awareness of fit, while simultaneously perceiving and identifying words, word-parts, and punctuation marks. Initially, these processes require much more conscious control and problem-solving, but for the mature reader they operate so automatically that they continue without conscious control and often appear effortless. Both code-emphasis and meaning-emphasis advocates agree upon this general characterization of complex processing, though they disagree about the role that anticipation plays and about the amount of visual detail that is processed while reading for meaning. Many cognitive psychologists, especially code-emphasis advocates, have focused their research primarily upon this synchronic view.

One thing that has not been well understood is the relationship between the high-speed, automatic processing of the mature reader and the processing that beginning readers must do. Over the years, both educators and psychologists have tried a number of ways of simplifying reading to make it easy for children to learn. A trend of the 1970s and 1980s had been to break reading into component parts so that students might master sub-skills in a step-wise fashion. This seemingly logical approach changes the nature of the process. It cuts the child off from useful sources of information and prevents him or her from orchestrating cues from several sources as good readers of all ages do. A component skills approach also gives emphasis to memorization, a type of learning which differs considerably from the complex parallel processing and problem-solving involved in reading (Ausubel, Novak, & Hanesian, 1978; Gagne & Briggs, 1974).

Experience with the intense tutoring of Reading Recovery makes it clear that learning component skills or parts is not the same as reading. Many children who have managed to learn almost all letters and sounds and to read and write several words still cannot read the simplest text. To successfully read texts, even beginning readers must divide their attention between meaning and other sources of information and make decisions in the same way that mature readers do, but within their limited repertoire of knowledge. The only way to learn to do this is to engage in reading activities in pursuit of meaning. Although code-emphasis advocates assume that attention to component skills is helpful, Clay points out that focus on acquiring item knowledge may have a negative effect on learning to read, especially for low-progress children: "The child cannot afford to spend much time practicing detail, and he may become addicted to such practice and find it difficult later to take a wider approach to the reading act" (Clay 1993b, p. 10).

Polanyi's notion of focal and subsidiary attention is helpful here (cited in Cazden, 1992, p. 14). Mature readers give focal attention to meaning and subsidiary attention to visual detail, language structure, and other sources of information. There is much that we do not know about how attention is distributed for beginning readers, but Clay's theories and Reading Recovery teaching experience suggest that learning to read is a matter of learning to give focal attention to meaning and subsidiary attention to cue sources of information. For many children this does not happen if the instruction asks the child to give focal attention to print detail and graphophonemic associations (the *code*).

Whole language theorists strongly support the importance of learning to read through reading (Butler & Turbill, 1984; K. Goodman, 1986; Goodman & Goodman, 1979; Harste, Woodward, & Burke, 1984; Holdaway, 1979; Smith, 1985) and some researchers and cognitive psychologists accept this idea as well (Adams, 1990; Gibson & Levin, 1975; Stanovich, 1994). On the other hand, advocates of the study of phonics and component skills in isolation give much less importance to the reading of continuous texts (Gough & Hillinger, 1980; Liberman & Liberman, 1990). Chall, Jacobs, and Baldwin (1990) have specifically recommended direct instruction on the code as the best approach for economically and educationally disadvantaged children. However, the effectiveness of Reading Recovery in accelerating the learning of thousands of children who began as the lowest readers in their classes serves as strong evidence against the need for an emphasis on phonics and word-learning in isolation for either educationally or economically disadvantaged children or for children with limited proficiency in the language of instruction (Clay, 1993b; Escamilla & Andrade, 1992; Pinnell, DeFord, & Lyons, 1988; Pinnell, Lyons, DeFord, Bryk, & Seltzer, 1994).

Reading is a Phased Thinking/Feeling/Communicative Process

In addition to its psycholinguistic complexity at any particular point in time, reading involves a complex processing that changes gradually over time (*diachronically*) influenced by psychological, linguistic, and social-communicative factors. Stated over-simplistically, any act of reading involves personal choice (emerging from a complex mix of interests, feelings, and ideas), activation of prior knowledge and schemata, engagement with the text, metacognitive control, generation of ideas and emotions, integration with existing knowledge and feelings, and judgment and evaluation. Although there may be cycles of engagement, the interplay of these processes changes as a reading event progresses over time.

Recently, many cognitive theorists and researchers have begun to take these processes into account, investigating the effects of prior knowledge, strategies, the assimilation and utilization of ideas, and with older readers—metacognitive knowledge (Baker & Brown, 1984; Brown, 1980). Other reading researchers have maintained a preoccupation with reading viewed synchronically — trying to unlock the processing in the mind of the reader at particular moments in time. They tend to undervalue this wider, kaleidoscopic view of reading as a communication or literacy event over time. As a result, their advice to practitioners has emphasized processing the code represented by print. Meaning-emphasis advocates, on the other hand, have made a strong contribution to our understanding of reading by bringing the communicative, change-over-time aspects of the reading process into prominent view. In fact, they may be guilty of a preoccupation with this wider, diachronic view of reading, undervaluing the evidence offered by cognitive psychologists from various research paradigms.

Reading Recovery theory and practice recognize the importance of meaning and the socio-communicative context for the emergent and beginning reader. Choice of books for rereading is largely under the child's control and new books are selected for the child with a strong sense of what will appeal to the child as well as what is within his or her capability. The book is introduced to the child so that he or she has a good sense of what it is about and so that paths are cleared for that child to be able to understand and read that book at that particular time. Assistance given during reading is carefully gauged to help the child maintain a focus on meaning and orchestrate cues from all sources (meaning, language syntax and phonology, print, pictures, and prior knowledge); meanwhile, the teacher keeps the task easy enough so that it is enjoyable and rewarding for the child.

Children Are Constructors of Their Own Knowledge

It seems illogical that children could learn to read by reading before they know how to read! Adults have rightly assumed that most children need their help; the question is: What kind of help works best and is most consistent with the notion of children as constructors of their own knowledge? Educators have used a variety of techniques to simplify beginning reading by exercising controls. The basal reader approach controlled the introduction and repetition of words used, for example, in Scott Foresman's *Dick and Jane Pre-primers* of the 1950s (Robinson, Monroe, & Artley, 1956/1962). Another approach has been to arrange for extensive repetition and feedback (e.g., *Programmed Reading*, Buchanan & Sullivan, 1973). A third has been to write texts in words that fit highly constrained patterns (e.g., *SRA Basic Reading Series*, Rassmussen & Goldberg, 1976). Even more extreme are programs such as *Distar* (Bereiter & Engelmann, 1983) which place strict controls on the language and gestures of the teacher, the child's responses, and the sequence of learnings. All of these approaches assume (a) that adults know best the sequence of learnings children must acquire and (b) that adult control over those sequences enhances learning.

Millions of children have learned through systems with built-in controls. But not all children do. In fact, each system produces failures. There is good reason to believe that the more rigid the program and the tighter the control, the higher the failure rate (Allington, 1991; Allington & McGill-Franzen, 1989; Clay, 1991). What seems to happen is that children who come to school with many early literacy experiences learn from highly controlled programs because they can fill in what is missing. Children with meager literacy backgrounds cannot do that. They may learn what the program teaches, which may not be enough; they cannot make sense of the program as presented (perhaps because the developer did not anticipate the difficulty of what is required); or they cannot find any motivation to learn it. Misled by their delayed start in learning and their apparently limited ability to learn through analogy, many people have assumed that the learning styles and needs of low-progress children must be qualitatively different. Yet, Reading Recovery experience tells us that these children, also, must learn by constructing their own knowledge.

Marie Clay (1991) points out the dangers of imposing adult controls on the tasks and materials of beginning reading:

> Attempts to control texts and learning sequences in these ways have probably made the learning task more difficult because important support systems within the language have been left out. Young children can and do learn more about the complex interrelationships within language than such programmes allow.
>
> Does it matter if texts are contrived . . .? For the more able children, perhaps not. They . . . are able to bridge the gaps between what instruction presents them and what they need to learn . . . . When less able children encounter difficulties, the reading programme is not questioned; rather it is the children who are labeled as having difficulties. (p. 187.)

Experiences such as lap reading and shared reading experiences with very young children suggest that such extreme control is unnecessary. With appropriate adult assistance, children can engage in reading and writing real stories even though they are in the very earliest stages of literacy learning. Appropriate assistance might be defined as: only as much as necessary so that the literacy experience can be successful and satisfying. Assistance is also appropriate if it allows the child scope to see relationships, make connections, and gain control at her or his own pace while at the same time fostering risk-taking and forward movement.

In both reading and writing, the Reading Recovery teacher supports a complete literacy experience—from book choice, to anticipation, to detailed processing, to comment upon meaning and enjoyment. What the child cannot do independently, the teacher does for the child, or she or he supplies just enough assistance (using techniques such as task sharing, modeling, prompts, and questions) so that the child can perform successfully (Wood, 1988; Wood, Bruner, &

Ross, 1976). Reading Recovery teachers learn to give support contingent upon what an individual child needs in order to read and write successfully and they learn to achieve a delicate balance between challenge and fluent, successful performance in their tutoring sessions (Clay, 1993b).

Adherents of both code-emphasis and meaning-emphasis positions tend to accept the notion that children construct their own knowledge. It seems likely that theorists from both camps would accept Cazden's (1992) suggestion that the ideal educational interaction involves both an active learner and an active teacher. The difference in their viewpoints hinges on varying interpretations of how the teacher and learner play active roles.

Code-emphasis people are influenced by research in the areas of learning and cognition, and they stress the importance of the child's active engagement during learning tasks. The learning principles they advocate encourage activation of the learner's prior knowledge, manipulation of materials, active exploration of features, opportunities for application, and transfer of learning. They usually make the assumption, however, that adults know best what the child should be learning, as well as the kinds of activities that will make the learning occur. So although they would place the child in an active role within learning tasks, the learning sequences are determined by the teacher or curriculum-makers.

Meaning-emphasis people, on the other hand, especially whole-language advocates, draw their learning paradigm from the literature on child language acquisition. They concede to the learner very considerable control over what is to be learned, the pace of learning, and the learning activities. Student choice is a fundamental tenet of their philosophical position, but their position about the role of the teacher in relation to the child's learning is less clear. The teacher is viewed as a facilitator of literacy activities and as a participant in the communicative cycles of literacy events, but there seems to be considerable ambivalence about how much coaching and intercession a teacher may engage in, almost to the point of believing that less is better.

Reading Recovery takes the position that there is nothing incongruous between, on the one hand, viewing the child as constructor of learning and on the other, adult assistance and intervention. But learning how to play the role of an active teacher without impeding the child's initiative and responsibility for learning is a very difficult process and is a major reason that the professional development of Reading Recovery is so intense and requires so much time. From the time that a child enters the program, teachers work to encourage that child's initiative and independence in learning. Reading Recovery teachers are asked to follow the child (Clay, 1991, 1993b), yet their curricular decisions about what to reinforce or teach are also based upon a developing understanding of Clay's theories of literacy acquisition, bolstered by their experiences teaching many children. Their instructional decisions (how to assist learning) are strongly contingent upon what a particular child knows, is noticing, and is doing at the time the teacher is working with him or her, yet guided by theory and the teacher's decisions about how best to support this child's learning at this time. Thus, Reading Recovery teaching represents a strong example of an active teacher and an active child.

The Focus of Teaching is Strategies

A key assumption of Reading Recovery is that children must acquire and use efficient strategies to get meaning from texts as they read for meaning. Building upon basic notions about directional conventions of print, the match between spoken and printed word-forms, and simple logical relations (e.g., recurrence, identity), children learn to search for and use information of various kinds in texts. Initially, they depend heavily upon cues from their knowledge of oral language structure and upon meaning cues supplied to them through pictures and the teacher's story introductions. Gradually they increase their ability to use print cues and phonological cues to generate, confirm, or alter their responses.

Reading Recovery teachers foster the development of strategies, including analogical thinking, and as children employ these strategies in reading, they are in effect teaching themselves about print. It is the problem-solving that children do as they pursue meaning through the reading and writing of whole texts that builds the store of words and word-parts that they can identify and recall. The teacher subtly encourages and solidifies these new and emergent learnings, but her or his main objective is to strengthen the learning processes at the child's disposal. The Reading Recovery teacher's unstated message to the child might be expressed as: *I am going to help you work out how to learn.* Learning to recognize words, word-parts, and sound-symbol associations becomes a by-product of the child's learning system and his or her daily efforts.

In contrast, reading programs that espouse direct instruction are based upon the unstated message, *We are going to teach you what you need to know.* The learning occurs primarily through telling. True, there is repetition, recall, feedback, reinforcement, and even many ingenious techniques to foster associations, but new learning is generally revealed to the student on a timetable controlled by adults.

Direct instruction is effective as long as the student is under tuition. Done well, it may be more efficient than instruction which allows the student to construct relationships as if they were personal discoveries. But it is not direct instruction that has given advantaged students their edge. These high progress children have developed self-extending learning systems that work well for them under a variety of conditions. They tend to fill in the gaps when exposed to programs with a narrow emphasis; they make connections quickly and learn easily through analogy (Clay, 1991). These characteristics were acquired before they entered school in homes that did not use direct instruction. If low progress learners are to catch up with such peers, they must acquire the same self-initiating systems of learning. Advocates of direct instruction claim that this is the most efficient way for slower learners to learn. For a sprint, they may be right; for a marathon, the opposite is true. In order for learning to be established as a lifelong process; motivation, momentum, and persistence must come from within.

Print Knowledge Emerges and Becomes Internalized

Whole language researchers have insisted that for adult readers, prediction plays a heavy role. They claim that the mature reader samples only as much visual information as necessary to confirm anticipated meanings (K. Goodman, 1967, 1989; Smith, 1985; Weaver, 1994). They object to instruction that isolates elements of print and provides practice on the sound-symbol associations. They down-play (if not deny) the importance of detailed knowledge of these print-language associations. Code-emphasis researchers disagree; people become good readers by becoming faster and more efficient at word identification, not by coming better guessers, and word identification is related to strong knowledge of sound-symbol associations (Ehri, 1989; Ehri &Wilce, 1985; Stanovich, 1986, 1994).

The research cited by the code-emphasis researchers cannot be ignored; better readers are faster and more accurate word-processors (Adams, 1990; Juel, 1991; Stanovich, 1986). But did they become better readers because they learned to be good word processors? Or did they become good word processors because they learned to be good readers? The theory and experience of Reading Recovery suggests that the latter is true, at least for a large number of children. As mentioned earlier, the problem-solving work that children do as they read and write for meaning leads to increasing knowledge of words and word-parts. One explanation of the accelerated learning phase that Reading Recovery children enter is their ability to learn words by using searching and cross-checking strategies. They learn to search meaning at several levels, language structural expectations, and cues from print and from the sounds of anticipated words—all while retaining the meaning of the story as their goal. They also learn to search their own knowledge of known words and word-parts and to reason by analogy from that knowledge to new items.

Researchers focused on the code or on phonemic awareness have argued that learning to read is quite different from oral language acquisition and that learning to read requires deliberate and sequenced instruction (Liberman & Liberman, 1990; Liberman, Shankweiler, Liberman,

Fowler, & Fischer, 1977). It has been assumed that those children who acquire with remarkable rapidity a knowledge of relationships between patterns of print and patterns of language have been precocious and rare (Clark, 1976; Durkin, 1966). Experience with Reading Recovery children indicates that almost all children are capable of acquiring this knowledge at a fairly rapid rate if they have developed a self-learning system and enjoy frequent, regular opportunities for literacy experiences. Whether this fact represents an amazing general ability of young humans to learn or a specific ability for language learning (including literate language) is something that merits considerable further research. What is clear, however, is that we could never be as successful with literacy instruction if children were not naturally endowed as learners. The tasks of teaching are to help children unlock this amazing ability and to establish conditions that foster and allow literacy learning to continue. When we try to do more than that we end up making it hard for those who haven't yet learned how to learn and we get in the way of those who can make rapid, natural progress.

One lesson from Reading Recovery experience is that for many children the initial task of learning how to learn words is very difficult. Two-dimensional, visual-perceptual analysis is quite different from previous experience and these beginners have no categories to help with the memory storage of the visual forms. Limited phonemic awareness and sound-symbol associations make it difficult to link what they attend to visually to other knowledge. By starting with what the child does know and proceeding slowly, Reading Recovery teachers help children develop these rudimentary learning processes so that accelerated learning is possible.

Words become known gradually, over repeated experiences and exposures. But research evidence (Zaporozhets & Elkonin, 1971, reported in Clay, 1991, p. 282-283) and Reading Recovery experience suggest that the speed at which they are acquired depends upon the extent to which the learner is contributing to the learning task. If the learner is passive, the number of repetitions required for learning is very high, for example, the controlled vocabulary and endless repetitions of basal readers was based on research indicating that at least 40 repetitions were necessary to acquire a word (Gates, 1961). But, if the child is using problem-solving strategies while reading with meaning very much in mind, he or she may learn a new word after four to six encounters. The knowledge may still be limited, dependent perhaps on a particular story context, but it seems to progress fairly quickly to the automatic and certain level. As most children progress through Reading Recovery, the time needed to acquire knowledge of words and word-parts seems to shorten at an almost geometric rate.

In other words, once the learning processes are in place, a child can continue to learn in less than ideal conditions. He or she no longer needs contingent teaching from a skilled tutor. This is the logic of the short-term intervention; this is why Reading Recovery children are discontinued (graduated) to continue their literacy learning in regular classrooms.

Readers Must Learn to Respond to Sound-Symbol Associations

Children must acquire and use sound-symbol associations in order to become readers. But in Reading Recovery this is not the central focus of teaching and learning. The Reading Recovery teacher recognizes and trusts the process of incidental learning, but she or he also assists it in several ways: (a) the teacher finds out what the child knows about words and letters upon entrance and helps the child use that knowledge as a bridge to new learning (e.g., if the child's name is Mark and he can write *Mark*, she calls attention to the similarity of Mark and Mother, first by telling or demonstrating, and then by asking or commenting); (b) during both reading and writing tasks, phonemic awareness is fostered by using Elkonin (1973) boxes and questioning techniques to help children hear and record sounds in words; (c) children are encouraged to learn one or two new words occasionally through repeated writing and unprompted recall— by the time that a child is flexible and fluent in writing about 30 or 40 high frequency words, he or she will have gained familiarity with most of the basic sound-symbol associations of English (Clay, 1991); (d) based upon careful observation and knowledge of children, the teacher makes comments or asks questions that help the child see relationships and develop networks of associations; and (e) children are engaged for two to three minutes daily in very simple puzzle-like activities with magnetic letters to further demonstrate these relationships and to let children continue to explore links that they have begun to see through reading and writing (Clay 1993b).

We see that Reading Recovery children acquire the knowledge of words and sound symbol-associations that is at least equivalent to most of their age-mates. However, this is done in the process of reading continuous texts with a focus on meaning and in the process of writing meaningful sentences and stories. The teaching interventions that assist and help solidify this learning are minimal and are based upon the teacher's awareness not only of what the child knows, but what he or she is beginning to notice as well (DeFord, 1991).

The difference between Reading Recovery and meaning-emphasis advocates is that the latter (whole-language) has faith that children will acquire almost all they need to know almost entirely through incidental learning as they engage in literacy activities under appropriate conditions. They acknowledge the utility of demonstrations and models, for example, as in invitational mini-lessons (Atwell, 1987), but they shrink away from more intrusive teaching moves, such as assisted performance, informing, prompting, and immediate feedback, that also occur in Reading Recovery. The difference between Reading Recovery and supporters of strong code-emphasis is that the latter make word-learning and sound-symbol associations the focus of their teaching, rather than the learning of strategies and processes that would allow eventual independence. They tend not to trust or recognize incidental learning. Often they operate on the principle: the stronger the dose, the greater the chance that all children will learn. According to Clay (1991; 1993b), this *overkill* approach is self-defeating. It creates failure situations for many children because the teaching is at too high a level, it creates boredom for the high progress learner, and it makes reading an unpleasant duty rather than a rewarding literacy experience.

Maintaining a Focus on Meaning Is Always Important

As explained before, code-emphasis researchers downplay the role of context and prediction in the reading process, basing their evidence primarily on (a) the high sensitivity of mature readers to visual detail in print and (b) the improbability of guessing the next word in any sentence or discourse string. But their evidence does not show that meaning is *not* operating or playing an important part. In fact, their data show that anomalies of any kind (distortions of spelling, syntax, or semantics) slow down the reader's processing and the more the meaning is disrupted by the anomaly, the more the processing is disrupted (Just & Carpenter, 1987; McConkie, 1979; Rayner & Pollatsek, 1989).

Experience with Reading Recovery teaching demonstrates that if the meaning breaks down, almost everything breaks down. For children with very limited knowledge of words and print, there is a necessary dependence on meaning and language structure in order to participate in literacy experiences at all. But throughout the program, what seems to distinguish independent readers from those who still need individual help is their ability to read fluently with meaning in mind, making short detours for problem-solving at the word level when necessary, but returning almost immediately to a discourse level of meaning.

Meaning plays a role in reading in three ways: (a) it is the goal and the motivation; (b) it is a source of information when searching for a response; and (c) it is used in confirming, rejecting, or self-correcting responses. Reading Recovery teachers usually respond to a child's reading difficulties (miscues, stoppages) by prompting first for considerations of meaning. As children progress, teachers balance their prompts for meaning, language structure, and print detail in relation to the pattern of the child's performance (Clay, 1991, 1993b).

Whole language advocates would agree wholeheartedly with the Reading Recovery emphasis on meaning. Code-emphasis researchers tend to assign less importance to meaning as part of the ongoing processing during reading, partly because print knowledge accounts for a much higher percentage of individual and group differences in their investigations and partly because of their belief that letter and letter-sound knowledge is a necessary foundation and prerequisite for reading.

A Theory of Change Over Time

It is significant that Clay's theories of reading and reading acquisition were developed on the basis of intense longitudinal studies of school children between the ages of five and six who were in the early stages of literacy acquisition. In addition to standardized formal measures taken at ages 5:0, 5:6, and 6:0, Clay's study involved weekly observations of 100 children's reading performances throughout an entire year (Clay, 1982). Evidence supporting code-emphasis theories of learning to read derives almost exclusively from studies which collect data at two, three, or sometimes five points of time; their research questions center upon the relative effects of specific variables, such as phonemic awareness, letter knowledge, ability to read pseudo-words, and reading comprehension (Bradley, Bryant, MacLean, & Crossland, 1989; Juel, Griffith, & Gough, 1986). Clay, on the other hand, observed children's processing as they were learning to read and write and she was able to record the diverse characteristics of individual children as learning progressed. As a result, her theories are based more strongly upon notions of (a) change over time and (b) unique contributions by individual learners than are other theoretical frameworks.

Children's reading behavior changes over time as their concepts about reading and writing emerge, as their knowledge about print increases, and as they learn how to use that knowledge strategically in the process of reading (which is also the process of learning to read). Initially, children respond to books and print globally, based upon their well-developed language capability, their experience with stories and narration, and their emerging literacy concepts. For example, they may tell a story from the pictures of a child's book, with almost no reference to print features (even if they realize what print is for). Soon they discover the relationship between oral language and print, and when they have some control over directional conventions, they can begin to match oral words with word boundaries while reading with a story in mind. What they may have learned about letters and written words helps them in these discoveries and the ability to match language to print in turn leads to new discoveries about letters and words.

As children acquire the alphabetic principle (with or without tuition), they begin to make new discoveries about sequences of letters and sequences of sounds within words and across related sets of words. Most children are able to learn about print through teacher-directed instruction; though in the process, some children become rather passive learners, dependent upon external guidance. It is the children who are able to use knowledge strategically and analogically who make rapid learning progress and who continue to advance their learning by the actions of reading and writing continuous texts while keeping meaning very much in mind.

Though what has been summarized might seem to fit nicely into a staged theory of reading acquisition, Clay's observations of the variability of children's progress toward literacy suggest otherwise. The notion of children as constructors of their own knowledge is consistent with the finding that development may be uneven and comparatively different from child to child and that many children form misconceptions about how reading and writing work. The broad outlines of literacy development can be traced (largely because the nature of the print conventions and the processes of reading and writing are relatively invariant), but the fine points concerning the progress of any individual cannot be easily predicted within those outlines or fit into stage theories of any specificity useful in instruction.

Although Clay's theories emphasize the role of meaning and language in learning to read, they also encompass the growing sophistication of children's knowledge about print. But this knowledge is quite complex, drawing upon phonological knowledge and awareness, perceptual learning, and an increasing intuitive awareness of complex relationships between print sequences and conventions and language and meaning. Code-emphasis research has uncovered the strong relationship between knowledge of the print-language coding conventions and measures of reading capability. Clay's theories do not deny the strength of that relationship. But they lead us to realize that reading, even in its earliest manifestations, is much more complex than the ability to apply sound-symbol knowledge. Furthermore, they lead to the realization that what produces that knowledge is the child's application of intelligent strategies as he or she engages purposely and enjoyably in meaningful activities rich in literacy opportunities.

Clay's theories also explain why beginning reading instruction which emphasizes word-learning and sound-symbol relationships can reduce the possibility that many children will become good readers. The low-progress children may learn to plod through spelling and decoding exercises and struggle through text when required, but they will not acquire the learning strategies or the rich tapestry of knowledge and abilities that literate reading involves. Clay's theories also suggest that in order to get started, some children will need a much stronger and more skillful intervention than classroom instruction can provide, no matter how rich the literacy activities and the teaching and learning interactions that occur.

Summary

Key concepts from the theoretical work of Marie Clay and the extensive teaching experience and results of the Reading Recovery program offer a rich source of information about the initial stages of literacy. This intense and richly documented intervention program for the lowest achieving first grade students offers insights that are especially relevant to the theoretical and practical debates between meaning-emphasis (whole language) and code-emphasis writers and researchers.

The principles from Reading Recovery theory and experiences presented here may help refocus these debates more productively by changing the focus of inquiry. The ideas presented here are:

1. *Reading is a complex, problem-solving process* that cannot be simplified by focusing the learners attention to one source of information at a time.

2. *Reading is a phased, thinking-feeling-communication process* involving motivation, the intentional pursuit of meaning, cycles of engagement, monitoring, and assimilation into and accommodation of existing knowledge structures.

3. *Learners construct their own knowledge* by actively pursuing meaning, relating new learning to old, and using strategies to solve problems.

4. *The focus of teaching is strategies.* By learning how to learn—as they explore the new worlds of literacy, stories, and print under expert tutorial guidance—young children develop a self-extending learning system that may serve them as long as they are active in literate activities.

5. *Print knowledge emerges and becomes internalized.* Meaning and language structure probably play no less a role in mature reading than in beginning reading. But print knowledge changes dramatically, even during the first year of literacy instruction. Once they have learned how to learn, young children have an almost uncanny capacity to acquire knowledge of relationships between letter patterns and language patterns, given adequate and appropriate reading and writing experiences.

6. *Children do learn to use letter-sound associations.* Children's miscues increasingly reflect attention to print and letter cues as they become more accomplished readers (Clay, 1982, 1991). But guidance in the acquisition of that knowledge should be delicately and sensitively attuned to what the child already knows and to how he or she is performing. Either a laissez-faire approach or an overkill approach is damaging to many children. Build on strengths, teach only as much as needed, and acquire literacy through the reading, writing, and rereading of continuous texts are principles of Reading Recovery that merit wider adoption.

7. *Maintaining a focus on meaning is always important.* If reading is not a meaning-driven, meaningful activity, it is not reading. Laboratory and classroom research studies must seriously investigate the effects of losing a focus on meaning and on language structure, both before and after the development of some sophistication in perceiving and processing patterns of print.

8. *Theories of beginning reading must recognize changes over time.* Although the results of learning to read involve knowledge of print code conventions and high-speed automatic word recognition, Clay's theories inform us that the beginnings of literacy involve language, a sense of story, and concepts about books and print at a rather global level. Reading capability emerges

and becomes a rich mixture of knowledge about print sequences, phonemic awareness, and meaning and syntactic relationships as children apply knowledge strategically in meaningful reading and writing experiences. Individual paths of progress are only roughly predictable because of the diverse opportunities and contributions to learning of each individual.

All leading theorists in the debate from either side would agree that prior knowledge, meaning, language cues, letter and word cues, punctuation and other print conventions, and phonological cues all play a part in that enormously complex process that is reading. Disagreements over emphasis, definitions, the inclusion of the broader social-emotional-communication considerations, and the translation of ideas into practice prolong a schism that presents unfortunate dilemmas for educational practitioners. Each side of the debate holds perceptions prejudiced by differences of value and belief. But, observations and reflections about the onset and early stages of literacy from the special vantage point of Reading Recovery teaching is a resource that should not be overlooked. It can help us move beyond entrenched positions to more productive research and to more helpful instructional practices in early literacy education. As Stanovich (1994) has urged, if we approach these issues with good intentions and try hard to overcome our biases, much can be learned from our collective thought and experience.

References

Adams, M. J. (1990). *Beginning to read: Thinking and learning about print.* Cambridge, MA: MIT Press.

Allington, R. (1991). The legacy of "slow it down and make it more concrete." In J. Zutell & S. McCormick (Eds.), *Learner factors/teacher factors: Issues in literacy, research and instruction.* Chicago: National Reading Conference.

Allington, R., & McGill-Franzen, A. (1989). School response to reading failure: Instruction for Chapter I and special education students in grades two, four, and eight. *The Elementary School Journal, 89,* 530-542.

Altwerger, B., Edelsky, C., & Flores, B. (1987). Whole language: What's new? *Reading Teacher, 41,* 141-154.

Atwell, N. (1987). *In the middle: Writing, reading and learning with adolescents.* Upper Montclair, NJ: Boynton/Cook.

Ausubel, D., Novak, J., & Hanesian, H. (1978). *Educational psychology: A cognitive view* (2nd ed.). New York: Holt, Rinehart and Winston.

Baker, L., & Brown, A. (1984). Metacognitive skills and reading. In P. D. Pearson, R. Barr, M. Kamil, & P. Mosenthal (Eds.), *Handbook of reading research* (Vol. 1). New York: Longman.

Bereiter, C., & Engelmann, S. (1983). *Distar: Direct instruction in arithmetic and reading.* Chicago: Science Research Associates.

Bradley, L., Bryant, P., MacLean, M., & Crossland, J. (1989). Nursery rhymes, phonological skills and reading. *Child Language, 16,* 407-428.

Brown, A. (1980). Metacognitive development and reading. In R. Spiro, B. Bruce, & W. Brewer (Eds.), *Theoretical issues in reading comprehension.* Hillsdale, NJ: Erlbaum.

Buchanan, C., & Sullivan, M. (1973). *Programmed reading.* New York: McGraw-Hill, Webster Division.

Butler, A., & Turbill, J. (1984). *Towards a reading-writing classroom.* Portsmouth, NH: Heinemann.

Cambourne, B. (1988). *The whole story.* Auckland, NZ: Ashton Scholastic.

Cazden, C. (1992). *Whole language plus: Essays on literacy in the United States and New Zealand.* New York: Teachers College Press.

Chall, J. (1983). *The great debate* (Rev. ed.). New York: McGraw Hill.

Chall, J., Jacobs, V., & Baldwin, L. (1990). *The reading crisis: Why poor children fall behind.* Cambridge, MA: Harvard University Press.

Clark, M. (1976). *Young fluent readers.* Portsmouth, NH: Heinemann.

Clay, M. M. (1982). *Observing young children: Selected papers.* Portsmouth, NH: Heinemann.

Clay, M. M. (1991). *Becoming literate: The construction of inner control*. Portsmouth, NH: Heinemann.

Clay, M. M. (1993a). *An observation survey of early literacy achievement*. Portsmouth, NH: Heinemann.

Clay, M. M. (1993b). *Reading Recovery: A guidebook for teachers*. Portsmouth, NH: Heinemann.

DeFord, D. (1991). Using reading and writing to support the reader. In D. DeFord, C. Lyons, & G. Pinnell, *Bridges to literacy: Learning from Reading Recovery*. Portsmouth, NH: Heinemann.

DeFord, D., Lyons, C., & Pinnell, G. (1991). *Bridges to literacy: Learning from Reading Recovery*. Portsmouth, NH: Heinemann.

DeFord, D., Pinnell, G., Lyons, C., & Place, A. (1990). *The Reading Recovery follow-up study* (Vol. II.). Columbus: The Ohio State University.

Durkin, D. (1966). *Children who read early: Two longitudinal studies*. New York: Teachers College Press.

Ehri, L. (1987). Learning to read and spell words. *Journal of Reading Behavior, 19*, 5-31.

Ehri, L. (1989). Movement into word reading and spelling: How spelling contributes to reading. In J. Mason (Ed.), *Reading and writing connections*. Boston: Allyn and Bacon.

Ehri, L., & Wilce, L. (1985). Movement into reading: Is the first stage of word learning visual or phonetic? *Reading Research Quarterly, 20*, 163-179.

Elkonin, D. (1973). U.S.S.R. In J. Downing (Ed.), *Comparative reading*. New York: Macmillan.

Escamilla, K., & Andrade, A. (1992). An application of Reading Recovery in Spanish. *Education and Urban Society, 24*(2), 213-226.

Gagne, R., & Briggs, L. (1974). *Principles of instructional design*. New York: Holt, Rinehart and Winston.

Gates, A. (1961). Vocabulary control in basal reading material. *The Reading Teacher, 15*, 81-85.

Gibson, E., & Levin, H. (1975). *The psychology of reading*. Cambridge, MA: MIT Press.

Goodman, K. (1967). Reading: A psycholinguistic guessing game. *Journal of the Reading Specialist, 6*, 126-135.

Goodman, K. (1986). *What's whole in whole language*. Portsmouth, NH: Heinemann.

Goodman, K. (1989). Whole language research: Foundations and development. *The Elementary School Journal, 90*, 208-221.

Goodman, K., & Goodman, Y. (1979). Learning to read is natural. In L. Resnick & P. Weaver (Eds.). *Theory and practice of early reading* (Vol. 1). Hillsdale, NJ: Erlbaum.

Goodman, Y. (1989). Roots of the whole language movement. *The Elementary School Journal, 90*, 113-127.

Gough, P., & Hillinger, M. (1980). Learning to read: An unnatural act. *Bulletin of the Orton Society, 30*, 179-196.

Harste, J., Woodward, V., & Burke, C. (1984). *Language stories and literacy lessons*. Portsmouth, NH: Heinemann.

Holdaway, D. (1979). *Foundations of literacy*. Portsmouth, NH: Heinemann.

Juel, C. (1991). Beginning reading. In R. Barr, M. Kamil, P. Mosenthal, & P. Pearson (Eds.), *Handbook of reading research* (Vol. 2). New York: Longman.

Juel, C., Griffith, P., & Gough, P. (1986). Acquisition of literacy: A longitudinal study of children in first and second grade. *Journal of Educational Psychology, 78*, 243-255.

Just, M., & Carpenter, P. (1987). *The psychology of reading and language comprehension*. Boston: Allyn and Bacon.

Liberman, I., & Liberman, A. (1990). Whole language vs. code emphasis: Underlying assumptions and their implications for reading instruction. *Annals of Dyslexia, 40*, 51-76.

Liberman, I., Shankweiler, D., Liberman, A., Fowler, C., & Fischer, F. (1977). Phonetic segmentation and recoding in the beginning reader. In A. Reber & D. Scarborough (Eds.), *Toward a psychology of reading*. Hillsdale, NJ: Erlbaum.

Lyons, C., Pinnell, G., & DeFord, D. (1993). *Partners in learning*. New York: Teachers College Press.

McConkie, G. (1979). On the role and control of eye movements in reading. In P. A. Kolers, M. E.

Wrolstad, & H. Bouma, (Eds.), *Processing of visible language* (Vol. 1). New York: Plenum Press.

Pinnell, G. (1990). Success for low achievers through Reading Recovery. *Educational Leadership, 48,* 17-21.

Pinnell, G., DeFord, D., & Lyons, C. (1988). *Reading Recovery: Early intervention for at-risk first graders.* Arlington, VA: Educational Research Service.

Pinnell, G., Lyons, C., DeFord, D., Bryk, A., & Seltzer, M. (1994). Comparing instructional models for the literacy education of high-risk first graders. *Reading Research Quarterly, 29,* 8-39.

Rayner, K., & Pollatsek, A. (1989). *The psychology of reading.* Englewood Cliffs, NJ: Prentice Hall.

Rassmussen, D., & Goldberg, L. (1976). *SRA basic reading series.* Chicago: Science Research Associates.

Robinson, H., Monroe, M., & Artley, A. S. (1956/1962). *The new basic readers: Curriculum foundation series.* Chicago: Scott Foresman.

Smith, F. (1985). *Reading without nonsense* (2nd ed.). New York: Teachers College Press.

Stanovich, K. (1980). Toward an interactive-compensatory model of individual differences in the development of reading fluency. *Reading Research Quarterly, 16,* 32-71.

Stanovich, K. (1986). Matthew effects in reading: Some consequences of individual differences in the acquisition of literacy. *Reading Research Quarterly, 21,* 360-401.

Stanovich, K. (1994). Romance and reality. *The Reading Teacher, 47,* 280-291.

Vygotsky, L. (1978). *Mind in society: The development of psychological processes.* Cambridge, MA: Harvard University Press.

Watson, D. (1989). Defining and describing whole language. *The Elementary School Journal, 90,* 130-141.

Weaver, C. (1990). *Understanding whole language: From principles to practice.* Portsmouth, NH: Heinemann.

Weaver, C. (1994). *Reading process and practice: From socio-psycholinguistics to whole language* (2nd ed.). Portsmouth, NH: Heinemann.

Wood, D. (1988). *How children think and learn.* Cambridge, MA: Basil Blackwell.

Wood, D., Bruner, J., & Ross, G. (1976). The role of tutoring in problem-solving. *Journal of Child Psychology and Psychiatry, 17,* 89-100.

ORAL LANGUAGE:
ASSESSMENT AND DEVELOPMENT
IN READING RECOVERY IN THE UNITED STATES

LANCE M. GENTILE
San Francisco State University

The role of oral language in literacy is well established (Clay, 1985, 1991; Enright & McClosky, 1988; Hanf-Buckley, 1992; McLaughlin, 1985). This article underscores:

1. The selection of English language learning children (ELL) for intervention in Reading Recovery using the Observation Survey (OS) but suggests oral language as a component of standardized and informal assessment;

2. Ways to pay *special attention* to oral language development for ELL children and create opportunities for talking across the components of a Reading Recovery lesson which may be more supportive, efficient, and cost effective;

3. The need for carefully designed studies related to the social and verbal interactions between the teacher and ELL children during Reading Recovery lessons; and

4. The need for research that investigates the effects of ELL children's learning to control basic sentence structures and their successful discontinuation from the program.

Clay's Record of Oral Language (ROL)

In New Zealand, an abundance of research has identified the differences among children who enter school at 5 years of age (Clay, 1985; Renwick, 1984). One of the major differences schools measure and prepare for is the level of a child's oral language. An assessment is used and when the results show a child does not possess oral language sufficient to begin formal reading and writing instruction, an oral language program of learning is recommended. In an early study, Clay (1985) advised:

> If we eased up a little on early reading and writing in the first six months of school not pushing so hard to get children further, earlier, where could we direct our energies? We could schedule time when children with poor language skills would be encouraged to initiate learning opportunities for themselves and then be encouraged to talk, to question, to explain to other children and to the teacher as she moves among them extending their expressions of ideas into an oral statement. (p. 36)

In children's first year of schooling, teachers provide intense, consistent, daily emergent literacy instruction by organizing specific talk-centered activities and interrelating oral language with reading and writing for those whose communication styles differ from the teachers' (Au & Mason, 1981; Cazden, 1988; Clay, 1985; Jamieson, 1977; Mackay, 1973). In the United States, teachers are challenged by a far greater diversity of socioeconomic problems and languages among children beginning school and efforts vary widely to address their oral language development (Peregoy & Boyle, 1993).

After years of researching the effects of oral language development on children's reading and writing, Clay, Gill, Glynn, McNaughton, and Salmon (1983) created a practical and useful instrument, *Record of Oral Language and Biks and Gutches*, to identify those needing oral language assessment and instructional modifications. Other formal measures of oral language are useful to Reading Recovery teachers (i.e., Student Oral Language Observational Matrix [SOLOM, Parker, Dolson, & Gold, 1985], Language Assessment Scales, [Duncan & De Avila, 1977], Basic Inventory of Natural Language [Herbert, 1977], or the Bilingual Syntax Measure [Burt, Dulay, & Hernandez-Chavez, 1975]).

However, Clay's focus in the ROL on basic sentence structures to develop oral language fluency supports her theory (1991) of how children relate language and print (p. 39). It examines the language structures ELL children control in their speech. These form the bulwark of much of what they read and write during Reading Recovery lessons. Furthermore, the ROL gives teachers:

- insight into ways young children control different sentence structures in English,
- useful ways of checking on a child's control of the language structures needed to do school work,
- a way to identify the most advanced structural level of oral language that a child might listen to and fully understand,
- a way to measure change in oral language competency due to specific instruction or from a child's environment, and
- a way to identify and select children whose language development may require special attention.

The ROL has two parts. Part I contains the basic levels and diagnostic sentences. Part II contains a series of pictures and questions related to the pictures that require a child to demonstrate control over inflections of English. Part II may be less important in Reading Recovery. It is not included here because research has demonstrated that typically inflection and pronunciation develop in the later stages of second language acquisition (Jackson, 1980; Mace-Matluck, 1981).

Part I: Levels Sentences and Diagnostic Sentences

The ROL has three sentence levels grouped on the basis of difficulty. The teacher reads these simple, declarative sentences out loud and the child is asked to repeat them. Clay (In Clay, et al., 1983) said, "research has shown that when we analyse a child's attempts to repeat a carefully constructed set of sentences we discover also those grammatical structures which he may be just beginning to understand but may not yet use in normal speech." (p. 10). An exact spoken repetition of each sentence by the child is scored as one point. There are two examples for each sentence level and seven sentences in each section making a total of 42 sentences across the three levels of Part I.

If a child scores less than 13 on the ROL she or he is unable to repeat Type A, simple sentences in Level 1 accurately. These sentences are made up of a subject, the verb to be, and some other simple statement. They do not have an object (e.g., My brother's knees are dirty. My father's radio is broken). For a complete description of Levels Sentence types from B through G the reader can refer to the ROL itself.

Diagnostic Sentences. Part I of the ROL also contains several diagnostic variations of the simple sentence types in the Levels Sentences that include:
- Imperative sentences,
- Questions,
- Negative sentences,
- Preposed phrases,
- Relative clauses, and
- Adverbial clauses.

There are 82 additional Diagnostic Sentences in Part I of the ROL which are not all inclusive but provide teachers a broader way of exploring a child's language beyond the Levels Sentences.

They are arranged hierarchically according to difficulty and are presented in the same manner as the Levels Sentences.

Clay et al. (1983) provide guidelines for analyzing children's oral language using their responses to the Levels Sentences and for applying information gleaned from the Diagnostic Sentences to the development of classroom instruction. She cautioned:

> In general, children scoring below 13 [on the ROL] will so far have acquired only limited control over the structures of oral English. They will be likely to have difficulty in following all but the simplest form of instructions given by the teacher and in following a story read to the class. These children should be considered for special attention in oral language development. (p. 29)

To paraphrase Clay's summary of the use of the Record of Oral Language: Teachers who use the ROL to gather insights about children's control of basic language structures may observe the extent to which children are gaining control of a standard dialect in addition to the one they already control and will be able to develop their own applications of the findings to suit their particular needs. But, in Reading Recovery in the United States is this too much to assume?

Oral Language Assessment for ELL Children in the United States

Researchers have long expressed the importance of fluent, structured oral language in the development of a child's literacy and particularly in relation to how it influences cognitive growth and the ability to arrange symbols logically and to think abstractly (Bruner, 1983). Large numbers of ELL children enter public schools in the United States. They are tested once at the beginning of kindergarten or upon entry into school and generally classified as Limited English Proficient (LEP), Non-English Proficient (NEP) or Fully English Proficient (FEP). (This article focuses on those children classified by the school as LEP and NEP. But unlike the ROL, the typical standardized oral language assessment results are limited and provide scant information that can be used to design a program of oral language instruction that supports children's growth in literacy (Peregoy & Boyle, 1993).

Consequently, Reading Recovery teachers must often depend upon the labels ELL children have earned from a single test, kindergarten teachers' judgement, and whether or not they appear to understand spoken directions during the OS as the basis for evaluating their emergent literacy and initiating instruction in the program.

Many ELL children are among those identified by Reading Recovery teachers as the lowest in reading and writing on the OS and qualify for immediate intervention. Often these children speak a dialect of English at home or another language in their homes and communities and apart from when they are in school may not hear or use standard English. Conditions at school in the United States may tend to militate against language development for children from these backgrounds.

Different cultures have different rules for speaking at home, and traditional schooling does little to erase differences in their oral language (Clay, et al.,1983). These children are often reluctant to speak with adults, and a teacher is at a loss to know how to get them to talk, so she or he may talk two-thirds or more of the time and *lead all the way* (Mackay, 1973; Jamieson, 1977). Clay (1991) said:

> If the child's language development seems to be lagging it is misplaced sympathy to do his talking for him . . . . The child who does not like to talk with the teacher or who has some difficulty understanding what the teacher is saying may be a child at risk. Be strong minded about talking with a child with whom it is difficult to hold a conversation. The human reaction is not to spend much time talking to such children. The educator's reaction should be to create more opportunities for talking. (p. 69)

Because many first grade classrooms in the United States are overcrowded, ELL children may have limited opportunities to participate whenever oral language instruction in English is conducted. Moreover, teachers' social, verbal interactions and attempts to engage them in conversation differ markedly from their interactions with standard English-speaking children (Hanf-Buckley, 1992). These conditions are cited frequently to support the decision to enroll them in Reading Recovery immediately because it is generally accepted that:

1. Regardless of ELL children's oral language deficiencies they should enter the program immediately if they can understand enough English to follow the directions for completing the OS and they score in the lowest group of alternatively ranked children in a first grade class.

2. Hypothetically, the oral language context of Reading Recovery lessons in which an expert adult user of English models and engages ELL children one-to-one in a variety of language-based learning activities and the material and activities she or he chooses for a particular child within the components of the lesson create what is necessary to accelerate these children's oral language and literacy.

3. Reading Recovery is not an ESL program.

Each of these positions is justifiable. In one recent study 75 percent of ELL children selected for Reading Recovery in California on the basis of only needing to understand the directions for the OS appeared to benefit immediately from working in the program and demonstrated accelerative learning (Kelly, Gomez-Valdez, Klein, & Neal, 1995). These researchers compared ELL children's rate of discontinuation from the program with that of English-only speakers (English) and Descubriendo La Lectura (Reading Recovery in Spanish / DLL) and showed almost identical percentages: 75 percent, 74 percent, and 78 percent respectively.

In this study, comparisons were made on the various tests of the OS, but oral language as a variable was not identified or treated. Asked how they accounted for such even results across the language groups, the authors repeated the generally accepted hypothesis: given the rich oral language context of Reading Recovery lessons in which an expert language user is modeling for and engaging the child in a variety of language use, Reading Recovery serves to accelerate a child's reading and writing development concomitantly with acceleration in oral language competence. This hypothesis needs to be tested and research expanded in the United States. Clay (1985) said:

> It seems oral language is used to facilitate progress in reading and writing but few if any activities are designed specifically to facilitate oral language control. Perhaps because language learning seems to be done so easily by many children in the majority culture we have forgotten to arrange for learning opportunities to learn more about the use of the language for talking. (p. 33)

Interrelating Oral Language Development with Reading and Writing Across Reading Recovery Lessons: Some Personal Observations, Questions, and Modifications

Thoreau (1927) stated, "As the least drop of wine tinges the whole goblet, so the least particle of truth colors our whole life. It is never isolated, or simply added as treasure to our stock. When any real progress is made, we unlearn and learn anew what we thought we knew before." One particle of truth colors my whole career teaching children and adults who speak a dialect of English or English as a second language to read and write in English or Spanish, training teachers to do the same and to provide more effective instruction for those who will either drop out of school or be pushed out because of basic literacy difficulties.

The truth is oral language is primary, interrelated with written language and it is the basis of verbal thought, social communication, and the complexities of reading and writing (Chomsky, 1972; Huey, 1908; Loban, 1963, 1976; Monroe, 1965; Purcell-Gates, 1991, 1992; Sulzby, 1985; Wells, 1981). Thanks to my work in Reading Recovery I have unlearned and learned anew what I thought I knew before.

My own observations of many Reading Recovery teachers working with ELL children in the United States support Mackay (1973) and Jamieson's (1977) research: teachers talk more than two-thirds of the time during a lesson and lead all the way. Single word or monosyllabic responses are routinely accepted without realizing the inhibiting effect this may have on a child's development in literacy. Attempts to clarify or expand children's oral language production are often weak and inconsistent and do not facilitate these children's learning by specifically linking what they can understand and say to what they read and write (Cambourne, 1988).

These observations may reflect personal experience or bias and, in the absence of empirical studies, should be viewed cautiously. But, Wells (1986) studied the social and verbal interactions between classroom teachers and children and concluded:

Teachers are unaware of the manner in which they interact with children and even when they become so by recording themselves and then transcribing and analyzing the resulting tapes, they do not find it easy to change interactional strategies built up over many years. For like the proverbial centipede, when asked to think about how they talk with children, some teachers find they become so self-conscious that they can no longer interact in a natural manner at all. The reason for this, I suspect, is that under normal circumstances, the focus of our attention is not on the verbal and nonverbal messages through which we communicate our intentions, but rather on the intentions themselves in relation to the specific activity in which we and our co-participants are engaged. (pp. 90-91)

The intention in Reading Recovery to accelerate children's learning and discontinue them as soon as possible may not encourage teachers in this country to pay enough attention to more varied verbal interactions nor expand their use of flexible prompts particularly when they have not been trained to develop oral language in the way teachers in New Zealand have. Where oral language development has not been a strong component of Reading Recovery teachers' background and training, supervisory models and explicit work during inservice classes may be required to help them become more aware of their communication patterns with ELL children.

Some questions occurred to me during my training as a Reading Recovery teacher leader while working with three ELL children. Can a Reading Recovery teacher trained to pay *special attention* to ELL children's oral language development and *create more opportunities for talking* change the manner in which she or he interacts with these children socially and verbally and support accelerative learning without disrupting the lesson or the research related to the program? For ELL children in Reading Recovery in the United States, is there a need to administer Part I of Clay's ROL to some of these children prior to their entry to the program and to measure the development of their oral language over time? Could this specific assessment of oral language among ELL children provide insights beyond what their ability to understand simple directions on the OS offers?

My academic background in language development and second language acquisition, emergent literacy, teaching a foreign language, and personally having had to study and learn a second language on foreign soil attuned my ear to the differences among these children's oral language competencies during the OS, *roaming,* and their early lessons. At one point in each of their programs they became stalled, seemingly unable to read increasingly more difficult texts or write more varied stories despite the fact I was trying to apply *correct* Reading Recovery procedures and prompts in these children's lessons. Another cautionary note is needed here because in my ignorance and novitiate role I may well have been more focused on the details of Reading Recovery procedures and missed the importance of process as it relates to these children's learning. Nevertheless, not only did their learning not accelerate but they began to regress. I examined their lessons carefully, looked at myself and seriously considered what I needed to change about me as a teacher and what I needed to do to adapt the program to meet their needs (Clay, 1993).

After altering the levels of texts and shared writing activities with limited success I decided to modify my verbal interactions with these children and focused on oral language development as an interrelated aspect of their reading and writing. Without adding to the burden of my teaching I incorporated more opportunities for these children to talk in their Reading Recovery lessons each day by:

1. Encouraging them to repeat whole sentences instead of accepting one word answers or monosyllabic responses.

2. Having them tell me what they or we would be doing at each transitional point of the lesson. For example they would say, "I am going to write on the board now," instead of saying "write," "writing," or some such limited utterance.

3. Encouraging the child after reading each familiar text to talk about the meaning, retell the story, and repeat the patterned language structure used in the text in our conversation.

4. Selecting and introducing texts that contained different high frequency language and syntax that would specifically scaffold a particular child's reading and writing development and by focusing heavily on meaning and structure as well as visual prompts and cues.

5. Using one of the familiar texts as a source of developing the child's daily story conversation and focusing on a specific sentence structure with the child to write a story based on this structure. After the child completed writing the story I repeated the structure and used it as a kernel sentence and substituted a simple meaning statement in conjunction with it. For example, if the child wrote, "I am going to the park today. " I would not only ask him or her to reread the story but afterwards say, "Yes, we can say, 'I am going to the park today or I am going to school today, or I am going home today.'" The child was asked to repeat each patterned substitution.

6. Asking the children to not just do the reassembly of the cut-up story at home but to bring it back in the envelope with the books they took home each evening. Before fluency writing I asked the children to quickly reassemble the story on the desk and read it.

7. Selecting the new book within lessons based on language they controlled or partially controlled which reinforced or strengthened these sentence structures.

8. By focusing on meaning, planting the targeted structure of language in their ear during the introduction of the new text, modeling for the child the language of the book and asking the child to read it and return to the text for a second reading "to get a flow of words and a real feel for the story" (Clay, 1993, p. 38).

At the end of this first year I made several observations:

1. Since I was aware of these children's oral language differences and the effects they were having on reading and writing in their program, it seemed natural and logical to interrelate oral language development across the lesson.

2. The length of the lesson expanded, but by not holding these children accountable for using structured language I was neglecting an important aspect of their development in literacy. The additional time allotted to the lesson may reflect my own ineptitude and warrants more carefully designed inquiry because some ELL results in other sites show comparability with the general population without adding time to the lesson (Kelly, et.al., 1995). More information is needed because there may be a variance between those ELL children who enter the program as LEP as opposed to NEP.

3. As children's control over basic sentence structures in oral language improved, so did their fluency and comprehension of the stories we read.

4. As the children used these structures in their writing they appeared to gain increased control over them in their oral expression and they began to accelerate their learning.

5. Each developed a self-extending system. All three ELL children were discontinued, though at different levels and at different points in their program.

During my field year I worked with three more ELL children. I supplemented the Observational Survey with Clay's ROL and the following two informal oral language measures at the start and finish of their programs.

1. During *roaming* I laminated pictures and asked the children to tell me a story about each one. I tape recorded these stories and responses to my questions during the narration then analyzed their expressive and receptive language level using the SOLOM (Parker,

Research in Reading Recovery

Dolson, & Gold, 1985).

2. I also asked the children to draw a picture about something we had read in *roaming* they particularly liked. Then I asked them to tell me about their drawing and I tape recorded and analyzed their oral language production using the SOLOM.

At the beginning of the program, two of the children scored less than 13 on the ROL and one scored 13, all three children scored between 5-11 (Phase I) on the SOLOM (NEP). I created the same opportunities for the children to talk more during the lesson that I established with the three ELL children I worked with during my training year.

The three children I worked with in my field year discontinued earlier than those I worked with in my training last year. All three successfully repeated 28-35 sentences from the Levels section of the ROL. They scored in the upper range of LEP between 19-24 (Phase III) at discontinuation (Gentile, 1995).

This work is preliminary, exploratory, and suggestive. No definitive conclusions can or should be made pending additional study and well designed investigations. Carefully controlled studies might generate more powerful instruction early in a child's program, but these initial efforts raise some interesting implications for further research and practice.

Implications for Further Research

Since reading and writing are derivatives of oral language, could it be that differences in ELL children's oral language development may account for some of these children's ability to accelerate their literacy learning? What effect might this have on the success and cost-benefit ratio of the program? On a similar note, would it be more cost effective and efficient to give some ELL children (those classified as NEP) intense oral language instruction first, then pick them up in the second round instead of placing them in the program immediately?

If oral language competency were identified and given special attention in a consistent way throughout the lesson, would more ELL children show accelerative learning and successfully complete the program? Absent of any adjustments to identify oral language differences and create opportunities for these children to talk more and relate what they say with what they read and write, might some of these children lack the foundation in language development to work effectively in the program early or make accelerated gains within the 12-18 weeks taken by the average child in the program?

These questions cast no aspersion on ELL children's cognitive ability, imply oral language differences preclude their entry into the program, nor that Reading Recovery becomes an ESL program when we identify and work to provide more opportunities to strengthen oral language in the context of their lessons. Rather, it may highlight what needs to be done about these children's oral language development in kindergarten and first grade.

When oral language assessment for ELL children in the United States is not included in Reading Recovery, might this inadvertently send the wrong message to teachers, i. e., since the Observational Survey does not contain oral language assessment and oral language is not tested, it is not assigned specific importance in the program?

Clay (1985) said:

Educators need to consider the recommendation that, because we know where we are going in early reading and writing and because teachers are doing a good job in this area, there is reason to pay more attention to oral language development particularly for children who enter school with less than average attainment in this area.

In New Zealand, studies confirm ELL children in Reading Recovery who successfully complete the program continue to develop their literacy (Clay, 1993). In his classic longitudinal study of kindergarten children over a thirteen year period from ages 5-18, Loban (1963) found those students in sixth grade who scored in the highest quartile of reading and writing were the same ones who scored highest on measures of oral language in the primary grades. He found the opposite to be true as well. Students who scored lowest in reading and writing in the sixth grade were the same who had scored in the lowest quartile in oral language in the primary grades. But, no such longitudinal study has been made of ELL children in Reading Recovery in this country.

When ELL children successfully complete Reading Recovery, longitudinal studies need to be conducted to examine the relationship of their oral language development to their continued growth in literacy across the primary grades. What differences are there in these children's oral language, their ability to read and write, and their continued success in school?

Finally, the social and verbal interactions between teachers and these children across their lessons need to be studied. Are there differences in the way teachers interact with standard English-speaking children and ELL children in Reading Recovery? What differences are there between teachers' verbal exchanges, expectations, time spent talking, attention to oral language development, and the selection and management of materials and activities for ELL children who successfully complete the program and those who do not?

According to Clay (1993), acceleration is the outcome of sound teaching. She notes:

As the child gains control of the various components of the reading process the teacher who is observing sensitively begins to realize that a faster pace up through text difficulty levels is possible. However for some children and some teachers this does not seem to happen. In this case, there is only one position to take: The program is not or has not been, appropriately adapted to the child's needs . . . some aspect of the teacher's teaching or some aspect of the reading process has not received attention. (p. 56)

Given the disparity between many ELL children's oral language development at home and in school in the United States and in light of Clay's admonitions:

• How can a Reading Recovery teacher's sensitive observation be complete without any assessment of ELL children's oral language competencies in standard English?

• How can a program be appropriately adapted to the needs of some ELL (LEP, NEP) children without the teacher paying special attention to the role of oral language development in Reading Recovery?

This article addresses these and other significant issues in Reading Recovery in California where a majority of the nations' second language learners reside, where the state ranks next to last in the nations' elementary school children's literacy, where one in four children lives in poverty and the socioeconomic differences among teachers and children are widespread, and where teachers work in the most crowded classrooms in the country and can face classes represented by 12 or more languages.

References

Au, K.H., & Mason, J.M. (1981). Social organizational factors in learning to read: The balance of rights hypothesis. *Reading Research Quarterly, 17*, 115-152.

Bruner, J. (1983). *Child's talk: Learning to use language.* London: W. W. Norton.

Burt, M., Dulay, H., & Hernandez-Chavez, E. (1975). *Bilingual syntax measure.* Orlando: Harcourt Brace Javanovich.

Cambourne, B. (1988). *The whole story: Natural learning and the acquisition of literacy in the classroom.* Richmond Hill, Ontario, Canada: Scholastic-TAB.

Cazden, C.B. (1988). *Classroom discourse: The language of teaching and learning.* Portsmouth, NH: Heinemann.

Chomsky, C. (1972). Stages in language development. *Harvard Educational Review, 42*, 1-33.

Clay, M.M. (1985). Engaging with the school system: A study of interactions in new entrant classrooms. *Journal of Educational Studies, 20*, 20-38.

Clay, M.M. (1991). *Becoming literate: The construction of inner control.* Portsmouth, NH: Heinemann.

Clay, M.M. (1993). *Reading Recovery: A guidebook for teachers in training.* Portsmouth, NH: Heinemann.

Clay, M.M., Gill, M., Glynn, T., McNaughton, T., & Salmon, K. (1983). *Record of oral language and biks and gutches*. Portsmouth, NH: Heinemann.

Duncan, S.E., & DeAvila, E. (1977). *Language assessment scales*. Larkspur, CA: DeAvila, Duncan, & Associates.

Enright, D.S. & McClusky, M.L. (1988). *Integrating English: Developing English language and literacy in the multilingual classroom*. Reading, MA: Addison Wesley.

Gentile, L.M. (1995, July 6). *Oral Language: Assessment and direct instruction in Reading Recovery in the United States*. Research paper presented at Annual International Reading Recovery Institute, Palm Springs: CA.

Hanf-Buckley, M. (1992). Focus on research: We listen a book a day; we speak a book a week: Learning from Walter Loban. *Language Arts, 69*, 622-626.

Herbert, C.F. (1977). *Basic inventory of natural language*. San Bernardino, CA: CHECpoint Systems.

Huey, E.B. (1908). *The psychology and pedagogy of reading*. New York: MacMillan.

Jackson, S.I. (1980). Analysis of procedures and summary statistics of the language data. In B.J. Mace-Matluck (Ed.), *A longitudinal study of the oral language development of Texas bilingual children (Spanish-English). Findings from the first year*. Austin: Southwest Educational Development Laboratory.

Jamieson, P.A.B. (1977). *Adult-child talk*. In G. MacDonald (Ed.), Early childhood education conference. Massey University, Wellington, NZ.

Kelly, P.R., Gomez-Valdez, C., Klein, A., & Neal, J. (1995, April 20). *Progress of first and second language learners in an early intervention program*. Research paper presented at Annual American Educational Research Association Conference. San Francisco.

Loban W. (1963). *The language of elementary school children* (NCTE Research rep. No. 1). Urbana, IL: National Council of Teachers of English.

Loban, W. (1976). *Language and development: Kindergarten through grade twelve* (NCTE Research Report No. 18). Urbana, IL: National Council of Teachers of English.

Mace-Matluck, B.J. (1981). General characteristics of the children's language use in three environments. In B.J. Mace-Matluck (Ed.), *A longitudinal study of the oral language development of Texas bilingual children (Spanish-English): Findings from the second year*. Austin: Southwest Educational Development Laboratory.

Mackay, R. (1973). Conceptions of children and models of socialization. In H. Dreitzel (Ed.). *Recent Sociology, 5*. London: Macmillan.

McLaughlin, B. (1985). *Second language acquisition in childhood* (Vol 2). Hillsdale, NJ: Lawrence Erlbaum.

Monroe, M. (1965). Necessary preschool experiences for comprehending reading. *Reading and inquiry. International Reading Association proceedings, 10*. Newark, DE: International Reading Association, 45-46.

Parker, D., Dolson, D., & Gold, N. (1985). *Student oral language observational matrix*. Sacramento: California State Department of Education.

Peregoy, S., & Boyle, O. (1993). *Reading, writing, & learning in ESL*. New York: Longman.

Purcell-Gates, V. (1991). Ability of well-read kindergartners to decontextualize/recontextualize experience into a written-narrative register. *Language and Education, 5*, 177-188.

Purcell-Gates, V. (1992). Roots of response. *Journal of Narrative and Life History, 2*, 151-162.

Renwick, M. (1984). *To school at five*. Wellington, NZ: Council for Educational Research.

Sulzby, E. (1985). Children's emergent abilities to read favorite storybooks: A developmental study. *Reading Research Quarterly, 20*, 458-481.

Thoreau, H.D. (1927). *The heart of Thoreau's journals*. Boston/New York: Houghton Mifflin.

Wells, G. (1981). *The meaning makers: Children learning language and using language to learn*. Portsmouth, NH: Heinemann.

Wells, G. (1986) The language-experience of five-year old children. In J. Cook-Gumperz (Ed.), *The social construction of literacy*. London: Cambridge University Press.

ABOUT THE AUTHORS

Billie J. Askew is a professor of reading at Texas Woman's University and Director of the University's Reading Recovery Regional Training Center. Prior to joining the university faculty, she taught in elementary classrooms and served as a public school administrator for a number of years. In addition to her continuing study of early literacy and early intervention, she is currently exploring the implementation of school programs, early writing processes, reading-writing relationships, and comprehension processes.

Diane E. DeFord is a professor in the Department of Education Theory and Practice in the College of Education at The Ohio State University where she teaches courses on reading and writing methods and evaluation. Diane has worked in this capacity for eleven of the thirteen years at OSU, and received the Ohio Governor's Award in 1988 for excellence in service and leadership to the state. She co-authored the book *Partners in Learning: Teachers and Children in Reading Recovery* and co-edited the book, *Bridges to Literacy*. In addition to these books about Reading Recovery, she has authored articles in professional periodicals and chapters in books related to teacher beliefs and children's developing and writing strategies. Most recently she has begun writing books for children with *Butch, the Outdoor Cat; Fritzie's Adventure;* and *The Amazing Galapagos Islands* published for primary age children.

Kathy Escamilla is currently an associate professor in the Division of Language, Literacy and Culture at the University of Colorado, Denver. Her area of specialization is bilingual education. She has been a bilingual classroom teacher, bilingual program director, and university professor. She has spent more than twenty-five years in the field of bilingual education and has published widely in the field. She is a past president of the National Association for Bilingual Education and has recently assisted with research projects related to the development and implementation of Reading Recovery in Spanish.

John W. Fraas teaches applied statistics in the education and business programs at Ashland University, Ohio. In 1986, he was the first professor to be appointed by the Board of Trustees of Ashland University to the position of Trustee's Professor, a position awarded to a professor who is recognized as an effective teacher and researcher. In addition to publishing numerous articles on applied statistics, he has written the textbook *Basic Concepts in Educational Research.*

Dianne F. Frasier currently works as an English/language arts consultant for Harris County Department of Education and as a Reading Recovery trainer for Texas Woman's University in Houston, Texas. Prior to her work in Houston, she was a Reading Recovery trainer at Texas Woman's University in Denton, Texas.

Janet S. Gaffney is an associate professor of special education at the University of Illinois at Urbana-Champaign. Her public school experiences include elementary and secondary teaching, reading specialist, Title I and special education teacher and coordinator. Jan's research and teaching are directed toward making a difference in the lives of students who are not demonstrating acceptable progress in reading and writing within their instructional programs. During her eight years of experience as a Reading Recovery trainer, she tutored children in Reading Recovery in local schools. Her publications and current research at the Center for the Study of Reading are focused on the effects of inservice education in the area of early literacy on teachers and on young children, particularly those who experience difficulty in learning to read and write. Her publications and research also focus on the contextual factors that support systems change. Dr. Gaffney had served on many journal editorial boards including *Cognition and Instruction; Exceptional Children; Literacy, Teaching and Learning;* and *Teacher Education and Special Education.*

Lance M. Gentile is a professor of language and literacy at San Francisco State University and a Reading Recovery Teacher Leader. He serves as a consultant to the San Francisco Unified School District supervising Reading Recovery/Descubriendo La Lectura teachers in training and in their development of children in Reading Recovery/Descubriendo La Lectura and its specific relationship to achievement in literacy.

Angela Hobsbaum has worked at the Institute of Education, University of London, for a number of years and in a variety of roles: training of primary teachers; working with preschool teachers; and running post graduate courses. She is the course tutor for the only Reading Recovery Teacher Leader training course in the UK. Since 1993, she has been one of the national coordinators of Reading Recovery in the UK, a job that offers challenges completely unlike those encountered in her previous academic work. Despite rumors to the contrary, Reading Recovery is consolidating its position in the British education system and is improving its achievement year by year.

Noel K. Jones directs the Reading Recovery program in the Wason School of Education at the University of North Carolina, Wilmington, where he trains Reading Recovery Teacher Leaders and teaches courses in language and literacy acquisition and reading education. Before coming to UNCW, he was a classroom teacher for fourteen years in four different states and served for five years as a reading curriculum director in Portland, Maine. Noel has worked with his colleagues at UNCW to incorporate elements of Reading Recovery training into graduate and undergraduate courses and to redesign the graduate program in reading education. He currently serves as chair of the standard and guidelines committee of the Reading Recovery Council of North America, and he continues to teach at least one child per year in Reading Recovery. He retreats in the summer to an old house in New Vineyard, Maine, where he likes to putter, read, write, and play tennis.

Adria F. Klein is a professor in the Department of Educational Research and Policy at California State University, San Bernardino. She has written several books, book chapters, and numerous articles on various topics including emergent literacy, Reading Recovery, reader's theater, integrated language arts, staff development, and technology. She is co-editor of *Literacy, Teaching and Learning,* journal of the Reading Recovery Council of North America. Adria teaches courses in language arts and literacy in the graduate Reading Education program, in addition to being a Reading Recovery Trainer of Teacher Leaders.

Carol A. Lyons is a professor of education at The Ohio State University, Columbus, Ohio. Dr. Lyons teaches courses in developmental reading, reading evaluation, corrective reading, cognition, learning and instruction, and Reading Recovery theoretical courses for teacher leaders and university trainers. Dr. Lyons has conducted research and published numerous articles in the field of Reading Recovery and learning disability, cognitive processing, and teacher development. She is the co-author of two books: *Partners in Learning: Teachers and Children in Reading Recovery* and *Bridges to Literacy.* Dr. Lyons is currently the President of the Reading Recovery Council of North America.

Susan Y. Paynter provides consultant service and technical assistance to literacy projects and other non-profit clients. She has been a Title I Coordinator, Reading Specialist, clinical instructor, classroom teacher, and university instructor and is a trained Reading Recovery teacher. She has served the Reading Recovery Council of North America and the University of Arkansas at Little Rock Reading Recovery program as a consultant. Susan has been instrumental in the implementation of Reading Recovery in consortium, local district, and university models throughout the United States. She has designed schoolwide, parenting and staff development programs supporting comprehensive literacy services in Texas, Arkansas, Mississippi, and many other Reading Recovery sites. Susan currently resides in Austin, Texas, and been president of the Texas Association for the Improvement of Reading (TAIR) and was a 1993 recipient of the Teacher Leader Award.

Gay Su Pinnell is a professor in the Department of Educational Theory and Practice in the College of Education at The Ohio State University, where she works extensively in field-based research projects and teaches courses in language arts and reading. In addition, she has completed several large investigations that have influenced educational practice and research and has written or edited numerous books and articles, including *Bridges to Literacy: Learning from Reading Recovery; Partners in Learning: Teachers and Children in Reading Recovery*; and *Guided Reading: Good First Teaching for All Children*. She is co-author of Scholastic's Literary Place. She is the recipient of the International Reading Association's Albert J. Harris Award, the Ohio Governor's Award, the Pi Lambda Theta Award for Service to Education, the Charles A. Dana Award for Pioneering Achievement in Education, and Ohio State's Distinguished Teaching Award. Gay served as the first President of the Reading Recovery Council of North America.

Kenneth J. Rowe is a senior research associate of the Centre for Applied Educational Research in the Faculty of Education at the University of Melbourne. In addition to his research and teaching commitments, Ken is a national training consultant and teacher from the Australian Consortium for Social and Political Research Incorporated. He teaches psychosocial research methodology and advanced statistical modeling (multilevel and covariance structure analysis). Ken's special interests include: conceptual and methodological issues in applied educational, epidemiological and psychosocial research/evaluation; the application of explanatory modeling techniques to substantive research/evaluation questions; educational assessment and psychometrics; and the rapprochement of quantitative and qualitative approaches to applied methodologies in educational, epidemiological and psychosocial inquiry.

Stanley L. Swartz is a professor of education, Faculty of Special Education, in the Department of Educational Research and Policy at California State University, San Bernardino, and Director of Reading Recovery in California and California Early Literacy Learning. He is the editor of two Dominie Press series of little books for emergent readers, Carousel Readers and Teacher's Choice Series, and is co-editor of *Literacy, Teaching and Learning*, the journal of the Reading Recovery Council of North America. Dr. Swartz is also the Director of the University Center for Developmental Disabilities.

Joseph F. Yukish is a professor of education and Reading Recovery Leader Trainer at Clemson University's Reading Recovery Teacher Leader Training Center. The research in this chapter was conducted while Yukish and Fraas were professors at Ashland University and worked with the development of Reading Recovery programs for Amish children in Holmes County, Ohio. Presently, Yukish trains Reading Recovery Teacher Leaders from South Carolina, western North Carolina, and Alabama. He has published seven children's books for emergent readers with Kaeden Press, Dominie Press, and Shortland Publications. Yukish wrote a two day workshop in Guided Reading for The Wright Group, trained trainers for them, and frequently presents Guided Reading workshops, in addition to the many inservice workshops he conducts for public school teachers and administrators. A longtime storyteller, Yukish has capitalized on his professional storytelling skills in working with children and adults in many settings. He is currently completing his second term as chair of the storytelling special interest group of the International Reading Association.